DARKEST BEFORE DAWN

DARKEST BEFORE DAWN

U-482 AND THE SINKING OF EMPIRE HERITAGE 1944

JOHN PETERSON

SPELLMOUNT

For Mum and Dad

And in memory of James Peterson, 1904–1980
who endured and survived the events in this book

First published 2011 by Spellmount,
an imprint of
The History Press
The Mill, Brimscombe Port
Stroud, Gloucestershire, GL5 2QG
www.thehistorypress.co.uk

© John Peterson, 2011

The right of John Peterson to be identified as the Author
of this work has been asserted in accordance with the
Copyrights, Designs and Patents Act 1988.

British Library Cataloguing in Publication Data.
A catalogue record for this book is available from the British Library.

ISBN 978 0 7524 5883 0

Typesetting and origination by The History Press
Manufacturing managed by Jellyfish Print Solutions Ltd.
Printed in India

CONTENTS

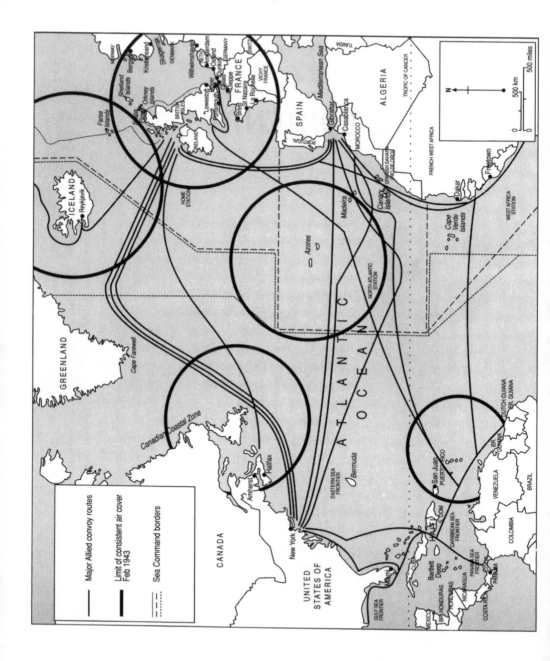

Legend:

- Major Allied convoy routes
- Limit of consistent air cover Feb 1943
- Sea Command borders

Map labels include: GREENLAND, ICELAND, Reykjavik, Faroe Islands, NORWAY, Kristiansand, Bergen, Skagerrak, DENMARK, Shetland Islands, Orkney Islands, Scapa Flow, Wilhelmshaven, NETH., Amsterdam, Ostend, GERMANY, Dunkirk, SWITZ., BRITISH ISLES, IRELAND, HOME STATION, Lowestoft, Portsmouth, Calais, Dieppe, FRANCE, Brest, St Nazaire, La Rochelle, VICHY FRANCE, SPAIN, PORTUGAL, Gibraltar, Casablanca, MOROCCO, Mediterranean Sea, ALGERIA, TUNISIA, TROPIC OF CANCER, SPANISH SAHARA (RIO DE ORO), FRENCH WEST AFRICA, Dakar, Freetown, WEST AFRICA STATION, Cape Verde Islands, Canary Islands, Madeira, Azores, NORTH ATLANTIC STATION, ATLANTIC OCEAN, Cape Farewell, Canadian Coastal Zone, Halifax, Amherst, Bermuda, EASTERN SEA FRONTIER, New York, CANADA, UNITED STATES OF AMERICA, Miami, GULF SEA FRONTIER, MEXICO, BR. HONDURAS, HONDURAS, NICARAGUA, COSTA RICA, PANAMA, PANAMA SEA FRONTIER, CARIBBEAN SEA FRONTIER, Bartlett Deep, CUBA, HAITI, San Juan, PUERTO RICO, VENEZUELA, COLOMBIA, BRAZIL, BR. GUIANA, DUTCH GUIANA, FR. GUIANA

Scale: 500 km / 500 miles

ACKNOWLEDGEMENTS

I have received help and advice from various people and organisations who have given me information, documents or photographs and I would especially like to acknowledge the assistance of the National Archives at Kew and the Tyne and Wear Archives Service. Being able to remotely search and order copies of documents and photographs that could only otherwise have been studied in person is an incredible service and we are very fortunate to have it.

I would like to thank Ian Wilson for what has been an inestimable and invaluable contribution to this book. From the very beginning he provided me with documents, photographs and ideas, some of which I could never have hoped to find without him. He has been incredibly generous in sharing information with me and this book would have been much poorer without his help.

I would also like to thank Leigh Bishop for the help and information he gave me, and for allowing me to use his stunning wreck photographs in the book. Seeing *Empire Heritage* in her final resting place helps to add another dimension to the story.

And finally, thanks to Shelley, without whose endless love and support this book would never have been written.

INTRODUCTION

Out in the blustering darkness, on the deck
A gleam of stars looks down. Long blurs of black,
The lean Destroyers, level with our track,
Plunging and stealing, watch the perilous way
Through backward racing seas and caverns of chill spray.
One sentry by the davits, in the gloom
Stands mute: the boat heaves onward through the night.
Shrouded is every chink of cabined light:
And sluiced by floundering waves that hiss and boom
And crash like guns, the troop-ship shudders … doom.

Night on the Convoy, Siegfried Sassoon

At 0350 hours, in the early morning darkness of Friday 8 September 1944 the sea moved with a moderate swell in the north-westerly force 4 off the north coast of Ireland near County Donegal. The moon had shone intermittently throughout the night and early morning; there had been some cloud cover but it was generally clear and visibility was good. Sunrise would be in another two hours. The cliffs of Malin Head, the most northerly point of Ireland, were black, rugged silhouettes, and there was no movement but that of the sea. The only sound inshore was of the wind and waves. Some fifteen miles out to sea, the night was disturbed by huge black forms moving in from the west. Enormous shapes of steel and the rumble of massive steam engines moved through the dim air, frothing bow waves spread across the water creating white-tipped trenches on the murky morning surface. This was the darkness before the dawn.

An enormous convoy of ships slid east from the Western Approaches towards the North Channel, the narrow strait between Scotland and Ireland on its way to Britain. They were at the final stages of a voyage that had taken them across the North Atlantic from the east coast of the United States and Canada. The main convoy was composed of no fewer than 98 vessels, a variety of ships of all types, shapes and sizes, sailing together for the protection of safety in numbers and surrounded by an escort of armed ships. Collectively, the motley group was called HX-305, one of the thousands of supply convoys that moved across the world and converged on Britain throughout the Second World War. In the holds of these ships lay the necessary supplies to sustain the British people in this desperate time and supply the Allied forces with fuel and weapons for the continuing conflict in Western Europe.

The majority of the ships were American, though there were also British, Dutch, Norwegian and Panamanian vessels amongst the convoy, sailing from New York or Nova Scotia to Liverpool, before dispersing to other ports across the country such as Manchester, Cardiff, Hull, Belfast and the Clyde, amongst others. They carried cargoes of grain, foodstuffs, lumber, paper, fuel and mail for the British population, alongside weapons, ammunition, trucks, tanks and oil for military use. In addition, they carried a large number of passengers, including many naval personnel who had lost their ships on previous voyages and who were heading back across the Atlantic to join new ones. They were known as DBS or 'Distressed British Seamen'. The most common reason for these men losing their ships was enemy action, and the most common perpetrator of those actions was the deadly U-boat.

By September 1944 U-boat activity in the North Atlantic was greatly reduced, having steadily tapered off over the previous fifteen months. Compared to the early days of the war, the U-boat threat was becoming negligible. Only a handful of merchant ships had been lost that year, a massive difference to the enormous losses suffered in 1940–1943 when U-boat successes had been at their height. In fact not a single ship had been lost to enemy action in an HX convoy since 22 April 1943, nearly seventeen months before. In previous years attacks had been much more frequent and deadly; for example, in 1942 the Allies had lost 124 ships in a single month and over 1,000 ships over the course of the year. Such losses represented an enormous number of men and shipping tonnage, lost forever beneath the freezing Atlantic Ocean, their holds full of supplies that would never serve their purpose. But by September 1944, as convoy HX-305 cruised east along the coast of County Donegal, successful U-boat attacks were at their lowest since the beginning of the war and developments in anti-submarine technology had given the Allies the upper hand. Also, the Allied invasion of Europe that had begun on D-Day had robbed Germany of her important U-boat bases along the Bay of Biscay. The subsequent breakout from Normandy and eventual liberation of France by the Allies meant that Germany had been forced to evacuate these bases and retreat her U-boats to her other occupied coasts such as Norway, or to Germany. This reduced her access to the Atlantic and meant a much longer trip for her U-boats trying to intercept Allied shipping as it moved through the Western Approaches.

But even though the Third Reich was rapidly unravelling and the Allies were edging ever closer to Berlin, the U-boat arm of the German Navy had proved itself notoriously determined and though the frequency and success of their attacks had certainly been diminished, the U-boats were still very much operational. In the previous two weeks at the end of August and beginning of September 1944, a number of unexpected and successful attacks had taken place in the coastal area where HX-305 was now sailing and three Allied ships had been sunk; a large American tanker, a Norwegian freighter and a Royal Navy corvette. Despite an extensive search the attacker had remained undetected and unidentified.

Whilst in Europe the war against Nazi Germany was slowly being won by the Allies, the men of the Merchant Navy had to remain ever vigilant, and could not for one moment forget the threat that the U-boats continued to represent. In late 1944, the tide had turned against Germany in nearly all the theatres of war, including the longstanding Battle of the Atlantic, but the Allied seamen were still sailing in almost constant danger.

That morning, as convoy HX-305 slid steadily eastwards, nobody looking out from amongst the vast scattering of ships could have known that they were not alone. There was nothing to tell them that they were being watched carefully by eyes from beneath the waves. In the calm of the dark September morning, a single periscope scanned silently across the vista in search of a possible target and a victim to add to the three that had already gone before. With just two days of the voyage left, the convoy moved steadily on, many of the ships' crews asleep below decks at this early hour. On the submerged vessel lying in wait, every man was awake.

The commander watching through the periscope finally selected a victim from amongst the ships as they moved past. He looked for a weak spot in the convoy, a way to get inside it, a way to get out again. The target he picked was a large ship, heavily laden and lying low in the water yet with a considerable superstructure. It was possibly a tanker, but sailing amidst the convoy it was just another shape in the night, nameless in the periscope crosshairs. The commander issued orders to the men waiting eagerly around him and the course was altered and set while preparations began deep in the innards of the long, sleek vessel. Slowly the U-boat began to turn, her whole body swinging round like a blade in the water to follow the path of the tanker, and to aim the deadly torpedo tubes moulded into her hull. The tubes were loaded whilst the distances were checked and various calculations made. Everything was set and confirmed whilst a constant watch was kept on the course of the unfortunate tanker, still unaware. The hydrophone on the U-boat scanned and listened to the surrounding wall of water outside. It locked carefully onto the sound of the enormous propellers turning beneath the ship. The U-boat rudder kept her turning until she pointed well to the east of her target; the extra angle on the trajectory was carefully calculated to give the torpedo time to get to the target. For such a calculation the distance to the target, the target's speed and the speed of the torpedo had to be vectored.

In the U-boat the crew were waiting, crowded around the commander at the periscope, watching him carefully. Even from behind the wall of water and layers of steel, they could hear the ships all around them ploughing through the darkness towards the North Channel. Everything was checked once more and then finally the order to fire was given.

The torpedo was pushed out into the darkness with a hiss of compressed air. Inside the U-boat a stopwatch began counting. Onboard the crew waited nervously as the seconds ticked away and everyone listened, their ears tuned to the ocean outside, for the sound of an impact. The stagnant air was thick with cloying diesel fumes and cooking smells along with the stink of unwashed bodies. Outside, the torpedo cut through the water just beneath the surface. At over seven metres in length, it was propelled by an electric motor capable of achieving a speed of 30 knots. At the front sat the deadly warhead, 280 kilograms of explosive power.

At 3.55 that morning, the torpedo struck its target in a perfectly aimed shot, and within seconds the fleet was plunged into chaos. The stricken vessel was a British merchant tanker called *Empire Heritage*. A large hole was blown in her side just above the waterline, and she immediately began to flood as the terrific blast from the torpedo ignited her massive oil tanks. The heavy ship could not possibly survive with her hull burst open and she subsequently became one of the biggest merchant losses of the war.

With news of the attack spreading through the convoy, a rescue ship called *Pinto* that was sailing nearby came quickly to her aid but within minutes of closing the wreck, she suffered a second torpedo from the same U-boat and went down in almost the same spot. As the convoy escorts tried desperately to reorganise a defensive screen, a third ship, the armed trawler HMT *Northern Wave* moved in, first to locate the attacker and then to rescue the men who had spilled out of the two sunken ships. She narrowly missed becoming a third victim as the enemy U-boat began her run for cover, which she eventually achieved without reprisal.

In under an hour, the peaceful September morning just north of County Donegal had been brutally shattered and the large convoy flung into disarray. As a desperate search began to find the attacker and save further losses, the two British ships settled broken on the seabed, and over a hundred men had lost their lives. Once more, it was brought home to the Allies that the U-boats could still pose a significant and deadly threat to their supply lines.

This is the story of convoy HX-305 told in full for the first time. It is the story of the two ships lost that morning – and others – of the men that survived, the subsequent inquiry and the aftermath of the attack. It considers the development of anti-submarine warfare by the Allies – some of which was prompted by the events described. It is the story of U-*482*, and of how a lone U-boat on her first active patrol managed to pull off one of the most extraordinary and dramatic U-boat attacks of the Second World War.

A FEW
CARELESS WORDS
MAY END IN THIS–

Many lives were lost in the last war through careless talk
Be on your guard! Don't discuss movements of ships or troops

I

THE BATTLE OF THE ATLANTIC

The Battle of the Atlantic was the dominating factor all during the war. Never for a moment could we forget that everything happening elsewhere – on land, sea and in the air – depended ultimately on the outcome of the Battle of the Atlantic.

Winston Churchill

In the years since taking power in 1933, Hitler's National Socialist Party had turned around the crumbling post-war Germany and made her into one of the most powerful countries in the world through a programme of military expansion and rearmament that had led to worldwide tension, mobilisation and eventually war.

What became known as the Battle of the Atlantic was in fact the longest continuously fought campaign of the conflict. After war broke out between Britain and Germany, it became clear that the biggest initial threat to the island nation was to her shipping. Britain was an island of 48 million people with an average annual import of some 55 million tonnes of raw materials; upwards of a million tonnes a week. Some of these materials were for use in factories for manufacturing and export, but most was simply what the population needed just to survive, let alone fight a war. Hitler knew that these supply lines were the key to achieving a quick finish to the war with Britain – and thus in Western Europe – and so his *Kriegsmarine* ('War Navy') began a focused operation to cut off the small island, shatter her merchant fleet, destroy her supplies and bring her to her knees.

Britain had the biggest Merchant Navy in the world with a fleet of around 18 million tonnes. These ships were continuously travelling all over the world, which meant that it would be an enormous and wide-ranging task to defeat them.

Though the war was fought in every corner of the globe, it was the supply lines pouring into Britain from the Atlantic that were the key to her survival. On one side of the battle was the Allied Merchant Navy, desperately trying to make it through to Britain with food and supplies, and on the other side were the U-boats, intent on preventing them. For Britain to survive, it was imperative that the ships crossing the Atlantic got through with the food, the weapons and the fuel to keep the country running. The celebrated pilots of the Royal Air Force could never have fought off the Luftwaffe in the Battle of Britain without the fuel for their aircraft and the ammunition for their guns. They could not have defended their coastline, or sent bombers across the English Channel without the necessary materials to build them. The tanks and guns for the Africa Campaign, the fuel for the evacuation of Dunkirk, the aircraft for the bombardment of Germany, the equipment for the invasion force for D-Day all came across the Atlantic in the holds of the Allied Merchant Navy ships. It is little wonder that Churchill acknowledged the Battle of the Atlantic as the dominating factor during the war.

Within twelve hours of the declaration of war on 3 September 1939 it became clear that Britain's greatest fears were to come true. The liner SS *Athenia* was torpedoed 200 miles out into the Atlantic on her way to Canada by U-*30*, who had mistaken her for a troopship. In fact she was carrying many civilians, of whom 118 died in the sinking. This tragedy was a sign of things to come. There grew an all-out tonnage war between the ships of the Merchant Navy and the Kriegsmarine as the U-boats began their campaign to starve Britain into submission. Later on, they would no longer be trying to simply defeat Britain – from mid-1942 when the war escalated with American involvement, the U-boats worked tirelessly to try and prevent the enormous movements of men, weapons and materials being shipped into Britain in preparation for the anticipated Allied invasion of Europe.

As the war progressed and it became clear that the U-boats were Germany's biggest hope in defeating Britain, production of the submarines escalated dramatically. At the outbreak of war Admiral Karl Dönitz who was *Befehlshaber der Unterseeboote* or Commander of Submarines, had just 56 U-boats in commission. This was nowhere near the number he wanted to begin his planned campaign but at least they were all new, and equipped with state-of-the-art submarine technology. Once war was declared U-boat production began immediately in nineteen different shipyards spread over eleven cities including Kiel, Wilhelmhaven and Hamburg. These shipyards would produce the 1,174 vessels that were ultimately launched during the conflict. Over the course of the war submarine technology developed rapidly and by 1945 the U-boat was a much more advanced fighting vessel than it had been at the start. But during the war years, the bulk of the U-boat fleet was made up of the Type IX and more importantly the Type VII, the latter a relatively small boat that varied in size from 630 to 760 tonnes. The Type VII was the most productive and widely used U-boat of the war, with almost 700 of them going into service. It was incredibly successful in theatre, totally unmatched as an attack submarine, and a combination of crew resourcefulness and endurance saw it succeed way beyond the parameters it was designed for.

In a time of war, all vehicles and crafts are used in any way they can to aid the war effort. From merchant ships to fishing boats, aircraft to motorcycles, cars and trucks, everything can be armed and armoured, and converted from its primary use to one of attack or defence. But a submarine is virtually unique in that it is exclusively a weapon, used for the stalking and stealthy attacking of enemy ships.

As an island nation, it is not surprising that in 1939 Britain had the largest Merchant Navy in the world. Somewhere in the region of 185,000 men crewed the ships that crossed the globe and it is estimated that during the war there were around 144,000 men at sea on any given date as they struggled to keep up the supply of food, men, supplies and munitions to Britain and the European front. Therefore there was enormous demand for merchant seamen and many experienced seamen chose to join the merchant marine over the Royal Navy. Life in the Merchant Navy would have been similar to life on a trawler or whaling ship. However, it was common for merchant seamen, fisherman or whalers to be part of the Royal Naval Reserve and many who were between trips at the outbreak of war were drafted straight into the Royal Navy. In 1938 the average age of a merchant seaman was 36 but there were also boys as young as fifteen or less aboard some of the ships, most of them from large ports areas such as London, Liverpool, Glasgow and the Tyne.

The men of the Merchant Navy – often referred to as 'the fourth service' – wore no distinct uniform like those in the Armed Services, and at most men on leave wore a small silver Merchant Navy lapel badge. This often resulted in sailors on leave being the victims of abuse from an ignorant public who seeing them without uniform mistakenly thought they were able-bodied men who were avoiding war service. In reality these were the men who were helping to keep the country alive and were often in much more significant danger than their uniformed counterparts in the armed services. In 1941 and 1942, 15,000 merchant seamen were lost as a result of enemy action and over the course of the war nearly 63,000 Allied and neutral merchant seamen lost their lives. It was a life spent endlessly crossing and re-crossing the seas, loading and unloading their cargoes, working four hours on and four hours off, never a full night's sleep or a full day's rest. And always there was a tenacious enemy lying in wait, ready to take the ship from beneath them. These men received little recognition for their dedication to duty. Ultimately many had no grave but the sea.

On top of these terrible human losses was the incredible tonnage of ships and cargoes being sent to the seabed by the enemy submarines. By the end of 1939, after fewer than four months of war, 147 ships had been lost; a total of 510,000 tonnes. This level of loss could not possibly be withstood by the British population, and the country was under immense strain as it continued to stand alone against Nazi Germany. It became clear that even a single U-boat was capable of inflicting levels of damage at sea that would have taken an entire army to achieve on land. Admiral Dönitz later wrote in his memoirs of the colossal impact a U-boat could make: 'How many soldiers would have to be sacrificed, how great an endeavour made, to destroy on land so great a mass of enemy war material?'

At the beginning of the war, the U-boats were under orders to observe 'Cruiser Rules', which meant that passenger ships were not to be attacked, and merchant ships were only to be attacked once fair warning had been given and the crews allowed to abandon ship, and even then only if they were within a reasonable distance from land. As time went on these rules were less and less adhered to, almost immediately in some cases – the *Athenia* being the earliest example. In some ways it is hardly surprising, as to follow the rules meant the U-boat having to reveal her presence, something which defeated the effectiveness of the surprise attack and which put her at unnecessary risk from counter attack.

Dönitz still did not have enough U-boats ready by the end of 1939 and it soon became clear to him that following the 'Cruiser Rules' was putting his precious submarines at unnecessary risk. For this reason in December 1939 Dönitz issued Standing Order 154, the first step towards what would be termed 'Unrestricted Submarine Warfare'. It was a controversial order that would later be used against him by the prosecution when he stood accused of war crimes at Nuremberg. Standing Order 154 read:

> Do not rescue crew members or take them aboard and do not take care of the ship's boats. Weather conditions and the distance from land are of no consequence. Think only of the safety of your own boat and try to achieve additional success as soon as possible. We must be harsh in this war. The enemy started it in order to destroy us, and we have to act accordingly.

Germany had already scored unprecedented success against the ships of the Merchant Navy, and there seemed to be little defence against the aggressive U-boats. And now with no restrictions on their attacks, things were only going to get worse for the merchant ships.

By September 1940 after a long twelve months of war, Britain stood alone. Her troops had been forced back to Dunkirk, Italy had joined the war against her and Norway had fallen to Hitler's forces giving Germany strategic bases right on the western coast of northern Europe. Finally France was defeated. Having the fourth largest navy in the world at that time, France's capitulation was a massive loss to Britain's war effort and the German occupation gave the Kriegsmarine potential bases right on the Bay of Biscay with direct access to the Atlantic. With control of France, the Kriegsmarine gained some 800 miles of Atlantic coastline, spreading from the Dover Strait right the way down to northern Spain. This meant the U-boats could now avoid the dangerous trip through the heavily mined and guarded English Channel and head straight to the Western Approaches where merchant ships poured into Britain every day. In effect, this doubled the active U-boat force by allowing each submarine to spend much longer on active patrol because they spent much less time travelling to and from port.

In the first months of the war, losses in the North Atlantic averaged some 80,000 tonnes a month, but with more operational U-boats than ever, the casualty rate had grown to losses of over 250,000 tonnes a month by the latter half of 1940; an enormous proportion of the ships that supplied Britain and three times what her crippled shipyards could manage to replace. It could not really be called a war of attrition because the attritional losses were on one side only. In the period from July to October 1940 an incredible 220 Allied vessels were sunk.

For the merchant vessels, U-boat detection technology was extremely primitive and to attack one was very imprecise because they simply could not be seen unless they were sailing on the surface. Therefore it was possible for a submerged U-boat to inflict enormous losses for proportionally little risk. In October 1940 there was a million tonnes of shipping sunk for every three U-boats that Germany had operational. Without doubt, the U-boat had become the primary weapon of the Kriegsmarine, and the destruction of the Allied Merchant Navy was their primary endeavour. In his memoirs, Admiral Dönitz later wrote that 'the most important task of the German Navy, and therefore of the German U-boat arm … was the conduct of operations against shipping on Britain's vital lines of communication across the Atlantic.'

The following is taken from an instructional handbook that was issued to the US Air Force during the war, highlighting the potential material losses created by the sinking of a merchant ship:

If a U-boat sinks two 6,000 ton ships and one 3,000 ton tanker, here is a typical list of the sort of losses we should incur: 42 tanks, 8 6-inch howitzers, 88 25-pounder guns, 40 40-mm. guns, 24 armoured patrol vehicles, 50 Bren guns or self-propelled gun mountings, 5,210 tons of munitions, 600 rifles, 428 tons of tank accessories, 2,000 tons of rations and 1,000 drums of petrol. Just think what we could have done with that lot, if the three ships had reached port safely! To inflict similar losses by air-raid the enemy would have to fly 3,000 sorties!

By the time they had direct access to the Atlantic from their French bases at ports such as Brest, La Rochelle and Lorient, the U-boats were able to attack at will, sinking merchant shipping on a daily basis with very little reprisal. It is little wonder that the men of the Kriegsmarine called this period in the autumn of 1940 'Die Gluckliche Zeit' or 'The Happy Time'. For the men of the Merchant Navy it was the beginning of the most concentrated period of loss that they would endure.

The closeness of the U-boats to St George's Channel at the south entrance to the Irish Sea meant that the Allies were now routing most of the shipping through the North Channel but still most of the attacks took place in the Western Approaches, the stretch of sea to the west of Ireland where the convoys passed through. Even in that targeted area there was a massive expanse of ocean to patrol and one of the biggest difficulties facing the U-boats was actually locating a convoy, particularly at night. To counter this problem, Admiral Dönitz initiated 'rudeltaktik', the formation of several U-boats into a single hunting unit or 'wolf pack'.

This meant several vessels, commonly between six and ten, under orders from BdU or Befehlshaber der U-boote (U-boat Headquarters) taking up positions along a likely convoy route and lying in wait for enemy ships. Then when one of the U-boats located a convoy they would report it and begin to shadow them without attacking. The other boats were then directed to the location while the initial spotter continued to track them so that they could report any changes of direction. Then when the rest of the pack was together they would strike simultaneously, often at night. The result was usually enormous damage to the convoy and it was often so sudden that the escort ships did not have a chance to react. In many cases the U-boats would manoeuvre right into the middle of a convoy before attacking so as to have a clear shot at several vessels at once, or they would position themselves behind the moonlight in the path of an incoming convoy, so that the convoy was bearing down on them. Then they could simply line themselves up and strike whenever the targets had moved within range. They usually chose to attack concealed under the cover of darkness, which also meant they could attack on the surface, thus avoiding detection by ASDIC, the early form of sonar that could only detect U-boats when underwater. It was an invention born from a combined Anglo-French scientific group who created a device that attached to the hull of a ship encased in a metal dome. It transmitted and received high-frequency sound waves sent in pulses that would ping and bounce back when they came into contact with any underwater object. The acronym ASDIC allegedly stood for 'Anti-Submarine Detection Investigation Committee', the name of the group who developed the device. In fact, no trace of such a committee has ever been found in the Admiralty archives; it was more or less a 1939 bluff by the Admiralty! The quartz piezoelectric crystals first used for underwater detection back in 1917 were referred to as ASDivite and the word supersonic was replaced with ASDics. So we are left with 'Anti Submarine Detection (or Division)' and no more.

For the Merchant Navy, the worst period of the entire war was the twelve months from June 1940 to May 1941 when they lost 806 ships; more than two a day. The majority were lost to the U-boats patrolling in the North Atlantic. Personnel losses were high because ships commonly sank in a very short time after a torpedo attack. Often a heavily laden ship with a hole blown in her side would flood incredibly quickly and begin to sink before the men on board had any chance to escape. It is estimated that 75 per cent of shipping sank within fifteen minutes of a torpedo impact but it was common for them to disappear within only two or three minutes. Any crew who were working deep below decks or were off duty and asleep at the time of an attack had very little time to get outside to a lifeboat. Those working in the engine room really had no chance. Therefore it became increasingly common for men to sleep in their clothes, even wearing a life belt so that they had every possible chance to escape in the event of an attack.

In June 1942 the Allies lost 124 ships, a total of 623,545 tonnes in a single month, the highest rate of loss in the war. Things were becoming increasingly desperate, and it was clear that to lose the Battle of the Atlantic not only meant the starvation and defeat of Britain, but also the prevention of any possible Allied invasion plans. If Hitler was to be defeated, it was vital that the ships kept getting through. Furthermore, the U-boat attacks had become far more aggressive, deadly and murderous under orders of the Führer himself. On 3 January 1942 he had ordered Admiral Dönitz, 'Merchant shipping will be sunk without warning with the intention of killing as many of the crew as possible.'

The early years of the war were the most successful for the U-boats, so they were inevitably the halcyon days of the U-boat aces, a time when the Third Reich elevated their most successful commanders to the status of national heroes. These original U-boat aces became household names throughout the Third Reich and their names are still synonymous today with the U-boat war, men like Otto Kretschmer, Wolfgang Lüth, Günther Prien, Erich Topp, Fritz-Julius Lemp and Joachim Schepke. These men became celebrities.

But the elevation of these men only made it a greater blow to the national morale when they were lost, as many inevitably were. As it turned out several of them were lost in quick succession providing a propaganda problem for Hitler's government. Günther Prien, the Bull of Scapa Flow, was lost in the North Atlantic on 7 March 1941. The loss was attributed to a depth charge attack by HMS *Wolverine*. Prien's loss was an enormous shock to the German people and to the other men of the U-boat arm. Just over a week later on 17 March 1941, during a wolf pack attack on convoy HX-112, Otto Kretschmer was taken prisoner after the destruction of his U-boat U-*99* following a depth charge attack by HMS *Walker* to the south-east of Iceland. In the same battle, Joachim Schepke was attacked by depth charges from HMS *Walker* and then rammed by HMS *Vanoc* after he was forced to surface. The vessel was totally destroyed and 38 of the crew killed, including Schepke who was on the bridge at the time of the ramming; he was reportedly severed in half by the collision. Three of the most famous and successful U-boat commanders of the war had been killed or captured in the space of ten days. Advances in Allied technology and tactics, as well as an increase in the availability of escort vessels meant the U-boats were finding that the hunt was not as easy as it was in the early days. After months of freely sinking massive quantities of shipping without reprisal, the U-boats found the enemy was fighting back.

Dönitz countered the problem of the escorts by sending his ships farther out into the Atlantic to hunt. The escort ships were only protecting the convoys in the closing stages of the voyage, joining up with them as they approached the west coast of Britain. So by sending the U-boats farther west they were able to attack undefended ships before the escorts arrived. It immediately changed the balance once more in favour of the U-boats. In early April, convoy SC-26 was attacked by several U-boats in the mid-Atlantic. The group of 22 ships which had left Halifax on 20 March en route to Liverpool came under attack over a period of three days, resulting in the loss of ten ships, with another three being damaged including the warship HMS *Worcestershire*. Only a single U-boat was lost in the battle.

Then on 9 May, another of the famed U-boat aces was lost when Kapitänleutnant Fritz-Julius Lemp was killed during the capture of U-*110*. Lemp had already gained some notoriety by torpedoing the liner *Athenia* on the very first day of the war. During an attack on a convoy, U-*110* was damaged by a depth charge attack by HMS *Aubretia*, which forced her to surface. Lemp gave the order to abandon ship but already they were under further attack by two nearby destroyers who thought they were preparing to fire the deck gun. HMS *Bulldog* and HMS *Broadway* began firing, causing further damage and casualties, only stopping when they realised the U-boat was sinking. HMS *Bulldog* moved in to capture the vessel as the crew abandoned ship but Lemp quickly realised that U-*110* was not sinking fast enough. He reportedly swam back to the submarine to destroy the code books and Enigma code machine, which he had assumed would be lost when she sank. He was not seen again, though German eyewitnesses later claimed he was shot in the water by a British sailor, presumably because he realised his intentions. HMS *Bulldog* captured the vessel and recovered the codebooks, logs and Enigma machine. This capture by the Allies helped towards the eventual breaking of the German codes by the code breakers at Bletchley Park and was one of the most significant intelligence coups of the war.

In response to the U-boats shifting farther west, the Allies decided to arrange escorts for the convoys for the entire duration of their voyages. The Canadian Navy began escorting the convoys for the western part of their trip, before meeting up with an inbound convoy and escorting them back.

Meanwhile, Allied anti-submarine tactics continued to advance, with sonar technology improving and weapons becoming more destructive and accurate. Direction-finding equipment was gradually beginning to pierce the U-boats' cloak of invisibility, and improvements in aircraft range plus the addition of Catapult Aircraft Merchantmen (CAM) ships, and increased coastal patrol aircraft made air coverage more extensive and effective. Also in the latter part of 1941 the breaking of the Enigma code meant the Allies were able to calculate and plot the location of the U-boats, and so reroute the convoys to avoid them.

Although the Allies were gradually beginning to detect and avoid the prowling U-boats, they were still not able to put up much of a defence, and with more German submarines coming into service there was still no tangible signs of an Allied victory. But before the year was out, the Japanese attacked Pearl Harbor.

The attack on 7 December 1941 brought the United States fully into the conflict, and meant that Admiral Dönitz immediately ordered his U-boats to cross the Atlantic and begin attacking shipping on the east coast of America. The operation was known as '*Paukenschlag*' or Operation *Drumbeat*. By early 1942 the Americans had also begun sailing their ships in convoy and losses quickly dropped. Once the potential for a turkey shoot faded, Dönitz redeployed his U-boats once more, withdrawing them from the east coast of the United States and returning them to the North Atlantic.

On 12 September 1942, U-*156* under command of Kapitänleutnant Werner Hartenstein torpedoed the enormous British liner *Laconia* (19,695 tonnes), in the South Atlantic between Ascension Island and Freetown, Sierra Leone, and brought about one of the most controversial – and remarkable – episodes of the entire Battle of the Atlantic. The ship was carrying 136 crew, 268 military personnel, 80 civilians, and 1,800 Italian prisoners of war guarded by 160 Polish soldiers. Upon realising there were Italians on board, who were still allies of Germany under Mussolini at that time, Hartenstein immediately began a rescue attempt and began signalling for assistance, first to BdU and then to any nearby vessels or aircraft. In a desperate attempt to make up for his mistake, he promised to cease hostilities against any vessel coming to assist regardless of nationality. At 0600 hours on 13 September 1942 Hartenstein broadcast the following uncoded message: 'If any ship will assist the ship-wrecked *Laconia* crew, I will not attack provided I am not attacked by ship or air forces. I picked up 193 men. 4, 53 South, 11, 26 West.'

U-*156* ended up with her hull literally covered in survivors, with the deck and conning tower packed with men clinging on to their only hope of survival. The U-boat had some 200 men aboard her and had helped another 200 into lifeboats while they waited for more help to arrive. Eventually on the 15th, U-*506* arrived on the scene and joined in the rescue, followed shortly after by U-*507* and the Italian submarine *Cappellini*. The U-boats began making their way towards land, towing the lifeboats behind them, now with hundreds of men in the lifeboats, and on and inside the U-boats.

Then at 1125 hours on 16 September, an American B-24 bomber flying from its base on Ascension Island arrived on the scene. The pilot spotted the U-boats and the lifeboats flying the flag of the Red Cross. He reported back to base and was instructed to attack immediately. At 1232 hours he began attacking, and the U-boats were forced to immediately cut the tow lines to the lifeboats and dive for cover leaving hundreds of men stranded in the water once again. The men who had been taken inside the U-boats were safe and soon afterwards ships arrived on the scene from Dakar and began picking up the rest of the survivors, but the incident still resulted in the loss of 1,658 lives out of the 2,741 aboard. The incident prompted a change in the way that the Kriegsmarine would deal with such situations for the rest of the war. In response Admiral Dönitz issued what became known as the 'Laconia Order':

1. All efforts to save survivors of sunken ships, such as the fishing out of swimming men and putting them on board lifeboats, the righting of overturned lifeboats, or the handing over of food and water, must stop. Rescue contradicts the most basic demands of the war: the destruction of hostile ships and their crews.

2. The orders concerning the bringing-in of skippers and chief engineers stay in effect.

3. Survivors are to be saved only if their statements are important for the boat.

4. Stay firm. Remember that the enemy has no regard for women and children when bombing German cities!

This order became one of the mainstays of the case against Dönitz at the Nuremberg trials. The issuing of the Laconia Order along with the equally controversial 'War Order No.154' – issued at the end of 1939 and ordering the use of unrestricted submarine warfare, where U-boats would sink merchant ships without warning and without stopping to rescue survivors – were the two points that resulted in Dönitz being found guilty of causing Germany to be in breach of the Second London Naval Treaty of 1936. At his trial, Dönitz was accused of being a war criminal on three counts and was found guilty on two of those counts resulting in a ten-year prison sentence, which he served in Spandau Prison, Berlin, finally being released on 1 October 1956.

Operation *Torch*, the Allied invasion of North Africa in November 1942, resulted in a significant increase in shipping as men and equipment were moved in to support the invasion, and this created a newly stocked hunting ground for the U-boats who saw another increase in successes, mostly owing to the fact there were simply more targets in the vicinity.

Although the U-boats were continuing to have enormous successes against them, the Allies were increasingly getting a grip on the situation. In October 1940 there had only been three U-boats lost for every million tonnes of Allied shipping sunk – by November 1942 they were losing seventeen U-boats for that same tonnage. There had been a distinct boost in the Allies' ability to fight back.

By early 1943, there was no doubt that the U-boats were up against a much more prepared and aggressive enemy, and there were disturbing reports coming into U-boat command from the returning commanders. They were beginning to find that they were falling victim to sudden air attacks, even when hidden at periscope depth, when previously they had been concealed below the waves. Even in darkness or in heavy fog, conditions that had previously been ideal for a hunting U-boat, the enemy aircraft seemed to be locating them with uncanny precision. Furthermore, the U-boats were finding that when they had located a convoy and had begun shadowing it until ready to attack, the escorting destroyers and corvettes were quickly detecting their position and they were having to break off almost immediately and dive for safety before a barrage of depth charges came down upon them. It was as though the Allied escorts could literally see them through the waves, and so they were no safer submerged than they were on the surface. The U-boat's most precious ability was the ability to hide, to prowl unseen and escape without trace; now it looked like that gift might have gone. It even became more difficult for the U-boats to locate the convoys and it began to seem as though the convoys were detecting them at a distance and adjusting their course to keep clear of them. Neither the U-boats nor Admiral Dönitz at U-boat Command could understand what had led to this loss of their invisibility. The truth was that several different factors were working against them.

By January 1943 Dönitz had some 400 U-boats under his command, seven times what he had at the start of the war, but this was no longer enough to ensure victory because of the dramatic technological improvements in submarine detection, defence and attack. By the beginning of 1943 it took 55 U-boats to achieve the success rate achieved by only 18 vessels in late 1940. And things were to get even worse for the German Navy that year. For the U-boat men, the fifth month of 1943 would be known as 'Black May'.

On 21 April 1943, Convoy ONS-5 departed Liverpool for Halifax, a group of 42 ships in twelve columns. Ahead of the group in the North Atlantic lay a record number of U-boats, as many as 36 spread over two patrol lines in the air gap below Greenland, an expanse of sea that lay outside the operational range of reconnaissance aircraft and so was safe from aerial attack. The Atlantic air gap became a major factor in the Battle of the Atlantic, 1,700 miles of ocean that was beyond the range of the aerial escorts on either side of the ocean. A considerable amount of time and resources was put into the development of long-range aircraft and other measures to bridge the gap. As ONS-5 headed west across the ocean there began an immense confrontation between the convoy and the U-boats that turned into a game of cat and mouse over several days and losses for both sides. By the time the convoy eventually reached Halifax on 12 May, it had lost thirteen ships but significantly it had destroyed six enemy U-boats and caused damage to seven others, figures higher than anything seen before in the Battle of the Atlantic. The U-boats suffered further heavy losses over the next few weeks and as the casualty list grew, things turned for the first time against the men of the U-boat arm. For this reason this period of the war is often quoted as the turning point in the Battle of the Atlantic; the first time since September 1939 that it seemed the U-boats were at a disadvantage. In the month of May 1943, the U-boat arm of the Kriegsmarine lost 41 boats, in most cases with all hands. A total of 1,785 crew were lost with only 183 survivors. Five U-boats were lost on the same day. The loss reports coming in to BdU and to Admiral Dönitz were unprecedented. They included U-954, lost off the coast of Greenland on 19 May following a depth charge attack from two British vessels. Dönitz's youngest son Peter was serving on this ship as a watch officer and died when it went down with all hands. His other son Klaus was also killed almost a year later, also at sea. Dönitz acknowledged on 24 May 1943 that 'Our losses…have reached an intolerable level.'

One of the U-boats attacked during 'Black May' was U-230 under Kapitän-Leutnant Paul Siegmann. On 12 May 1943 the U-boat was detected as it was attempting to intercept and attack convoy HX-237. They were pursued by the convoy escorts and were forced to dive to the seabed where they were subjected to an intense ten-hour attack from the ships up above. An officer on U-*230*, Herbert Werner, who wrote the book *Iron Coffins* about his experiences, gave an account of the incident; one suffered by many thousands of submariners and one that few survived to describe.

> We sat helpless 265 metres below. Our nerves trembled. Our bodies were stiff from cold, stress and fear. The mind-searing agony of waiting made us lose any sense of time and any desire for food. The bilges were flooded with water, oil and urine. Our washrooms were under lock and key; to use them would have meant instant death, for the tremendous outside pressure would have overwhelmed the outflow.

Dönitz's Allied counterpart Admiral Sir Max Horton, Commander-In-Chief of the Western Approaches, had also realised that the U-boat losses were reaching 'an intolerable level'. He wrote at the end of May 1943: 'The heavy casualties inflicted on the enemy have greatly affected his morale and will prove to be a turning point in the Battle of the Atlantic.'

In addition to the massive casualties being inflicted on the U-boats, in July 1943, for the first time in the entire conflict, the number of new Allied ships being built exceeded the number being lost. This was largely due to the American-built 'Liberty' ships, cargo vessels built in enormous numbers to an originally British design that had been amended to make them faster and cheaper to manufacture. By the end of the war 2,751 Liberty vessels had been produced and supplied to Britain under the Lend-Lease Act of 1941. This act was passed in March 1941 before the United States entered the war, and gave the President the right to sell, lease or lend other nations materials that were vital to their defence. It allowed them to remain outside the conflict and yet assist where they saw fit.

Now with so much working against them, Dönitz pulled his U-boats out of the North Atlantic and redeployed them to areas where successes were easier and had considerably less risk. In his memoirs Dönitz would admit that by this date, 'We had lost the Battle of the Atlantic.' The U-boats then began operating in the central Atlantic and the Indian Ocean but although there was much less danger to the submarines, there were far fewer vessels available to sink and so it was impossible for them to make any tangible impact on the Allied war effort.

In the North Atlantic, the difference in casualties between 1942 and 1943 is quite startling. In 1942 merchant losses were at a peak of 1,006 ships – in 1943 this had dropped to 285. By contrast the U-boat losses increased from 35 in 1942 to 150 in 1943. U-boat Command was left reeling in May 1943 as day by day U-boats were losing contact and simply disappearing. In that single month they lost almost as many U-boats as the entire previous year.

Year	Merchant Losses	U-boat Losses
1939	47	6
1940	375	18
1941	496	19
1942	1006	35
1943	285	150
1944	31	111
1945	19	54 *

*This figure indicates losses through enemy action only

In the summer of 1943 the Allies began a campaign to destroy the U-boats as they made their way to or from their ports on the Bay of Biscay. It was a long and often futile 'search and destroy' operation as bomber crews endlessly scanned the sea for a glimpse of a periscope or a trace of bow waves. However, it did bring some success and resulted in 218 U-boats being attacked, with 27 confirmed as destroyed and a further 31 damaged.

It was clear that the U-boats were now fighting a losing battle and that unless some new technology arrived to circumvent the Allies' radar capabilities or defeat their aircraft, they could not possibly maintain their struggle. But new developments *were* underway. The Germans had been continuously working on the improvement of both their vessels and weapons since before the war. There were two new U-boat designs that, if they entered the action, could drastically alter the balance once more in the Battle of the Atlantic.

The *Elektroboot* series designed by Hellmuth Walter was conceived to operate fully submerged without the need to surface. This could potentially nullify the air threat. The first of these electric boats was the Type XXI followed by the short range Type XXIII that only went into production in 1944. They were impressive ships, able to travel faster submerged than the Type VII could travel on the surface, meaning they could outrun most of the vessels likely to be hunting them. Their weapons systems were upgraded meaning reloading was much faster and more efficient; their torpedo tubes could be reloaded in around a quarter of the time it took to reload the tubes in a Type VII. So the technology already existed and it was only a question of whether the older submarines could keep the fight going long enough for the new models to make it into production. Dönitz knew that to carry on the fight against a superior enemy could mean horrendous losses for the U-boat service but he believed he had to maintain attacks until the new ships were ready.

Torpedo technology also developed significantly in the war years. In the beginning, they were unreliable weapons, air-driven with an erratic magnetic firing mechanism that was prone to failure. Often they would fail at the point of firing, or would launch but simply never reach the target. In other cases, the firing trajectory would be right, the calculations correct, they would strike the target but the explosive warhead would fail to detonate. Admiral Dönitz once said of them: 'I do not believe that ever in the history of war have men been sent against the enemy with such a useless weapon.'

As the technology advanced, the air-driven torpedoes were replaced with electric motor-driven versions, armed with contact detonators to set off the warhead. They became more reliable and more deadly, and a range of different torpedo types was developed for use against Allied merchant ships. The LUT torpedo could be launched with a pre-programmed course set to make it criss-cross a convoy path so that if it missed it would double back and keep going until either it hit a target or ran out of power and sank. The GNAT torpedo, named the Zaunkönig T5, was another new development. The British acronym GNAT stood for German Navy Acoustic Torpedo. The torpedo contained two hydrophones that would home in on the propeller sound of a target and guide itself towards it. Because it was only sensitive to targets moving between 12 and 19 knots, it was particularly dangerous for convoy escort ships, which tended to move in that range. In the first operational use of the T5 torpedo, during attacks on convoys ON-202 and ONS-18 in September 1943, the Allies lost six merchant ships and three of the escorts.

In January 1944 after continued high losses amongst the U-boat arm, Dönitz gave up on the *rudeltaktik* wolf pack tactics and returned to sending the boats out on independent patrols. It was clear to him that they stood no chance of winning the Battle of the Atlantic; he had too few boats and the Allies had grown much stronger with the increased number of ships and the significant developments in anti-submarine technology. All that was left for the German submariners was to fight on in defiance, in the vain hope that the new U-boats would be ready in time and that they could take back the advantage.

The first Type XXI U-boat was not launched until 12 May 1944 when U-*2501* went into the sea in Hamburg. With her launch there was once again a glimmer of hope for the U-boat crews. But it would take time to get production up so that the new boats could be delivered in significant numbers and another technological development was introduced to try and improve things temporarily. It was called the *schnorkel* or snorkel, and it began to be retro-fitted to some old Type VII and Type IX U-boats from mid-1944 onwards as well as to all newly built ships. In terms of wartime U-boat developments it was to become one of the most significant as for a while it gave the U-boats back their invisibility. The snorkel was, simply put, an exhaust pipe that lay along the top of the U-boat hull and was connected to her engines below. When the U-boat submerged the tube could be raised so that it was out of the water and so allowed the diesel engines to operate underwater by allowing them to take in and expel air. Normally U-boats had to run on their electric motors when underwater and had to regularly surface to charge them using the engines. The snorkel meant that they could use their engine all the time and reduced the need to surface, which made detection by the enemy much less likely; a ship could stay out of sight throughout an entire patrol. In the last year of the war, the snorkel-fitted U-boats managed to carry out around 400 successful attacks, in which over 200 merchant ships and convoy vessels were sunk. When summarising U-boat operations in September 1944 the BdU recorded in the war diary:

> The effect of the schnorchel was certainly decisive, and operation in the Channel without it would have been quite out of the question. Only a few months ago it would have seemed impossible that a boat could operate for 42 days without breaking surface once. Only by means of the schnorchel was it possible to operate close to the English coast again and to bridge the intervening gap between the operation of the new and old types of boats.

But despite a flurry of success, the snorkel was not enough for the U-boats to truly regain their advantage in the Battle of the Atlantic; the new boat designs would simply arrive too late to have any significant impact and the snorkel itself was not without operational problems. Although it could provide a tremendous advantage to a U-boat by allowing it to remain invisible to patrolling aircraft, the snorkel could also cause devastating problems for a submarine. To operate the device successfully it was vital that the submerged ship was sailing at the correct depth and maintained this depth throughout. If the U-boat was positioned too high in the water, then the snorkel stuck out too far and could easily be spotted by an enemy ship or more likely, by air patrols. If the U-boat was running too deep, there was the chance that the head of the snorkel would dip beneath the water, causing the head valve to shut off. This instantly cut the air supply to the engines and as a result they began sucking in the air inside the ship. The result was a vacuum that caused pain in the ears of the crew and was capable of bursting eardrums.

The snorkel had the additional disadvantage of cutting the running speed of the U-boat to just six knots with the snorkel extended; any faster and it was likely to be torn off. Also, the U-boat became more or less 'deaf' with the diesel engines running underwater compared to the relative silence of the electric motors. Though it was harder to detect, the U-boat was a much slower and noisier machine with the snorkel in operation.

Following the Normandy Landings in June 1944, Germany lost her bases on the Bay of Biscay and her U-boats were pushed back and forced to operate from the remaining occupied territories such as Norway. Dönitz began an inshore campaign, sending his snorkel-fitted ships to the coastal waters of the United States and back to the North Channel into Britain in a last attempt to sink as much shipping as possible. Even the English Channel was no longer a very feasible hunting ground by the late summer of 1944 because it was no longer within easy range of the submarines forced to operate from the occupied territories. BdU acknowledged in September 1944:

> Operation of type VIIC in the Channel will as a rule no longer be possible, as the outward and return passages alone last 7–9 weeks, and by that time as far as one can see the boats would no longer be in a condition to operate in such a difficult area. For these therefore, there only remain the coastal waters around England such as the Moray Firth, Minch, and North Channel, as well as waters off Reykjavik.

The extra distance that they had to travel from Norway and around the coast of Britain before they reached their area of operations meant that the U-boats could spend much less time on patrol before they had to return to port for fuel and supplies. In August 1942 it was estimated that a U-boat would spend on average 60 days at sea in each 100-day period, and that 40 of those days would be spent in the area of operations. But by December 1944 they were only spending 37 days at sea in each 100-day period and of these only 9 were spent in the area of operations.

Despite the increasing difficulties faced by the U-boat crews they still managed to keep up the fight and successes did come, even in the limited coastal waters. But they would never reach the levels of the early war years and they came at a terrible cost. Ultimately 783 U-boats were lost during the war and around three-quarters of the men in them.

On 25 August the Allies finally liberated Paris. Their forces had already regained control in the Mediterranean and Africa, and the Germans were steadily being beaten back towards Berlin. The situation had improved for the Allies right across the world and it was widely believed that the end of the war had crawled into view. But as convoy HX-305 moved into the Western Approaches towards the end of their journey across the Atlantic, the U-boat war was still far from over. There were still many battles to be fought before absolute victory and for the men of the Merchant Navy the danger was still present. The U-boats had been weakened, but their resolve was strong and the threat they represented could never be ignored, even as the war was drawing to a close. It was a lesson that convoy HX-305 was soon to learn.

Type XXI 'electrc boat'; the double hull gave it almost three times the space for batteries of the conventional U-boat and she was designed to replace the Type VIIC. Insufficient numbers were delivered to alter the final outcome of the Battle of the Atlantic.

II

THE ALLIED CONVOY SYSTEM

Our object must be to locate the convoys and destroy them by means of a concentrated attack … the finding of a convoy on the high seas is a difficult task. Our operations therefore must be concentrated against those areas in which the enemy sea lines of communication converge and join – namely, off south-west England and in the vicinity of Gibraltar.

Admiral Dönitz War Diary entry, 1 October 1939

The Battle of the Atlantic was the longest fought campaign of the Second World War, lasting from the first few days of the conflict right up to the Nazi capitulation in May 1945. Following the lessons learned during the First World War, and realising from the very beginning the threat to her shipping from enemy U-boats, the British government initiated a convoy system for the protection of her merchant ships. Although it was to be without question a safer method of sailing, many of the merchant captains did not welcome the convoys, as it went against the way they were used to operating. A merchant seaman was used to sailing alone, and resented being hemmed in by other vessels invading his sea space. They did not like the loss of their independence, the regulation of their ship and their route. Their speed was to be set by some other authority, their cargo decided, their course set, and though it proved effective and advantageous, the convoy system was disliked by the majority of the captains.

Following the occupation of France, Germany now had U-boat bases along the French coast, bringing them much closer to the Atlantic convoys and saving them a week's travel per trip as the U-boats no longer had to sail all the way around from northern Germany.

Of course with the U-boats now based so close to the southern entrance to the Irish Sea, it became far too dangerous for the merchant ships to enter Britain by that route. The Allies began redirecting all their convoys through the North Channel, the narrow stretch of water that separates Ireland and Scotland. Armed escort ships began to accompany the convoys more and more, stretching farther westward to lend support to shipping as it moved in through the Western Approaches. It was not until after the D-Day invasion four years later and the subsequent liberation of France that it became safer once more for ships to use the southern approach through St George's Channel. With their French bases lost, the German U-boats had to transfer back to their own bases or those in their other occupied territories. Therefore by August 1944 most shipping was once again coming into Britain by the southern approaches, west of Land's End.

In April 1941 Prime Minister Winston Churchill said, 'In order to win this war Hitler must either conquer this island by invasion or he must cut the ocean lifeline which joins us to the United States.' Without the resources for an invasion, and with his Luftwaffe beaten back by the RAF pilots during the Battle of Britain, Hitler was left with only one of those options – cut the supply lines, starve the country. It became clear that the U-boat was the only tool Germany had that could achieve the defeat of Britain. It was to prove a tool that cut deep.

And so as the war got underway, and the U-boats began their deadly assault on the British merchant ships, it was imperative that the Allies take swift and effective action. Following its success during the First World War, the convoy system was the clear solution, and was put into operation right from the outset.

The convoys were given a code made up of letters that denoted where the shipping was travelling to or from, followed by a number particular to that trip. For example the *Empire Heritage* was travelling in convoy HX-305 so it is identified as travelling from Halifax, Nova Scotia (and later New York) to Britain. Incidentally, though both Halifax and New York were the western terminals for the HX convoys, New York handled around 80 per cent of the traffic. The numbering merely tells us that it was part of the 305th such convoy on that route. There were over 200 different convoy routes used during the course of the war, all with their own unique prefix. Some other coding examples of more prolific routes are PQ, which signified an Iceland to northern Russia route, ON standing for Outbound North meaning a convoy leaving for North America from Liverpool, and SC or Sydney, Nova Scotia to Britain. Some routes ran regularly throughout the war whilst others were only used for a brief spell or sporadically when the need arose. Then as the war developed and the occupation of different territories changes, the convoys evolved, like the FXP convoy, which only ran from June to October 1944 ferrying invasion forces across the English Channel.

The convoys could be made up of a very diverse selection of vessels, meaning all shapes, sizes and potential speeds, and to stay together they had to maintain a collective course and speed. On the HX convoys the speed was initially set at nine knots though this increased to ten knots in mid-1941. The favoured formation for a convoy was a broad one where possible, meaning that a small group of eight ships, for example, would sail in a 'row' rather than in four 'columns' of two. Early in the war the average convoy was around 35 ships, usually formed into between six and nine columns of around five ships each. In open sea they were usually formed into a rectangular pattern, with the various cargoes distributed carefully throughout; ships carrying raw materials would normally be positioned around the outside of the group, with the escort ships such as destroyers or corvettes outside them. More explosive or dangerous cargoes such as ammunition or fuel oil would be deployed inside the body of the convoy, along with troop transports or passenger vessels.

Overall control of the convoy itself rested with the convoy commodore who usually sailed in the middle column of the convoy. He was a civilian, usually a retired naval officer or a merchant captain nominated from the Royal Naval Volunteer Reserve. There would also be a nominated vice-commodore, usually the master of one of the ships in the convoy. However there was also the senior officer of the escort who was responsible for the safety of the convoy and so could insist on certain procedures if he felt it was necessary. Beyond that, control of the entire group, including the escorts lay, with Western Approaches Headquarters in Liverpool who took command of all convoys once they were east of a certain point in the North Atlantic.

The HX convoy route was actually the longest continuous series of the war, as ships made the crucial Atlantic crossing throughout the conflict. HX-1 sailed from Halifax, Nova Scotia on 16 September 1939 just two weeks into the war, and the last, HX-358, set sail on 23 May 1945, nearly two weeks after the German surrender. They remained in a numerical order until HX-229, which was split into convoy HX-229 and HX-229a, to try and clear some of the congestion in New York harbour, leaving there on 8 and 9 March 1943 respectively. HX-229 was subjected to a horrific U-boat assault that saw thirteen ships lost and others damaged – the worst losses of any HX convoy during the course of the conflict.

There were also some variations on the HX convoys such as the HXF groups, the F standing for 'fast'; these convoys were specifically for quicker ships. The varying speed parameters became important from April 1944 when many of the escort vessels had transferred away from the convoys in preparation for supporting Operation *Overlord*, the Allied invasion of Europe. The convoys would be suffixed F, M or S depending on their fast, medium or slow speed. There were also some BHX convoys where a feeder convoy sailing from Bermuda joined the main convoy as it left Halifax. In total there were 377 HX convoys, made up of 17,744 ships. Incredibly, of these convoys only around 38 suffered a direct enemy attack proving the relative effectiveness of the convoy system. In total there were 110 merchant ships lost from the entire HX convoy system throughout the war, 96 of these from U-boat attack. This total only includes those lost whilst in convoy. In addition there were 60 stragglers lost who were sailing alone plus 36 sunk either prior to the escort arriving or after scattering.

In mid-1944 the average HX convoy size increased to between 60 and 100 ships, mainly because so many of the escort vessels were relocated for the Allied invasion of Europe. With fewer escorts some of the convoy routes were suspended, such as the ONS (Outward North Slow) and the SC (Sydney, Cape Breton) and merged with the ON and HX convoys respectively. This increase made for some exceptionally large movements of ships and when convoy HX-300 departed New York for Liverpool on 17 July 1944 it contained an incredible 167 ships in 19 columns, including 14 columns of 9 and 3 of 10; it was the largest convoy of ships ever assembled post-sail.

HX-305 left New York on 25 August 1944 made up of 98 vessels of which two were lost in the attack by U-482. In fact they were the only two ships lost from an HX convoy for the whole of that year. Obviously other convoys were crossing the globe in all directions, facing the same threat of attack, and many of them took a much higher proportion of losses.

Year	Number of HX convoys	Ships lost in convoy
1939	22	1
1940	91	48
1941	70	21
1942	54	8
1943	53	27
1944	55	2
1945	32	3

Below is a selection of some of the major convoy routes than ran during the Second World War. There were many more than this used; some covered only small coastal routes, some were temporary convoys to supply the changing theatres of war, and some ran throughout the conflict. In some cases the speed and type of a ship would determine which convoy it sailed in because some were designed specifically for a certain type of ship such as tankers, merchant ships or military transports.

Convoy Code	Route	Notes
AS	USA – Suez	Military transports
AT	New York – UK	Military transports
CT	UK – Canada and USA	
CU	Caribbean – UK	Tankers
ET	Africa – Gibraltar	
EXP	UK – France	Invasion convoy June – October 1944
FN	Southend – Scotland	
FS	Scotland – Southend	
FXP	France – UK	Invasion convoy June – October 1944
GAT	Guantanamo – Trinidad	
GUS	Port Said – USA (Slow)	
HG	Gibraltar – UK	
HX	Halifax – UK	Ran throughout the war
JW	Loch Ewe – Russia	Replaced PQ convoys late 1942
KJ	Kingston – UK	
KMF	UK – Mediterranean (fast)	Mainly military
KMS	UK – Mediterranean (slow)	Mainly military
MKF	Mediterranean – UK (fast)	
NA	North America – UK	Military transports
OB	UK – North America	
OG	UK – Gibraltar	
ON	UK – North America	Replaced OB convoys in 1941
OS	Outward Southbound	
PQ	Iceland – Russia	Replaced by JW late 1942
QP	Russia – Iceland	
RA	Russia – Iceland (later UK)	
RS	Gibraltar – Freetown	
RU	Reykjavik – Loch Ewe	
SC	Halifax – UK	Slower merchant ships
SG	Sydney (NS) – Greenland	
SH	Sydney (NS) – Halifax	
SL	Sierra Leone – UK	
SR	Sierra Leone – Gibraltar	
TM	Trinidad – Mediterranean	Tankers
TO	North Africa – Caribbean	Fast Tankers
UC	UK – America/Caribbean	
UGS	USA – Gibraltar (later Port Said)	
UR	Loch Ewe – Reykjavik	
US	Australia – Suez	
WS	UK – Suez and Bombay	
XK	Gibraltar – UK	

Empire Heritage with boilers firing (above) and tied up between trips (below). In the above view her lifeboats are clearly visible. She sank so quickly they were never lowered.

III

EMPIRE HERITAGE – THE MERCHANT SHIP

The Merchant Navy, with Allied comrades, night and day, in weather fair or foul, faces not only the ordinary perils on the sea, but the sudden assaults of war from beneath the waters or from the sky.

Winston Churchill, July 1941

Empire Heritage began life as the *Tafelberg*, an enormous 13,640-ton steam ship built by Armstrong, Whitworth and Co, in Newcastle-upon-Tyne. It was begun in 1929 for the Kerguelen Sealing and Whaling Co. Ltd, a subsidiary of Irwin and Johnson based in South Africa. She was fitted out especially for Antarctic whaling with a strengthened hull for working in ice and massive tanks for transporting whale oil to Europe. She was the first twin-screw whaling factory steamer and at her launch was the largest factory ship in the world and the largest ship to have ever sailed under the South African flag. She was launched on 29 April 1930. In his book *A Whaling Enterprise – Salvesen in the Antarctic*, Gerald Elliot wrote of these ships:

> The great expansion of the late twenties brought in an entirely new type of floating factory. Specially designed and built for their purpose, they were bigger than the converted liners and broader in the beam. They had their machine rooms aft, with the stern slip going up between the twin funnels, and the bridge and crew accommodation placed well forward at the bow, leaving a large midships section for the whaling 'plan' deck where the whales were cut up, and a spacious factory

area below it for the processing machinery. Below that again was large tank storage for fuel oil and whale oil.

Following the outbreak of war in September 1939 *Tafelberg* ('Table Mountain' in South Africa) headed south to the Antarctic for the 1939/40 season. Whaling factory ships were particularly valuable to the war effort as they were built to carry enormous quantities of whale oil and so were put into service as fuel oil tankers. Also, once their large factory decks were cleared of their machinery and whaling equipment they could be filled with tanks, trucks and even aircraft. They had plentiful crew accommodation and so were ideal for transporting passengers between ports. They were usually very heavily laden and their size and shape also made them prominent targets. They had extra decks that raised their profile high above the surface; their working decks were some 14 feet above the waterline, and so they were probably the most conspicuous ships in a convoy. Also they were often positioned on the flanks of a convoy and so lacked the relative safety of the ships inside the group. It is no coincidence that by the end of the war some 27 floating factory ships had been sunk and most were amongst the very largest vessels to be lost in the war.

Lieutenant–Commander John Chrisp spent the 1953/54 whaling season aboard the Christian Salvesen factory ship *Southern Venturer* as a whaling inspector and experienced first-hand the life and work of the whaling industry. He returned for the 1954/55 season and during this time he wrote his book *South of Cape Horn*. He describes his first sight of a whaling factory ship:

> She was like no other ship I had ever seen; and in 25 years in the Navy I had come across some pretty peculiar vessels … Her two funnels were not placed centrally but far aft, and were not in line but one beside the other. Her stern was cut away, and a gaping tunnel, big enough to house a couple of trains, ran from the water-line deep into her innards. Her bows were blunt, her freeboard was high, her draught was shallow. Derricks and winches, cranes and stanchions, masts and aerials sprouted in confusion from every unlikely inch of her decks. She offended every concept of grace; she violated every law of naval architecture.

R.B. Robertson, a medical doctor who spent the 1949/50 season on a factory ship, made similar observations in his book *Of Whales and Men*.

> For seamen who have not seen a factory ship, I would describe her thus: Imagine two large oil tankers stuck together beam to beam, so that their funnels are abeam, and not fore and aft. Place the two in an immense blunt-bowed hull, with a wide, shallow draft and a freeboard of prodigious height. Then cut off the stern of this

Siamese ship, carve a great obscene-looking hole where the sternpost was, and run a tunnel that could accommodate two railway trains from the waterline between the two screws at a gently sloping angle up to the main deck, just forward of the funnels…In her superstructure, a factory ship is divided in two – the reason being that two vast areas of deck space, each capable of accommodating two or more ninety-foot whale carcasses, must be left clear in the middle of the ship; below this clear space is the factory, a maze of machinery, occupying three decks and a floor space measurable in acres; and below that again are the tanks, capable of accommodating twenty thousand tons or more of oil, and reaching down to the bilges. The engines that drive the ship are abaft the factory space; and the bridge, stores, offices, and administrative part of the ship are forward of the factory space.

These ships were designed so that a whale could be pulled up the stern ramp using an enormous claw made of 2 tonnes of cast steel, and pulled along the massive deck of the ship with powerful winches and lines of thick steel cable that lay across the deck and hung from the winches above. It was this very same deck space that was so valuable for carrying cargo during the war years. The blubber was then removed and dropped down holes in the deck to the boilers below. This was boiled up to extract the valuable whale oil then stored in huge tanks below deck. In the war these same tanks could be put to use for the transporting of massive quantities of fuel oil. The whale was pulled along to the next set of cranes around the centre of the ship; known among the whalers as 'Hell's Gate', an apt name for the place where much of the goriest work took place. There is no need to describe the many procedures involved in the processing of a whale, but the factory ship dealt with them all quickly and efficiently, and all without having to tow the whales to shore.

The Tyne and Wear Archives have a contemporary brochure for Armstrong, Whitworth & Co. that shows a photograph of *Tafelberg* along with the ship profile and deck plan, and a breakdown of technical information. It lists her principal features as:

A factory deck fitted with 34 Meat and Bone Digesters, 18 Blubber Digesters, 4 sets Hartmann Apparatus; 4 bone saws on upper deck, 2 40-ton Winches for hauling whales up slipway. Blubber Cutters. Separate rooms on upper deck for refining oil. Workshops. W.T. Installation. Oil cargo capacity, 651,104 cubic feet.

At that time she was equipped with eight lifeboats, each designed to accommodate 55 people. She was modern and well-equipped, and a major asset for the Kerguelen Sealing and Whaling Company Ltd.

When *Tafelberg* left the Bristol Channel on 28 October 1939 to begin the whaling season, the convoy system was already in place, and she headed for South Georgia via Aruba as part of convoy OB-26. Then, after the season ended in the spring of 1940, she returned to Britain via the US, leaving as part of convoy HX-60 on 23 July 1940. She was listed with a cargo of fuel oil destined for the Clyde.

On 28 January 1941 she was sailing through the Bristol Channel, near to Barry in South Wales, when she struck a mine that was floating in the water, causing significant damage to her hull. She eventually became beached to the west of Cold Knap Point and stuck there. After several weeks she was refloated and towed around the coast to Whitmore Bay where she was grounded so that temporary repairs could be carried out, but she became stuck on a sand bar and was further damaged, with her back finally being broken in the process. She was eventually torn fully in two as weather ravaged the damaged wreck, and reportedly became a favoured playground of local children for many months. It was some considerable time before she could be patched up, the work being determined by the state of the weather. Often the welders were forced to work up to their waists in water as they struggled to seal up the damaged ship. Eventually watertight bulkheads were fitted over the open hull ends, and the two halves were towed separately around to Cardiff for proper dry-dock repair. The first half went on 25 July, the second half two weeks later on 12 August. She was eventually rejoined and made seaworthy once more, but she returned to service as a different ship, re-launched as the steam tanker *Empire Heritage*.

The 'Empire' prefix that the newly rebuilt ship received was given to vessels during the Second World War that had been built or requisitioned for the Ministry of Shipping, later the Ministry of War Transport, specifically for war service. Over the course of the war, over 1300 vessels of all shapes and sizes sailed with the Empire prefix, including tankers, cargo ships, coasters, colliers, tugs, tramp steamers, landing craft, in fact almost every conceivable type of craft. Of those serving, 196 were lost over the course of the conflict, the last being *Empire Gold*, an 8,028-ton steam tanker, lost on the morning of 18 April 1945 after being torpedoed by U-*1107*. She was sailing in convoy HX-348 with a final destination of Antwerp, when she was hit twice along with another ship, the *Cyrus H. McCormick*, around 70 miles west of Brest. Of the 47 men aboard, only four survived. For her attackers, this was their first and last taste of success. Twelve days later, on 30 April, U-*1107* was lost close to the port of Brest after a bombing run from an American Catalina aircraft.

The Empire ships provided a much-needed boost to the tonnage required to keep the war effort going, but they were not enough and outside assistance was required to bridge the growing gap between ship losses and production output. The

US began production of Liberty ships, as previously mentioned, cargo vessels built to British specifications but turned into a mass-producible design by the US shipyards that began turning them out in incredible numbers. They were built under the lend-lease agreement between the US and Britain, where ownership remained with the US Navy. It is estimated that 2,751 ships were turned out of eighteen shipyards between 1941 and 1945. They were welded together instead of riveted and were assembled from prefabricated parts in a production line type operation that meant they were constructed at an amazing speed; the average ship took just 42 days from start to finish. Initially they were mostly named after famous Americans but it later became common for names to be put forward by any public groups who raised more than $2 million in war bonds. They became the major American shipping output of the war. Around a million tonnes of cargo shipping was produced in the US in 1941 but this had risen to around eight million in 1942. A target of sixteen million was set for 1943 but in actual fact somewhere closer to nineteen million was produced. This enormous amount of new shipping was largely crewed by the many 'distressed' seamen who had lost their previous vessels. As losses increased at sea, so did the casualty rate but there were still huge numbers of men rescued and landed back in port that were then without a ship. This meant that by 1943 there was an estimated surplus of 10,000 fully trained seamen, just waiting for a ship to join. The convoy ships were often home to seamen hitching a lift to join a new vessel.

Before the Lend-Lease agreement and the Liberty ships, there were the Ocean ships, a predecessor to the Liberty operation, also ordered by the British Government and constructed in shipyards on the east and west coasts of America. They were again built to a British design, and used the same welding techniques that would be used on the Liberty ships. They were 441 feet long, 7.174 gross tonnes, with a speed of 11 knots. There were a total of 60 such ships delivered between October 1941 and November 1942, all named with the prefix 'Ocean'. Seventeen of them were lost in action.

Likewise Canada made an enormous naval contribution from her shipyards, providing what would be known as the Fort and Park ships, the former used as a prefix and the latter as a suffix. Unlike the American-built vessels, they were riveted in the more traditional manner. The Fort ships were coal powered and the Park ships were oil burners. They were built to the same specifications as the Liberty ships and achieved a similar speed of eleven knots. These shipbuilding programmes, along with the Empire ships, created a supply of new vessels that could fill the gaps in the supply line, sustain and increase the flow of much needed food and supplies into Britain, and ultimately transport the men and equipment required for the invasion of Europe. It was these ships that destroyed Dönitz's dream of Britain's capitulation in the face of starvation.

After her conversion to an Empire ship, the *Empire Heritage* was 512 feet long (156 metres) and was a massive 15,702 tonnes having gained more than 2,000 extra tons in weight. Also in preparation for her war service she was armed with six 20mm Oerlikon cannons, a 12-pounder gun and 4 p.a.c rockets.

After her requisition by the War Ministry she had been placed under the control of the Christian Salvesen Company of Leith whose own ships had all been requisitioned around the same time. She returned to service in February 1943 under the command of James Campbell Jamieson, a senior master of Salvesen from Sandness in the Shetland Islands. He had begun the war as master of the *Salvestria*, another of Salvesen's floating factory ships that became the first of the company's losses during the war. Jamieson was only the second British man to be appointed manager of a floating factory ship; generally they had been managed by Norwegians. He was given the position after helping Salvesen get one of their ships, the *Saluta*, out of Tonsberg harbour where she was blockaded during a Norwegian union strike in 1936. It was his success in getting the ship away from the port that led to his promotion to 1st Officer and then manager of the *Salvestria*. On 27 July 1940 she activated an acoustic mine near Rosyth and sank, the first casualty of what would be a series of losses for the company. Jamieson went on to command the *Southern Princess*, another Salvesen ship before taking command of *Empire Heritage,* his last ship.

On 8 June 1944, Captain Jamieson was awarded the OBE for Meritorious service at sea in the King's Birthday honours list. He was given his medal at St James's Palace and the award was published in the *London Gazette* (no. 36547) two days later.

During the war Salvesen lost many of their ships and a great many of their finest officers and seamen; 418 of their men were lost at sea, and over 100 of these were lost as passengers on other ships – men who had already lost their ship and were being transported home in order to join another one. Twenty-three of Salvesen's men received decorations for gallantry or meritorious service and another 13 were given commendations. Out of the 26 Salvesen-owned ships that were taken for war service, 16 of them were lost, including all six of their factory ships. Many more were lost or damaged out of the ships that the company managed, and those that survived were left in a terrible state of repair after the ravages of war. Of their 63 whale-catchers, 57 were requisitioned for war service, mainly as minesweepers or convoy escort vessels. Nine of these were lost.

During the war Salvesen operated seven floating factory ships, three of their own plus *Southern Princess* and *Southern Empress* which they acquired from Unilever, the British-owned *Svend Foyn*, and the *Empire Heritage*. As already mentioned, *Salvestria* was lost to a mine in July 1940, *New Sevilla* was torpedoed in

September that same year and *Strombus* hit a mine in October. Then in October 1942 *Southern Empress* and *Sourabaya* were torpedoed on their way from New York to Britain, and in March 1943 the *Southern Princess* was also lost to a U-boat attack. It was not uncommon for merchant seamen to find themselves a victim more than once and several of Salvesen's men experienced multiple attacks. The second mate of *Empire Heritage* had previously served on the *Salvestria*, *Strombus* and the *Southern Princess* before surviving the attack by U–482. Olaf Hansen and Chief Engineer William Skinner of the *New Sevilla* survived her sinking only to be lost two years later on the *Southern Empress*. Dr Luigi Togneri, the ship's doctor on *New Sevilla,* also escaped her sinking, and later was one of the many that went down with *Empire Heritage.*

Being under the management of Christian Salvesen, *Empire Heritage* also had many of their regular whaling men in her crew. Among them was Able Seaman James Peterson, a Shetlander, who spent the years on either side of the war working for the company at their whaling operations in South Georgia. James was one of ten children born to Henry and Barbara Peterson of Braewick, a small crofting community about ten miles north of Lerwick, Shetland's main town. The ten children were born between 1898 and 1920 with James being the fifth child and third son, born on 7 May 1904. The second child and second son was John Thomson Peterson, born on 9 February 1900 and killed in the First World War on 25 January 1918 aged just seventeen. Most of the other children remained in Shetland, though the eldest, Henry, later emigrated to Australia and settled in Sydney, and Barbara, the third eldest, later settled in Vancouver.

During the war years James got engaged to a fellow Shetlander he had met whilst in Edinburgh, Betsy Margaret Pennant, originally from Uyeasound on the island of Unst. She was working there as a doctor's housekeeper at 15 Walker Street Edinburgh between the west end of Princes Street and the Haymarket. Later they would be married and settle back in Shetland, and James would continue working with Salvesen in South Georgia when the whaling operations recommenced at the end of the war.

In fact the whaling did not finish with the outbreak of war, and had actually carried on though with limited expeditions in 1939 and 1940. As it became more dangerous and the need for shipping became more pressing, there were barely any expeditions in 1941, after which all whaling ceased until the end of the war. The Admiralty could not spare the necessary naval escorts to protect the whaling ships and it was decided that the factory ships were of more use as tankers and for transporting tanks and vehicles, while the smaller whale catchers could be better used for patrol work and minesweeping. According to his discharge book, James Peterson sailed from Leith aboard the steamship *Coronda* on 29 September 1939, less than a month into the war, and was discharged on 6 November in South Georgia to begin the whaling season, which ran over the British winter. This was the second ship to be given that name; the first had actually been the very first Salvesen ship to begin Antarctic whaling in 1907 when she sailed from Leith to the Falkland Islands to set up the whaling station at New Island. They expanded to South Georgia the following year and Coronda Peak, which overlooked the whaling station at Leith Harbour on the island, was named after the ship. Incidentally Dr R.B. Robertson wrote in *Of Whales and Men* that 'Leith Harbour is the foulest place I have seen in a far-travelled life. I have been in Indian and African villages where sanitation is an unknown word, and where the villages raise themselves some inches higher every year on their own excreta; Leith Harbour is filthier than these.'

The tough conditions that the whalers lived and worked under give an indication of why they were such a resilient and dependable breed of seamen.

James then joined another ship, *New Sevilla*, on 7 December and remained with her during the season and for the journey home, being discharged in Tilbury, London on 2 May 1940, with the war now fully underway. The *Coronda* was later struck by a bomb whilst en route from Iceland to Liverpool with a cargo of herring oil in September 1940. The ship blazed for five hours before the fire was finally extinguished and the damaged ship was taken under tow and beached in the Firth of Clyde. Twenty-one crewmen were killed in the attack, and buried on the island of Bute whilst the ship was later repaired and put back into service, continuing for the rest of the war.

James Peterson once again joined the *New Sevilla* on 12 September 1940, ready to begin the next whaling season. It always ran over the British winter to exploit the milder summer season in the southern hemisphere. *New Sevilla* was a converted liner (previously *Runic II*) that had been changed into an oil-burning factory ship with a stern slip. He joined her at Birkenhead, but this time they never made it to South Georgia. On the evening of 20 October she was attacked while sailing in convoy OB-216, just west of Scotland. The convoy had been spotted by the commander of U-*138*, a young Latvian Oberleutnant named Wolfgang Lüth, who went on to become the second highest scoring U-boat ace of the war. A torpedo struck *New Sevilla* under her funnel and tore open a hole in her with a second exploding in her engine room shortly after. Lüth went on with his attack against other ships in the convoy, sinking three of them while *New Sevilla* remained afloat though fatally damaged and without power. She was eventually put in tow with a view to being salvaged, while other ships in the convoy gathered up the survivors. Alongside James Peterson were between 70 and 80 other Shetland seamen, around a fifth of the total crew. In total 412 of the crew were rescued and landed in Belfast before being transferred back to England. Fortunately only two were lost, one of whom was a Shetlander, carpenter John T. Smith, but with so many aboard, the consequences could have been tragic for the small island community. As it happened, the damage to *New Sevilla* proved to be too much for her to bear, and after some 20 hours in tow, she sank just nine miles off the Mull of Kintyre.

It is worth expanding on the incredible contribution that the men of the Shetland Islands made, not only in the Second World War but in naval history as far back as the Battle of Trafalgar. Following a visit to Lerwick Harbour in 1803, Captain Fanshaw of HMS *Carysfort* wrote: 'The great advantage is that every Shetland man and boy understands how to handle an oar and manage a boat.'

It was this inherent seamanship that led to Shetland becoming a target for the feared men of the Impress Service, whose job was to scour the country for males to fill the ships of the Royal Navy. Shetland was already a favoured recruitment port for the whaling ships sailing to the Davis Straits. Maintaining the required numbers in the Navy was proving difficult and in 1795, Prime Minister William Pitt introduced the Quota Act, which meant that every county or district had to provide a certain number of men for service; the number determined by the overall population of the area. According to her size, Shetland had to provide around 100 men but many more than that volunteered and as their skills at sea became apparent, the Navy demanded even more. Therefore by the Battle of Trafalgar in 1805, it was estimated that there were some 3,000 Shetland men serving in the Royal Navy, an enormous proportion of the total male islands population, and proportionately more than anywhere else in the country. There were at least three Shetlanders amongst the 800-strong crew of Nelson's flagship HMS *Victory*, and another four even rose to the rank of admiral in other ships of the fleet, a quite incredible accomplishment at a time when wealth and social position were more important than skill and intelligence when gaining promotion. Their natural ability clearly shone through and could not be denied.

During the Second World War 3,300 Shetlanders, men and women, served their country throughout the armed services and Merchant Navy. According to the Shetland Roll of Honour, 357 of those lost their lives. Of that figure, 248 were lost in the Merchant Navy and another 36 in the Royal Navy, meaning 284 or 80 per cent of the total were lost at sea. A further 400 were in the RAF where 22 lost their lives.

Prior to the war many Shetlanders were employed by the whaling industry, working each season for Christian Salvesen & Co. Ltd down in South Georgia. At the outbreak of hostilities some who were in the Royal Naval Reserve were drafted into service while many others naturally went into the merchant service, going with their ships, which had also been drafted. With such a large number of men being spread across the Merchant Navy during the war, there were Shetlanders in every corner of the globe, and they were present at some of the most significant events of the war.

In the early months of the war there were Shetlanders aboard the *Royal Oak* when it was torpedoed by Günther Prien in Scapa Flow, they were aboard the *Jervis Bay* in the battle to defeat the *Admiral Scheer*, they were on the *Hood* when she was lost in the battle against the *Bismarck* and *Prinz Eugen*. They served in the ships of the rescue service and the escort ships. They were on the tanker *Ohio* during Operation *Pedestal*, the heroic Allied convoy that got through to Malta when she was under siege by Axis forces. They were there at the defeat of the *Scharnhorst*, when she was sunk on Boxing Day 1943 by British ships to the north of Norway. They served on the dangerous PQ convoys to northern Russia including the notorious PQ17, which sailed in the summer of 1942 and lost 25 of its 36 ships, all to enemy action. They were in the crucial convoys HX-229 and SC-122, amongst the most infamous voyages of the Battle of the Atlantic. They were at D-Day, and in the Mediterranean, in Africa and the Far East. From such a small island the Shetland seaman spanned the globe, experiencing the war in all situations, environments and conditions.

After the loss of *New Sevilla*, James Peterson then went on to serve on the tanker *Empire Norse*, (ex-*Anglo Norse*) during 1941 and 1942, crossing and re-crossing the Atlantic as part of the SC/ON Atlantic convoys. According to his papers, he was discharged from the *Empire Norse* at Glasgow on 17 September 1942, and remained ashore until joining the newly refurbished *Empire Heritage* the following January.

The first convoy voyage of *Empire Heritage* began from Cardiff on 27 February 1943 sailing to Milford Haven and then Belfast, before crossing the Atlantic carrying British merchant seamen to crew some of the newly-built Liberty ships being constructed in the US. She left Belfast with convoy ON-170 on 3 March 1943, though *Empire Heritage* detached from the convoy two days later and returned to the Clyde. The remainder of the outbound convoy of 49 merchant ships carried on and arrived in New York on 20 March.

Empire Heritage was then assigned to convoy ON-174, which departed Liverpool on the 20th, the same day her original convoy landed in New York. This group of 40 merchant ships crossed the Atlantic in nineteen days, arriving in New York on 8 April 1943. She returned to Britain just over two weeks later with convoy HX-236. The group of 24 ships departed New York on 24 April 1943 and arrived in Liverpool on 9 May. James Peterson was then discharged from the ship on 14 May in Liverpool; his book was stamped and signed by the Master and fellow Shetlander, James Campbell Jamieson. He was re-engaged two days later on the 16th for the next trip, this time having been promoted to bo'sun, a foreman of the general crew. At this time the Merchant Navy ships and crews were pushed to the limit of their endurance as ships arrived in port and were quickly turned around once their cargo had been offloaded. The same thing happened once they were loaded at the other end, and they were speedily loaded and then departed again laden with men, equipment and supplies for Europe. There were often short spells spent in port, maybe only a day or so to load up before returning to the perilous Atlantic.

Empire Heritage left Liverpool and joined up with convoy ON-186, a group of 39 merchant ships which had originated in Milford Haven on the Welsh coast on 24 May. This was the beginning of James's longest period of engagement in his discharge book; joining *Empire Heritage* in Liverpool on 16 May 1943, he would not be discharged until 25 May 1944 in Glasgow, a period of more than a year, and that was after being re-engaged only two days after a period of engagement that ran from 23 January to 14 May.

They arrived in New York on 7 June 1943 after just over two weeks at sea. *Empire Heritage* remained there for just over a fortnight, and departed again on 23 June 1943 as part of convoy HX-245, an assembly of 84 ships that arrived in Liverpool on 7 July. She was simply listed as carrying 'valuable cargo'. HX-245 was a fairly large convoy and after leaving New York the initial convoy rendezvoused with groups from Halifax and St John's for the trip across the Atlantic. However, several of the vessels experienced mechanical problems and six ships had to return to port with defects including engine room problems and leaking boiler tubes. There were two collisions between ships in the convoy in dense fog. On the night of 27 June 1943 the ships *Clausina* and *Skaraas* collided in the darkness with both ships damaged. *Skaraas* suffered damage to her port bow and lost an anchor, while *Clausina* was damaged on her starboard quarter. Fortunately there were no casualties and the ships were able to carry on at normal speed as all damage had been above the waterline. The second collision was more serious and took place in the early evening of 1 July. The merchant aircraft carrier (MAC) *Empire Macalpine* was landing aircraft when she collided with the *Empire Ibex* causing damage to both ships. The damage to the smaller vessel proved fatal and two days later the *Empire Ibex* sank, with all her crew having been safely transferred to the rescue ship *Perth* the previous day. The rest of the convoy including the *Empire Macalpine* carried on and arrived in Britain four days later.

By the end of the month *Empire Heritage* had returned to sea with convoy ON-195. The convoy had once again started from Milford Haven, on 31 July, and by the time it was through the Western Approaches it had gathered 50 merchant ships plus escorts. Most of the convoy was destined for New York but it also included vessels headed for Australia, who would eventually detach and join up with other convoys heading there. This time the ships arrived in a little under two weeks, making New York on 13 August. Again the turnaround was fast and they were originally scheduled to return to Britain in convoy HX-253 on 20 August but were held over to the next convoy and left New York with HX-254 a week later. On this trip she carried fuel oil and the captain of the *Empire Heritage* James Campbell Jamieson acted as vice commodore for the fleet. Again, several ships were forced to turn back with engine defects though the convoy proceeded without attack and made an average speed of 8.7 knots. They finally arrived in Liverpool on 12 September.

Less than two weeks later they were heading back across the Atlantic in convoy ON-203, a group of 62 merchant ships plus escorts that departed Liverpool on 22 September 1943, and arrived in New York on 10 October. At this point, *Empire Heritage* took a break from the ON/HX convoy route and instead made the trip, sailing independently, down the east coast of America from New York to Hampton Roads in southeast Virginia. There she joined convoy UGS-24, the convoy route from Hampton Roads to Port Said in Egypt.

UGS-25 left Virginia on 24 November 1943 and made the trip across the Atlantic and into the Mediterranean to Port Said, with *Empire Heritage* detaching from the convoy and sailing to Bizerta. After delivering her cargo at the Tunisian port she departed and joined the closing stages of UGS-26, which had left Hampton Roads on 5 December. They arrived in Port Said on 30 December. Over the next month she stayed in North Africa, sailing independently from Suez to Aden and from Aden to Bombay and then to Abadan, arriving there on 10 February 1943.

Empire Heritage then sailed on one of the small convoy routes, PA-69 from Bandar Abbas to Aden, on 16 February 1944. This trip along the Persian Gulf from Iran to Yemen took only eight days, and they arrived in Aden on 24 February – but not without incident. The group of 19 ships was spotted and stalked by U-*510*, under the command of U-boat ace Kapitänleutnant Alfred Eick. On 22 February when the convoy was 200 miles from its destination port of Aden, U-*510* made two attacks, torpedoing three ships in the convoy. The American steam tanker *E. G. Seubert* (9,181 tons) with a cargo of 79,000 barrels of fuel was hit by a single torpedo on the port side that exploded in one of her tanks and started a fire while blowing a deck gun clear over the side. She listed to port and capsized soon after with only one of her lifeboats having been launched. Of her crew of 70, only six were lost, the rest being picked up by two vessels and later landed in Aden. The British motor tanker *San Alvaro* (7,385 tons) also took a torpedo and the explosion started a fire which quickly spread and she had to be abandoned. One gunner was lost in the attack and the remaining 52 crew were picked up by HMAS *Tamworth*, which then sank the burning wreck using her guns and depth charges. Finally, the Norwegian motor tanker *Erling Brøvig* (9,970 tons) was hit amidships by a single torpedo that nearly broke her in two. She was taken in tow and was eventually beached near Aden where her cargo of oil was transferred and temporary repairs could be made. Her entire crew of 45 survived the attack and having abandoned the ship, they reached Aden in the lifeboats. On the PA convoy route, PA–69 was in fact the only convoy in the series to be attacked by a U-boat. *Empire Heritage* and the rest of the ships carried on and arrived in Aden on 24 February.

Her next trip saw *Empire Heritage* returning through the Mediterranean and back across the Atlantic with convoy GUS-33, the GUS prefix denoting a slow convoy from Port Said to the United States; the opposite direction to the UGS convoys. The initial convoy group departed from Port Said on 5 March 1944 with other ships joining them the following day from Alexandria. As on her outbound trip, *Empire Heritage* made the trip in two stages and detached from the convoy to sail into Augusta on 11 March with eight other vessels, while the remainder of the convoy carried on, mainly to their final destination of New York or Chesapeake Bay where they arrived on 3 April. The UGS/GUS convoys could be incredibly complex owing to the amount of traffic coming and going from the various ports en route. For example, after leaving Port Said, convoy GUS-33 had ships joining it from, or breaking away to, Alexandria, Augusta, Malta, Bizerta, Tunis, Bone, Tripoli, Algiers and Oran, and all within the first week of the voyage. *Empire Heritage* remained in Augusta until she could rendezvous with the next GUS convoy, GUS-34, which left Port Said on 15 March. She joined the group a few days later and sailed with them all the way back to the United States, arriving in Hampton Roads on 14 April 1944.

From there *Empire Heritage* headed back up the coast to New York City where she returned across the Atlantic on 5 May 1944 as part of the large 94-ship convoy, HX-290. She carried a cargo of fuel oil in her tanks and a deck cargo of AFVs (armoured fighting vehicles). The trip went without incident and they arrived back in Britain on 19 May. *Empire Heritage* then sailed independently from Liverpool to the Clyde, arriving on 24 May to prepare for her next Atlantic crossing.

She joined convoy ON-239 on 3 June 1944 and headed again from the Clyde to New York, while the largest seaborne invasion in history was preparing to cross the Channel three days later. The enormous convoy of 96 merchant ships sailed west, arriving on 22 June.

On 3 July *Empire Heritage* departed New York City for Liverpool as part of the even bigger HX-298, a convoy of some 115 vessels when joined by some from Halifax and Sydney in Nova Scotia. On this occasion *Empire Heritage* also carried the fleet Commodore, A.N. Hakking. This huge group of ships carried a diverse range of cargoes including sugar, meat, fruit, oil, metal, lumber, grain, mail, ammunition, with some ships listed simply as carrying 'general' cargo. The ships arrived in Britain on 18 July, with *Empire Heritage* proceeding to her destination port of Glasgow via Liverpool, arriving there on the 22nd.

She only remained there for a week before departing again for the outbound trip across the Atlantic on 25 July. Convoy ON-246 was made up of 107 merchant ships plus eighteen escorts. They arrived in New York on 9 August. They remained there for two weeks and departed again for Britain on 25 August. This was convoy HX-305. *Empire Heritage* sailed with a cargo of 16,000 tonnes of fuel oil and 1,947 tonnes of deck cargo including Sherman tanks and dump trucks. It was this final trip that brought her under the deadly periscope crosshairs of U-*482*.

The table below shows all the known movements of *Empire Heritage* during the war, from her first convoy in March 1943 to her final, fatal passage in September 1944.

Convoy	From	Departed	Destination	Arrived
Independent	Cardiff	27/2/43	Milford Haven	2/3/43
Independent	Milford Haven	2/3/43	Belfast	3/3/43
ON-170	Liverpool	3/3/43	New York	Returned
ON-174	Liverpool	20/3/43	New York	8/4/43
HX-236	New York	24/4/43	Liverpool	9/5/43
ON-186	Liverpool	24/5/43	New York	7/6/43
HX-245	New York	23/6/43	Liverpool	7/7/43
ON-195	Liverpool	31/7/43	New York	13/8/43
HX-254	New York	27/8/43	Liverpool	12/9/43
ON-203	Liverpool	22/9/43	New York	10/10/43
Independent	New York	11/11/43	Hampton Roads	12/11/43
UGS-24	Hampton Roads	14/11/43	Port Said	Returned
UGS-25	Hampton Roads	24/11/43	Port Said	
			(EH to Bizerta)	21/12/43
UGS-26	Hampton Roads			
	(EH from Bizerta)	5/12/43	Port Said	30/12/43
Independent	8/1/44	Suez	14/1/44	Aden
Independent	14/1/44	Aden	22/1/44	Bombay
Independent	3/2/44	Bombay	10/2/44	Abadan

Independent	13/2/44	Abadan	16/2/44	Bandar Abbas
PA-69	Bandar Abbas	16/2/44	Aden	24/2/44
Independent	Aden	25/2/44	Suez	4/3/44
GUS-33	Port Said	5/3/44	Hampton Roads	
			(EH to Augusta)	4/4/44
GUS-34	Port Said			
	(EH from Augusta)	15/3/44	Hampton Roads	14/4/44
HX-290	New York	5/5/44	Liverpool	19/5/44
Independent	Liverpool	23/5/44	Clyde	24/5/44
ON-239	Liverpool	3/6/44	New York	22/6/44
HX-298	New York	3/7/44	Liverpool	18/7/44
Independent	Liverpool	21/7/44	Clyde	22/7/44
ON-246	Liverpool	25/7/44	New York	9/8/44
HX-305	New York	25/8/44	Liverpool	10/9/44
				(EH lost 8/9/44)

EMPIRE HERITAGE – SPECIFICATIONS

Type	Steam Tanker
Built at	Armstrong, Whitworth & Co. Ltd, Newcastle
Owner	Christian Salvesen & Co. Ltd
Completed	1930
Requisitioned	1943
Length (feet)	512
Beam (feet)	72
Gross Tonnage	15,702

IV

U-*482* – THE U-BOAT

The only thing that really frightened me during the war was the U-Boat peril.

Winston Churchill

U-*482* was one of the Type VIIC vessels, widely regarded as the workhorse of the German Kriegsmarine fleet in the Second World War. U-boat design was constantly evolving during the late 1930s and into the war years and the Type VIIC was in many ways a perfect fighting machine for the time. In 1937 after two years of production on the Type VIIA – of which only ten were produced – the VIIB emerged, larger and more powerful with better armaments and an additional rudder for improved manoeuvrability. Extra saddle tanks were fitted to the vessels giving a much greater fuel capacity and therefore range; they could travel an extra 2,500 nautical miles at cruiser speed. Production for this model was still only a meagre 24 ships. When production began on the Type VIIC in 1940 following the outbreak of war, the design had evolved further to provide the Kriegsmarine with one of their most successful weapons against the Allies.

Between 1940 and the end of the war, 568 Type VIIC vessels were produced, and they were constantly being refined to make them better and more deadly. The first commissioned Type VIIC was U-*69* in 1940. They were similar in power to the Type VIIB but were larger and so slightly slower, but later in the war modified units were designed that contained much lighter machinery and thicker pressure hulls. Also in 1944/45 many Type VIIC vessels were fitted out with snorkels that allowed the vessels to stay submerged for greater distances. Two other variations were made of the Type VII though both in small numbers.

The Type VIID, which was designed for mine laying and of which only six were built, and the Type VIIF, used as a supply vessel.

TYPE VII U-BOAT SPECIFICATIONS

Displacement (tons)	769 (surfaced) 871 (submerged)
Length (metres)	67.1
Beam (metres)	6.2
Height (metres)	9.6
Draft (metres)	4.74
Power (hp)	3,200 (surfaced) 750 (submerged)
Speed (knots)	17.7 (surfaced) 7.6 (submerged)
Range (miles)	8,500 (surfaced) 80 (submerged)
Torpedoes	14 (4 bow tubes/1 stern tube)
Armaments	1 88mm deck gun (220 rounds)
Crew	44–52 personnel
Maximum depth (metres)	220 (crush depth 250)

Life on board a U-boat was a cramped, stagnant affair, and within days of leaving port the crew became pale from a lack of sunlight. Water was conserved for drinking only, there was little washing, and of the two toilets aboard, one was usually used to store food and supplies leaving the other one to be used as it was intended, and with up to 50 men sharing the one convenience, the effect can be imagined. Each man shared a bunk with another man on the opposite watch, and had only a small locker for personal possessions; soap, razors and aftershaves were considered a waste of space. This cramped airless space gradually filled with the fumes from the engines, increasing carbon monoxide as the oxygen diminished, the aromas of cooking and the smell of the sweaty occupants creating an odour unique to a U-boat. The vessels often suffered from leaks and so a layer of condensation usually clung to the inner surfaces causing fresh food to quickly spoil and go mouldy, food tins would begin to rust and the men would experience terrible headaches and skin problems. Kapitänleutnant Peter Cremer of U-*333* wrote in his log of one voyage: 'The atmosphere is foul from the stench of rotting food and the high proportion of carbon monoxide in the air.'

U-boat crewmen were normally young, mostly in their early twenties, and the commander only in his late twenties. The oldest man aboard U-*482* was 29 and the youngest still 18. It was an incredibly strange and uncomfortable life, not to mention extremely dangerous.

U-*482* was built at Kiel in construction yard 317. She was launched on 25 September 1943 and was commissioned on the first day of December that year. She was put under the command of Kapitänleutnant Hartmut Von Matuschka, a 29-year-old German Count whose family had risen to prominence amongst the nobility of nineteenth-century Prussia, though the Matuschka family history reached back much further.

Hartmut was the second of four brothers born to Graf (Count) Heinrich von Matuschka (1887–1935) and Anna von Heydebrand und der Lasa (1891–1964). All four of the sons inherited the title of Graf along with the secondary title of Freiherr (Freeman) von Toppolczan und Spaetgen. The eldest brother Friedhelm was born in 1913, Hartmut in 1914, Siegfried in 1917 and Volkhart in 1921. All of them except Hartmut were born in Potsdam and all four of them served as officers in the armed services during the war. Friedhelm and Volkhart joined the army with Volkhart serving as a Panzer officer on the Eastern Front where he was twice wounded in action. Siegfried entered the Luftwaffe and Hartmut joined the Kriegsmarine. Friedhelm and Volkhart both survived the war, Friedhelm passing away in 1979 and Volkhart in 2000. Siegfried served as an Oberleutnant (1st Lieutenant) in the Luftwaffe and was killed on 16 April 1943 in a dogfight over the English Channel near to Abbeville in Northern France. At the time he was serving as Staffelkapitan or Squadron Leader and was flying a Focke-Wulf 190A, a plane which he had flown successfully many times on operations over the Eastern Front. Siegfried was credited with 29 kills during his career and was considered a German fighter ace, being awarded in his short career the Iron Cross 2nd Class, Iron Cross 1st Class, the German Cross in Gold, and the Honour Cup of the Luftwaffe; an award which was established by Reichsmarschall Hermann Goring in February 1940 for 'special achievement in the air war'. Hartmut may have been inspired by the impressive honours achieved by his younger brother and encouraged to strive for similar success in the Kriegsmarine. Siegfried was killed shortly after Hartmut began his U-boat training.

Incidentally, the family was also related to Michael Graf von Matuschka (1888–1944), a German politician who was later arrested and executed for suspected involvement in the 'July 20 Plot' to assassinate Adolf Hitler, better known as Operation *Valkyrie*. Michael was born in Schweidnitz in Silesia in 1888 and studied law at Lausanne, Munich, Berlin and Breslau, finally qualifying in 1910. He joined the Prussian Army and was wounded on the Eastern Front in 1915 where he was captured by the Russians and ended up a prisoner of war in Siberia, though he escaped in 1918 and returned to Germany. Following the war he became the County Commissioner of Oppeln and was later elected to the German Landtag as a member of the Centre Party. He later went on to work at the Prussian Ministry of Interior in Berlin and in the administration of Silesia where he met the Deputy

Regional Commissioner Fritz-Dietlof Graf von der Schulenburg, a member of the German Resistance and an important figure in the plot against Hitler. Schulenburg persuaded Michael to agree to take the post of Regional Commissioner in Silesia in the government that would be formed once Hitler had been removed. Schulenburg himself was to be State Secretary. When the plot failed the conspirators were rounded up by the Gestapo with Schulenburg arrested on the very day of the attempt on the Führer's life. He was tried on 10 August 1944 and hanged the same day at Plotzensee Prison in Berlin. In total some 5,000 people were arrested on suspicion of having some connection to the 20 July plot as the Gestapo sought to crush all resistance within the Reich. Michael Graf von Matuschka was arrested and tried on 14 September 1944 and killed the same day, also at Plotzensee. This was less than a week after the attack on *Empire Heritage* and just three days after young Hartmut finally emulated the success of his brother Siegfried and was awarded the German Cross in Gold for his achievements as a U-boat commander.

Graf von Hartmut Matuschka was born in Blasewitz, a historical part of Dresden, on 29 December 1914 and brought up in the dark days following the First World War when Germany was a country in ruins. Prior to entering the submarine arm of the navy and taking command of U-482, Hartmut had served as a range-finding officer on the *Prinz Eugen*, the heavy cruiser that fought alongside the *Bismarck* at the Battle of Denmark Strait on 24 May 1941. He was on duty aboard the German ship when it scored the initial hit on HMS *Hood,* which caused an enormous fire before the *Bismarck* finally destroyed the celebrated British battleship with the loss of 1,417 men, leaving just three survivors. Fritz Otto Busch describes the young officer in his book *The Story of the Prince Eugen*: 'Count Matuschka, the slim First Lieutenant and range finding officer, was leaning against the armoured wall and giving instructions through the headphone, calmly, slowly and distinctly, his thin aristocratic face bent over the microphone.'

The two German ships knew that other enemy ships were closing in and *Bismarck* had been damaged by at least three shells causing water to leak into her fuel oil and later slowing her down. The two German ships separated, with *Bismarck* heading for St Nazaire for repairs while *Prinz Eugen* set a course for Brest in France. The loss of HMS *Hood* was a nightmare for the British, from both a naval and a propaganda point of view. All available warships were redirected to hunt down the *Bismarck* at all costs. Over the next three days there were several air and sea attacks on the German battleship but without much success, though a Swordfish biplane from the carrier *Victorious* scored a single hit causing the first fatality on board. Then on the evening of 26 May the carrier *Ark Royal* despatched another Swordfish attack and this time a torpedo scored a hit that jammed the ship's rudder making her un-manoeuvrable. The following morning two of the chasing British ships, *Rodney* and *King George V*, caught up with her and began a relentless attack. She suffered massive casualties and damage and most of her officers were killed when a shell exploded on the bridge. She remained afloat and unwilling to surrender. Eventually the order was given to scuttle her and abandon ship. Though many survivors were picked up it is believed that some 2,100 lost their lives. The *Bismarck* slid beneath the waves and even in her defeat achieved a legendary status as probably the most famous battleship of all time, the naval equivalent of the *Titanic*.

Prinz Eugen made it to Brest on 1 June, her crew devastated at the news of the *Bismarck's* demise. That first night in port she was damaged by an RAF bomb that landed near the main artillery command centre killing 60 of her crew. Shaken by the loss of his greatest ship, Hitler had ordered all the main battleships back into home waters in February 1942 to defend the German territories in Western Europe and Norway. *Prinz Eugen* made the dash back to Germany along with the *Scharnhorst* and *Gneisenau* amongst other smaller vessels. It was known as Operation *Cerberus* after the three-headed dog in Greek legend that guards the gates of Hades. Once back in German waters, *Prinz Eugen* was ordered to Norway on patrol. On 23 February the British submarine HMS *Trident* fired a torpedo at the German battleship scoring a hit on her stern. The explosion caused massive damage, forcing her to divert to Trondheim for quick repairs before returning to Kiel in May to receive a new stern. This kept her from active service until the following January.

Following the loss of the *Bismarck* and the damage at Brest, this third blow may have been what made the 27-year-old officer Graf von Hartmut Matuschka reconsider his naval career. Perhaps he grew frustrated at the pace of the surface war; the *Prinz Eugen* had seen little action since the Battle of Denmark Strait. Or perhaps it was the fact that his brother in the Luftwaffe had won such honours after achieving great successes while he had been forced to sit idle. In February 1943 after just over three years with the *Prinz Eugen*, Matuschka volunteered for the U-boat service. By this point in the war the service was desperate for new commanders as most of the old set that had been there at the outbreak of war had been killed or captured. Many young officers from other areas of the Kriegsmarine volunteered and after a two-week selection exam were entered into a course of intensive training as the next generation of U-boat commanders. The rigorous training lasted roughly a year. Crews were sent on hundreds of training missions where they learned to handle their vessel in all waters, both surfaced and submerged, and how to shadow and attack enemy convoy vessels. One U-boat commander said of the training: 'The knowledge acquired during this single year of training, in which the crews were tested to the limits of human endeavour, was the foundation ... upon which the future structure of the U-boat arm was built.'

The first voyage for the newly built U-*482* and her crew was a short run from Kiel on 6 August 1944, arriving at Horten just two days later. This was followed by another short trip from there on 14 August, arriving at their base in Bergen on the 16th. Later that same day, U-*482* departed Bergen on her first active patrol; her destination the North Channel, the area to the north of Ireland where the Atlantic convoys came into Britain. She was attached to the 9th Flotilla.

The construction details of U-*482*, one of a batch of six Type VII ships ordered from Kiel at the same time, highlight what could be the considerable time between a ship being ordered and leaving on her first active patrol.

U-*482* CONSTRUCTION

Construction Yard	Deutsche Werke AG Kiel
Yard Number	317
Ordered	5 June 1941
Keel Laid	13 February 1942
Launched	25 September 1943
Commissioned	1 December 1943
First Active Patrol	16 August 1944

U-*482* was one of the first vessels to have success with the new 'snorkel' device when she made her patrol in August/September 1944. She left Norway and headed towards Shetland, passing submerged between there and the Faroes and then south to the coast of Ireland, surfacing only to make radio contact. She travelled there and back making a total voyage of 2,729 miles with only 256 of those travelled on the surface. That was all made possible by the snorkel. Matuschka wrote in his war diary, 'Snorkelling is useful and is highly regarded by the crew.'

As well as the snorkel device, U-*482* was fitted with a 10cm radar detector and armed with the latest torpedo technology including acoustic torpedoes that could home in on the sound from ship propellers, and pattern torpedoes as previously described, that could be programmed to turn around if they did not hit a target and zigzag back along a course until either it found a target or ran out of fuel. This made a particularly deadly weapon if fired into the middle of a convoy.

U-*482* carried Bold Canisters, known by the Allies as Submarine Bubble Target (SBT). This was a device designed to confuse enemy sonar or ASDIC by creating a cloud of bubbles that could resemble a submarine on radar screens. This could be very difficult to distinguish from the real thing, giving a fleeing

U-boat more chance of escape. It was a metal canister, 3.9 inches in diameter, which was filled with calcium hydride. The U-boat launched the canister from a special tube, and a valve on the device allowed seawater to seep in and mix with the chemical compound, creating copious amounts of gas that resulted in clouds of bubbles. The valve also controlled the buoyancy of the canister and kept it at the right depth until the chemical was depleted. The resulting effect could last for almost half an hour, and so keep a hunter occupied with depth charge attacks whilst the enemy slipped quietly away. The device came into wide use in 1942 and was developed and improved as the war continued. In the later years when the U-boats had all but lost their advantage of invisibility, the Bold Canister could be the difference between escape or rapid destruction and death. The last model, the Bold 5, was designed for use at depths of up to 200 metres.

The U-boat was equipped with anti-aircraft weapons though they were never brought into use on her first patrol, mainly because she spent so much of the time submerged. They were tested for the first time just before U-*482* returned to Norway at the end of her patrol and were found to be inoperative. Matuschka wrote in the war diary:

> The Flak weapons were used for the first time on the day before last of the undertaking. All failed. The fault with the 20mm weapons lay with the rusty ammunition from the upper deck container … as the boat had only tracer bullets and came up almost only at night for a short time, it was not tested for malfunction … the cause of malfunction could only be checked through testing in peace and quiet or on entering harbour.

When U-*482* left Bergen in August 1944, she was being sent out with as good a chance as the Kriegsmarine could give her. Although the Type VII was now an ageing model they were yet to launch a better vessel, and she was armed and equipped with the best technology that Germany had. She was up against a formidable opponent, one that would be looking for her and that had the technology to hunt her down and destroy her. Despite this, her crew were staunch and her commander unwavering. It was their first active patrol and they were determined that they would have success. And so they did.

U-*482* left Kiel in early August 1944 and sailed to Horton in Norway, leaving there on the 14th and heading north towards Bergen to begin their patrol. They sailed west through the North Sea and awaited orders from BdU. On the 16th they received their orders, which were also recorded in the BdU war diary for that date.

> In order to spread out the 11 boats at present proceeding from Norway to the Atlantic, U-*482, 296, 680* are to sail between the Shetlands and Faroes into the

North Atlantic. The boats are intended for operations off North Minch and the North Channel. The boat received instructions to proceed with caution as according to experience the enemy intensifies his air activity on confirming the presence of U-boats on the Norwegian coast.

On 18 August, with U-*482* in position AF79 on the Kriegsmarine grid, BdU sent out orders allocating various U-boats into positions. 'The following positions were allocated: 'U-*224* operational area off Reykjavik, U-*296* North Minch, U-*482* North Channel, U-*680* Moray Firth'.

And so Matuschka took U-*482* across the North Sea, north of Shetland and moved down the west coast of Scotland towards the North Channel. She was one of several new Type VII snorkel-fitted boats sent out from Norway to various patrol areas in British coastal waters. Over the next twelve days, she sailed through the AF grid area to the north of Scotland and down through the AM area to quadrant AM53, arriving there on 30 August. Over the course of this journey Matuschka recorded sighting three aircraft and a group of destroyers, but never close at hand and never were they detected on the way to their patrol area. AM53 was the area right at the entrance to the North Channel, west of Islay in Scotland and north of County Donegal in Ireland. It was here that Matuschka and his men found their first victim.

The Kriegsmarine grid system was a very simple and unique way of tracking both their own and enemy shipping at any point across the globe, and gave them the ability to vector their U-boats toward or away from the enemy. They created a grid that covered the whole world, with each square or quadrant allocated a unique two-letter code, for example AB, AC, AD and so on in the North Atlantic. The grid went in horizontal bands with the first letter changing the further south you went, with the second later changing from left to right. So a ship sailing from the east of Canada and sailing east in a straight line would begin in AH, and sail through AJ, AK, AL and AM, which would take them to the west of Scotland. Then each quadrant was divided up into nine smaller squares which were then divided again into nine even smaller squares, like a Sudoku grid. These were numbered 11, 12, 13 up to 19, and then 21, 22, 23 to 29, right up until 91, 92, 93 until the last square, which was 99. This gave the first two numbers after the two-letter code. Then each of these squares was divided up again in the same way to give a smaller and more accurate position. Though it appears complicated, it was a surprisingly simple and effective way of dividing up the world map, and because it did not mention the standard coordinates of longitude and latitude, even if the Allies intercepted a signal, they could not determine a position without knowledge of the grid system.

When U-*482* attacked her first victim, they were in position AM5397, which meant they were in quadrant 97 or the seventh smallest square, in the ninth larger square, in square 53 of the AM quadrant on the map. The grid below shows the AM53 grid divided up into the nine larger squares (numbered in bold) and then the nine smaller squares in each. AM5397 can be found third from the right, bottom row (underlined).

QUADRANT AM*53*

1	2	3	1	2	3	1	2	3
4	**1**	6	4	**2**	6	4	**3**	6
7	8	9	7	8	9	7	8	9
1	2	3	1	2	3	1	2	3
4	**4**	6	4	**5**	6	4	**6**	6
7	8	9	7	8	9	7	8	9
1	2	3	1	2	3	1	2	3
4	**7**	6	4	**8**	6	4	**9**	6
7	8	9	7	8	9	<u>7</u>	8	9

The first victory came on 30 August 1944, two weeks after leaving Bergen. U-*482* had moved silently into her patrol area, lying in wait for a target to present itself and at around 1530 hours convoy CU-36 sailed into view, CU being the prefix for convoys travelling from Curacao to Britain. Five of the ships began to break away from the main convoy and changed course for their destination, which was Loch Ewe in Scotland. They were the steamships *Erin*, *Memnon* and *Cape Nome*, and the tankers *Crown Point* and *Jacksonville*. They formed into a short column and at the end of the column was the large tanker *Jacksonville*, newly completed that year in Oregon at the Swan Island Shipyard. She was hefty at 10.448 tonnes and was heading from New York to Loch Ewe, having departed on 19 August.

Her cargo was an enormous 141,000 barrels of 80-octane gasoline. It was later noted that conditions at the time were choppy and visibility was good, the depth of water was around 35 fathoms. Aboard *Jacksonville* there were six armed guards on lookout duty with two on the bridge, two on the bow and two on the stern. The ships *Erin* and *Crown Point* were just ahead of the *Jacksonville*. This was only the third trip across the Atlantic for the brand-new tanker, having already sailed from New York with convoy CU-32 back in July, and back across with UC-32 at the beginning of August. U-*482* was lying submerged nearby and had spotted the little group as they broke away from the main convoy. The U-boat began to stalk the tanker as she made her turn for the Scottish port. Shortly before 1600 hours the convoy was about 50 miles north of Londonderry, near the Donegal coast at position 55.30/07.30W. Kapitänleutnant Matuschka was watching carefully through the periscope and turning his boat to line up the forward torpedo tubes with the hull of the tanker as she completed her turn towards Loch Ewe. The torpedoes had been armed and the firing calculations made as the U-boat crew waited in silence for their first chance to score a victory.

A later report dated 5 September 1944, written by the commanding officer of the armed guard aboard the *Cape Nome*, described the situation:

> At 1545 on 30 August 1944 convoy CN was in approximate position 55-50N and 07-30W within sight of the Irish Coast (distance about 20 miles) with orders for diversion having been received a few minutes previously ... The *Jacksonville* had completed its turn just a moment or two before, being in a position a few hundred yards from the point of turn when an explosion was heard.

The U-boat fired two torpedoes on different trajectories from her bow torpedo tubes. As the tanker completed her turn and continued north towards Loch Ewe the two deadly warheads were cutting through the water towards her. Three-and-a-half minutes later at 1555 hours there was a deafening explosion as the first torpedo tore into the starboard side of the tanker and exploded in the number 7 tank, immediately igniting the enormous fuel cargo.

> I was standing in the starboard passageway of the bridge deck at the time. The alarm brought all hands to battle stations. As I ran for the ladder to the flying bridge I saw the *Jacksonville* 500 to 800 yards astern, with a narrow flame 40 to 50 feet in height and about 25 feet in width (fore & aft) just from the centre line of the main deck just aft of the bridge house at an angle of 60 degrees from the horizontal on the port beam. About 30 seconds after the first explosion a muffled explosion or rumble was heard simultaneously with the complete envelopment of the

Jacksonville in a flame which extended the entire distance forward a width of 100ft or more on each beam narrowing toward the bow in a rounded edge. The height of the flame was 200 to 300 feet.

In seconds the entire ship was ablaze with flames shooting 300 feet into the air as the crew made a desperate scramble to escape. After another 33 seconds the second torpedo struck, this time breaking the vessel in two and removing almost any chance of escape for the stricken crew. Not a single lifeboat had the chance to launch, and those who made it onto the deck could only jump overboard, hopelessly clutching a lifejacket for survival. But even these few were mostly caught up in the massive blaze surrounding the ship as burning gasoline poured from the ruptured hull. The suddenness of the attack and the resulting fireball made it very difficult for witnesses on the nearby ships to determine exactly what happened, which resulted in several conflicting statements. One witness thought the torpedo had struck the ship between the poop deck and amidships but could not determine on what side it had hit. He also thought the second explosion was from the fuel tanks or the ship's magazines. Some claimed the torpedo had hit on the port side, others claimed it was starboard.

Marcellus R. Wegs, a gunner in the armed guard aboard the *Jacksonville* later gave his account of the attack:

> One Wednesday afternoon about 3:45, one of my buddies and I were cleaning one of the 20mm guns on the aft port side when a very loud explosion arose from the bow, pieces flying everywhere with smoke rolling up as a big cloud. When the smoke cleared away it looked like the forward gun was gone along with the two men on watch. My buddy and I watching for fire started to put the gun together we had started to clean. Before we had done very much more the second torpedo struck amidships, exploding the gasoline and fire was everywhere. I grabbed an armful of life preservers, threw them down on the 38 gun deck and took one myself. I proceeded to run through the flames to the stern, one deck lower that I was. My buddy followed me until we came to our quarters. He went inside and after that he never had a chance, anyway I never saw him nor any of the others since.

An enormous ball of fire rapidly consumed the ship to the extent that just moments after the torpedo had struck the tanker was no longer visible behind the screen of smoke and flames. The officer aboard *Cape Nome* continues his account:

> In about one minute from the time of the explosion all that was visible where the tanker had been last seen was the huge flame attended now by columns of smoke at

the lower edge around and at the top. Approximately 2 or 3 minutes later at a point 20 degrees to the left of her course fifteen feet of the bow could be seen to move slowly into view from the huge column of smoke and flame.

The sudden and unexpected daylight attack, combined with the explosive cargo aboard the American tanker meant that in a matter of seconds the newly built ship was turned into a mass of burning metal and could be seen for miles around. The crew of U-482 must have been ecstatic to see this mighty ship explode right before them. It was their first taste of the success they had been training for. For Kapitänleutnant Matuschka it must have brought back memories of the day he watched HMS *Hood* burn after the attack by the *Prinz Eugen*.

Gunner Marcellus Wegs continued to describe his efforts to escape the blazing tanker. By now even the surrounding waters had began to burn because of the leaking fuel.

I kept on running to the stern with my one arm in my life preserver. Had I put it on I would have burned on top of the water. Jumping in I swam beneath the flames underwater until I couldn't go any further so I came up and was still in the flames. I fought the fire off, but couldn't breathe for fumes and smoke. Feeling that I would rather drown than burn, I swam underwater some more and came up the second time, right at the edge of the fire. I kept swimming on top then, gasping in the fresh air, and as I got about 20 feet from the fire, I took off my five buckle overshoes and shoes and tied my life preserver on right. I was almost exhausted. I knew I was burned, but I never knew how bad, although I could hardly see because of it.

The witness aboard the *Cape Nome* realised that the chances of finding survivors were slim.

No lifeboats or life rafts were observed at any time. Neither were any men seen swimming in the water at any time in the proximity. The great mountain of smoke could be seen on the horizon extending high in the sky for hours thereafter being blown slightly in an ENE direction.

From a crew of 78 men there were only two survivors. One was Frank B. Hodges, a fireman who was in the mess room drinking coffee when the first torpedo struck. The other was the gunner Marcellus R. Wegs who was a strong swimmer and had worked as a lifeguard prior to the war. As their crewmates perished around them, these two men somehow managed to survive though both suffered serious burns.

Frank Hodges later described how he dashed out of the mess room at the first explosion and found that the ship was already ablaze. He ran to the boat deck to try and get his lifejacket but the flames and smoke began to engulf him, and so he turned to the stern rail and threw himself overboard without any flotation device. He surfaced to find the sea on fire all around him, and had to keep diving under to escape the flames, surfacing every so often to try and find a clear patch of water. Fortunately the attack had occurred in broad daylight so he was able to navigate his way to the windward side of the ship but found the flames were shooting high into the air above the burning vessel, and the sea was ablaze in all directions. There were several dead men in the water nearby, many of them clutching lifejackets that they had not had time to put on. Hodges later recalled that he could not recognise any of the men he came across in the water as they had been badly charred by the fire.

Marcellus Wegs who had only joined the service on 14 March 1944 later told his story to the *Democrat-Message* newspaper. His account was printed several months after the attack, once he had been repatriated to the United States, and while receiving treatment for rheumatic fever brought on by the time spent in the cold water of the North Channel. Ironically the naval hospital he attended was in Jacksonville, Florida. He described his rescue.

> A destroyer escort vessel, one of five that was escorting us across, came back imme-diately and by that time I had some burned life preservers and some torn pieces to hang on to. They threw off a raft to me, but due to the water being so rough and me almost frozen I was unable to reach it. I then saw a man swimming back towards the burning ship. I hallo'ed five or six times at him – he was almost uncon-scious – but he heard me and I encouraged him to swim. He said he had a leg broken so we stayed together. I told him to take his shoe off and he did and we got along pretty well then. The skin was all peeled off his face, his hair burned off and I couldn't recognise whether he was navy or merchant marine. Finally I asked his name and he said 'Frank Hodges', I knew then he was merchant marine.

Both men were eventually picked up by the USS *Poole* after an hour and a half in the water. The two enormous halves of the burnt and broken tanker actually remained afloat despite the massive damage but the aft section was later sunk by the escort ships using depth charges and the drifting forward section sank some fifteen hours later. Frank Hodges later said he had no recollection of being picked up by the destroyer and was told that he was delirious by the time he was eventually taken on board. He was taken to Londonderry and then to Belfast where he was treated for burns and other injuries. Marcellus R. Wegs continued his account in the *Democrat-Message*:

The destroyer escort stopped and picked us up then. I started to climb the ladder they let down for us. I reached up two rungs and fell back in. Then one of the gunners from the vessel leaped over the side and tied a line under my arms and the rest pulled from top side while he pushed from underneath. I reached top side but was unable to stand up. Everything turned black and I fainted. They took me below, removed my clothing, gave me plasma and wrapped me in blankets. When I came to, I was all bandaged up and couldn't see, and I was sure sick.

Like Frank Hodges, Marcellus Wegs had little recollection of being rescued and was also delirious by the time he was taken from the water. On his return to the United States he was awarded the Purple Heart for being wounded in the line of duty.

In the confusion created by the burning ship, U-482 crept silently away from the scene, her crew rejoicing in their first success. In a later report into the incident it was noted that the attacking U-boat had not been sighted or detected at any time. Escort ships circled the burning tanker for a considerable time, looking for survivors and any trace of the attacker but to no avail. The stony seabed below made it near impossible to make any accurate sonar detection. Coastal waters such as these could be notoriously difficult to scan because of the distortion caused by rocks, currents and even old wrecks which all showed up and helped cover a legitimate target. Because no contact was made there were no depth charges launched. A biplane appeared to join in the search for the attacker but also without result. It was noted in the report into the attack that it was believed the U-boat had watched the first four ships turning when the convoy detached and used this to line up the attack on the fifth ship when she completed her manoeuvre. They also made the assertion that because the order for detaching from the main convoy had been issued to the relevant ships by radio, it was possible that the attacking U-boat had intercepted and decoded the message.

Just hours after witnessing the sinking of the *Jacksonville* from his own ship, SS *Georgia*, first engineer Robert Goodwin composed a poem entitled 'A Tanker's Hit'. The third verse is particularly poignant and describes the feelings of those who were so close to the stricken ship, but who could do nothing for the men aboard.

Have you ever seen a tanker hit?
It's not a pleasant sight;
The ship from stem to stern is lit
With fires that burn so bright.

Smoke pours from her into the blue
And forms a mighty cloud,

Then turns into a ghastly hue –
A ship that was so proud.

Then men on ships about do stand
And sadly watch her burn;
There is no way to lend a hand,
Just watch, and wait your turn.

So down into a watery grave
She takes her gallant crew;
And all of those who had been brave,
A trip to heaven drew.

That same day BdU recorded a radio intelligence report in the war diary. 'English unit reported tanker torpedoed at 1555 in AM53 (U-*482*).'

Following the devastating attack on the *Jacksonville*, the hunt began. HMS *Hurst Castle* was one of 30 escort ships that had been ordered out to look for the U-boat and protect the rest of convoy CU-36. The corvette was sent out from Lishally near Londonderry to join in the search. Meanwhile U-*482* had turned west away from the detached section of the convoy and on 31 August the crew lay on the bottom to avoid detection by the ASDIC scans from the destroyers hunting for them up above. They lay still and quiet in the darkness, with the terrible sound of warships crossing the sea overhead.

During the night of 31 August, Kapitänleutnant Matuschka spent some time watching a large Swedish steamer, which turned out to be the SS *Gripsholm*, a liner employed by the International Red Cross as a diplomatic exchange ship. The 18,000-ton ship was built in 1924 by Armstrong, Whitworth & Co. Ltd of Newcastle, and belonged to the Swedish-America Line and operated their New York to Gothenburg service. Then in 1940 she was employed by the Red Cross and spent the rest of the war carrying refugees, prisoners of war and repatriated citizens across the Atlantic. These ships were supposed to be given safe passage and left unharmed by either side, as they carried citizens of all the warring countries in either direction across the Atlantic. When U-*482* came across her she was busy exchanging injured passengers, and effectively a sitting duck. But Matuschka identified the vessel and left it safe and sound before proceeding with his patrol. The *Gripsholm* continued in her role with the Red Cross until 1946, when she returned to her normal service. Interestingly, in 1954 she was sold to the North German Lloyd Line and renamed *Berlin*, operating their Bremerhaven to New York service. She was finally scrapped in Italy in the mid-sixties, some twenty years after her encounter with U-*482* in the North Channel.

After a tense day of avoiding her hunters, Matuschka once again found an opportunity to boldly attack, quite a feat with the sea dotted with enemies intent on his destruction. It was early in the morning of 1 September 1944, less than two days after the destruction of the *Jacksonville*. From the spread of ships in his periscope, Matuschka locked on to a Royal Navy corvette and began to make preparations for an attack. It was the HMS *Hurst Castle*. Like the *Jacksonville*, the *Hurst Castle* was a new vessel, having only launched that same year on 23 February in Dundee. She had been built there by Caledon Shipbuilding & Engineering Co. Ltd and had only been commissioned on 9 June meaning she had been in active service for less than three months. Over 40 Castle-class ships were built, first appearing late in 1943 as an improved version of the older Flower-Class corvettes. They were slightly larger (1,010 tons) and were around 47 feet longer, better equipped with ASDIC as well as new radar technology and the Squid mortar for attacking enemy submarines. The Squid was a development of the Hedgehog spigot mortar bombs that exploded on impact and proved highly successful in sinking U-boats.

With the *Hurst Castle* having been ordered to join in the search for the *Jacksonville* attacker, it was horribly ironic that at 0822 hours U-482 fired a single Zaunkönig T5 torpedo (a GNAT) at her and scored a direct hit. The corvette was badly damaged by the torpedo and sank with the loss of sixteen of her 105 crew; the youngest casualty was just sixteen years old. They were northwest of County Donegal in position 55.27N/08.12W. The GNAT torpedoes were designed to run straight for a distance of 400 metres, after which the acoustic homing technology would activate to target the enemy. Each torpedo was fitted with two sets of magnetostriction hydrophones, designed to locate, track and target the sound of the victim's propellers. Of course, this could result in a fired T5 torpedo turning back towards the sound of the U-boat that had fired it, and at least two U-boats were destroyed in this way. So the practice was for the U-boat to dive immediately after firing and go silent. These acoustic torpedoes were deemed particularly useful against fast moving convoy escorts as they would be drawn towards her propellers, and so the T5 acquired the nickname '*zerstörerknacker*' or 'destroyer cracker'.

Another ship that had joined the search for the attacker of the *Jacksonville* was HMS *Ambuscade*, which had been in the Clyde when sent out to join the hunt. She began an ASDIC sweep along with the other escort vessels when the *Hurst Castle* was torpedoed off their starboard side. The *Ambuscade* broke off her search to pick up the survivors of the sunken corvette, moving to the site where the corvette had sunk, and deploying scrambling nets over the side for the survivors to climb aboard from rafts or from the freezing sea. She later landed them in

Moville in Northern Ireland, before returning to the search for the still-unidentified U-*482*. The extensive search continued for several days, now for the perpetrator of both attacks, but no enemy vessel was detected and so once again U-*482* escaped unseen. HMS *Hurst Castle* was the first of only two Castle-class ship sunk by enemy U-boats during the war, the other being HMS *Denbigh Castle*, lost on 13 February 1945 after being torpedoed by U-*992*.

Later that day, the Count recorded hearing extensive depth charge attacks nearby, dropped from both ship and aircraft. The assault continued for several hours while the U-boat maintained a slow speed and a steady depth of around 85 metres. Finally he dropped to the seabed and waited for the attack to pass. It was shortly after midnight before U-*482* finally rose up to periscope depth and began moving once more. Kapitänleutnant Matuschka noted in his war diary that they found navigating their way around the area relatively simple. 'Navigation is not difficult because radio signals are used on English and Irish coasts, according to nautical radio stations and light signals are burning on Irish coasts as in peace time.'

It was now 2 September 1944. U-*482* had spent much of the time in the patrol area lying close to the seabed to avoid detection and only occasionally moving up to snorkel depth under cover of darkness so that the diesel engines could be run and the batteries recharged. They knew that showing any more of the boat above the water than the few feet of snorkel pipe would mean certain doom in these guarded waters. The day passed with the U-boat lying low, the crew listening carefully to the black abyss around them and occasionally lifting to the surface to peep cautiously through the periscope. Matuschka was simply waiting for his victims to come to him. He would not have to wait for long.

It was later that evening that Matuschka and his men once again got lucky. They were proceeding with the boldness that Admiral Dönitz demanded from his U-boat crews. Despite their extraordinary good fortune so far and the vast Allied hunt that they had avoided, there was no feeling amongst the crew that they were pushing their luck. So when a new opportunity arose to attack, Matuschka and his men would not miss their chance. They crept up to periscope depth later in the evening and around half an hour before midnight heard the first sounds of ships approaching. Matuschka put up his periscope and found they were in the middle of a convoy, sailing westbound in the moonlight. He selected a target, logging it as a 5,000-ton freighter and fired a single T5 torpedo, the same type of acoustic torpedo that he had used with devastating effect against the *Hurst Castle*. The crew waited in silence, counting off the seconds and listening for the sound of detonation.

This time the victim was a Norwegian ship called the *Fjordheim*, a freighter of 4,115 tonnes that had joined the westbound convoy ON-251, sailing from

Swansea on 29 August and stopping in Belfast Lough before leaving again on 1 September to join up with the main convoy, which had left Liverpool that same morning bound for Halifax, Nova Scotia. The freighter had a crew of 38 aboard and a cargo of 4,000 tonnes of anthracite that had been taken on at Swansea.

The *Fjordheim* and her convoy had left the North Channel and were moving west of Northern Ireland in position 55.55N/09.28W, ready to head out into the Atlantic. Already their fate was sealed. Matuschka had the freighter in the sights of his periscope and the torpedo had been sent with its deadly cargo ready for delivery. The single shot slammed into the starboard side of the *Fjordheim*, towards the rear of the ship, just between hatches 4 and 5. The torpedo exploded, shaking the vessel and sending an enormous blast rippling through her that blew apart the ship's hatches. In seconds, the deck was awash with water and lumps of the cargo. As the ship flooded with seawater, she began to go down by the stern and the crew moved quickly to abandon ship. All four lifeboats were rapidly manned and launched, with the crew trying to get clear as fast as possible to avoid the suction caused by the sinking freighter. It was common for the very hot boilers in a sinking ship to explode as the freezing seawater reached them, and this was what happened to the *Fjordheim*. The cold water flooded through the freighter as she sank through the waves, eventually reaching the scorching boilers and causing a second vicious blast around six minutes after the torpedo had struck. The *Fjordheim* sank fast.

Of the 38 crew, 32 were in the launched lifeboats and another man was picked up from the water soon after. Two more were later picked up by the nearby steamer *Empire Mallory,* which had launched a lifeboat to search for survivors. This left three men lost in the sinking. Two of them were stokers on the ship and were likely trapped beneath decks when the torpedo hit. The 33 survivors from the lifeboats were later picked up by HMCS *Montreal* and eventually transferred to the convoy rescue ship SS *Fastnet* along with the two from *Empire Mallory*. These 35 men remained on the rescue ship and carried on towards Halifax with the rest of the convoy where they arrived on 17 September.

Kapitänleutnant Matuschka and his crew did not realise his torpedo had actually hit the target, though they heard the sound of the explosion. The time the acoustic torpedo had taken to connect with the Norwegian freighter was beyond his expected time to detonation and so he thought that his torpedo had been a miss and had simply detonated at the end of its run. It was common for a U-boat to dive immediately after launching a T5 torpedo for reasons given earlier and so having not seen the sinking freighter or any evidence of her loss, he did not acknowledge or record the kill until much later confirmation. Even in his later transmission with BdU when listing his successes, Matuschka does not mention the freighter or any sinkings on that date.

Over a period of just four days U-*482* had sunk three Allied ships, and without coming close to any danger herself, despite the extensive search for her after the loss of the *Jacksonville* and *Hurst Castle*. The U-boat had managed to remain undetected by a combination of boldness, skill, unusual good luck and the poor ASDIC conditions in the coastal waters. But Kapitänleutnant Hartmut Von Matuschka was not finished yet; he still had torpedoes stowed aboard ready for use.

At 1700 hours on 7 September they came across the hospital ship MS *Oranje* while sailing towards the Irish coast. The *Oranje* was built in Amsterdam and was launched on 8 September 1938 weighing 20,117 GRT. Designed to sail between the Netherlands and the Dutch East Indies, she was capable of sailing at 26 knots and on her launch was the most powerful motor liner in the world. She was converted to a hospital ship during the war and served all over the world before returning to life as a passenger ship. Fortunately Kapitänleutnant Matuschka identified the ship correctly and did not make her another victim of his first patrol.

U-*482* remained in her patrol area to the north of Ireland and it was several more days before she located another victim. She remained submerged, moving slowly and silently along the coast, using the snorkel when the crew dared to run the diesel engines and keep the batteries charged. Not until 8 September did they get another opportunity to attack, as the massive convoy HX-305 moved out of the Western Approaches of the Atlantic and towards the North Channel. The events of this next confrontation are given in detail later on but it is worth noting here that this first active patrol by U-*482* became the most productive by any Type VII U-boat for the whole of that year, a success that was quickly noted by Admiral Dönitz.

Shortly after the details of this patrol became known, and U-*482* had begun the long trip back to Bergen, the young U-boat commander was notified that he had been awarded the Iron Cross First Class, having already received the Second Class after the Battle of Denmark Strait in the *Prinz Eugen*. The following is taken from an Allied Ultra intercept of a communication between U-*482* and U-boat command, followed by their reply. Note how Matuschka does not list the *Fjordheim* amongst his victims, because at this point he still did not realise that she had been sunk.

11 September 1944

From: Matuschka (*482*)

To: COMSUBS

Return cruise. Sunk the following: On 1/9 in AM 5612 DD from search group. From inbound convoys: On 30/8 in AM 5397 tanker of 7000 tons; On 8/9 in AM 5387 freighter of 5030 tons; tanker of 6000 tons. T5 SS shot on freighter of 5000 tons. Detonation after 2 minutes, 47 seconds.

11 September 1944

From: COMSUBS

To: Matuschka (*482*)

Hurrah for such an excellent achievement. I award you the Iron Cross First Class.

Matuschka later received a second communication informing him that he had been awarded the German Cross in Gold, a higher accolade.

After this considerable success and with all torpedoes expended, U-*482* headed for home and arrived back in Bergen two and a half weeks later on 26 September 1944 after a six-week patrol that covered some 2,729 miles, of which over 90 per cent was spent submerged, proving the worth of the new snorkel technology. In his memoirs, Admiral Karl Dönitz wrote of the snorkel, following the success of U-*482*:

> I ordered that, in future, no boat was to be sent into the Atlantic which was not equipped with a schnorchel. Thereupon U-boat Command, having equipped the boats with this device, sent them for the first time since 1940 close to the English coast. The first report received showed very positive results. U-*482* (Lieutenant-Commander Graf von Matuschka) had taken station in the North Channel, to the north of Ireland and, according to British reports, had there sunk the corvette HMS *Hurst Castle* and four merchantmen.

His enthusiasm regarding the snorkel was understandable, not only because of the success of U-*482*, but because at a time when the rate of U-boat losses had become much more frequent, things suddenly seemed to be improving; in October 1944 only one snorkel-equipped vessel was damaged out of the 41 on patrol around the north coast of Britain.

However, despite the stealth advantages the snorkel provided to a U-boat, it also meant the submarine travelling at a much reduced speed, and most of the time was spent travelling at just 2 or 3 knots or often just lying on the bottom to avoid detection. Progress was slow with the U-boat perhaps increasing speed to 5 knots for a single period of a few hours each day in order to recharge her batteries. Then occasionally she might surface at some period during the night to air out the boat and possibly increase speed to cover some extra distance, but probably for less than an hour at a time. This made for slow, tentative progress during which boats rarely managed more than 50 miles a day.

Matuschka himself put his success on this first patrol largely down to the snorkel, claiming that by staying submerged it had meant they had not once been sighted by air patrols. This is certainly true to some extent, as at no point were they positively identified by the Allies, nor accurately located by ASDIC and the defensive depth charge attacks made by the searching escort ships were never close enough to be dangerous and showed no sign of being targeted. Even if they had been spotted or detected at some point there is no evidence amongst any Allied reports to show U-*482* was ever positively identified during her first active patrol.

Of course, merely surviving in these dangerous and heavily patrolled waters was an extremely difficult task at a time when the Allied counter measures were at their most effective. Survival relied on intense planning, careful action and maintained focus on the part of the U-boat commander and his crew. Even the smallest operational error could cost the U-boat its most precious commodity – stealth. For the U-boat to operate successfully meant that every man aboard had to fulfil his duties accurately and safely. Kapitänleutnant Matuschka wrote in the war diary: 'Conduct on first patrol into enemy waters was good, everybody everywhere worked reliably, breakdown of machinery etc was quickly mended and therefore success was made possible.' He went on to praise the leading engineer who acted 'quietly and calmly in critical situations and who had to fulfil difficult demands due to all the snorkelling.' He also praised the mechanics that had repaired the periscope after it had received some damage and a pump that had become jammed through rusting. The crew had worked well together despite the pressure of living under constant danger. Lying in the abyss beneath the waves, the crew might not see an attack coming, and it could come at any time. A U-boat crew could never be sure that they had not been detected by the enemy and that a ship or aircraft was not already heading for their position to seal their fate. In his patrol report Matuschka wrote:

> ... the stay in the strongly observed and defended operational area under the coast, the unending listening, taking bearings from Saw buoys, Destroyers, Wabos, Asdic, not knowing if one was observed and by whom, was mentally exhausting. Experience, getting used to pressure and lastly courage through success (formerly achieved) helped one to accept it all with equanimity.

Despite these pressures, U-*482* had been remarkably successful on her very first patrol. Even Matuschka himself was surprised at how well things had gone. In a letter dated 29 September 1944, after his return to Bergen, Matuschka wrote: 'After our first patrol we have returned in good shape to the north. Our task had led us to the west coast of England and given us quite unusual success.'

U-*482* remained in Bergen for the next seven weeks while the crew went on shore leave. Hartmut von Matuschka returned home during this time, flushed with success. The crew were all young men; on her second patrol, the oldest man on U-*482* had just turned 30, while the youngest was eighteen. They were all new to this incredible success and must have felt invincible. And it was not only the fact that they had sunk so many ships, but the timing and positions of those ships that made their success so extraordinary. By September 1944 anti-submarine technology had made attacks in British coastal waters seemingly impossible, but with the fitting of the snorkel to their U-boat, Matuschka and his men seemed to have turned the tide all on their own. They had proved that the inshore waters could once more provide an excellent hunting ground; they had proved that it could still be done.

They all returned to Bergen in November to begin preparations for their next patrol when once again they would be sailing west towards the North Channel. It was hoped that they would match their previous success and once again manage to upset the continuous stream of merchant shipping that poured into Britain.

U-*482* began her second active patrol, departing Bergen on 18 November 1944, this time attached to the 11th Flotilla. The full story of this second fateful patrol is given in detail later on. We can note here that U-*482* had already carried out the most successful Type VII U-boat patrol of 1944, sinking five ships from three separate convoys, and sending a massive 32,671 tonnes into the abyss. Of course it must never be forgotten when listing ships and tonnage that there were also men aboard those vessels, and U-*482*'s devastating first patrol resulted in the loss of 234 Allied seamen.

COUNT HARTMUT VON MATUSCHKA

Name	Graf von Hartmut Matuschka, Freiherr von Toppolczan und Spaetgen
Date of Birth	29 December 1914
Birthplace	Dresden-Blasewitz, Saxony

NAVAL CAREER

8 April 1934	Entered the navy as an Offiziersanwärter (Trainee Officer)
1 July 1935	Promoted to Fähnrich zur See (Petty Officer)
1 January 1937	Promoted to Oberfähnrich zur See (Midshipman)
1 April 1937	Promoted to Leutnant zur See (2nd Lieutenant)
1 April 1939	Promoted to Oberleutnant zur See (Lieutenant)
January 1940	Joined the *Prinz Eugen*
24 May 1941	Served at the Battle of Denmark Strait as Artillery Officer

1 April 1942	Promoted to Kapitänleutnant (Lieutenant Commander)
March 1943	Transferred to the U-boat service and entered training
March 1943– September 1943	U-boat commander training
September 1943– October 1943	U-boat commander torpedo training
November 1943	At Kiel during the final stages of construction of U-*482*
December 1943– November 1944	Commander of U-*482*

AWARDS

September 1941	Iron Cross 2nd Class (while serving as an Artillery Officer on the armed cruiser *Prinz Eugen*)
September 1944	Iron Cross 1st Class (while serving as Commander of U-*482*)
September 1944	German Cross in Gold (while serving as Commander of U-*482*)

U-*482* PATROL HISTORY

Departed	Arrived	Duration (days)	notes
Kiel 6/8/44	Horten 8/8/44	3	
Horten 14/8/44	Bergen 16/8/44	3	
Bergen 16/8/44	Bergen 26/9/44	42	first active patrol
Bergen 18/11/44		7	lost 25/11/44

U-*482* SUCCESSES

Date	Ship	Tonnage	Nationality	Convoy
30/8/44	*Jacksonville*	10,448	USA	CU-36
1/9/44	HMS *Hurst Castle*	1,010	UK	CU-36
3/9/44	*Fjordheim*	4,115	Norway	ON-251
8/9/44	*Empire Heritage*	15,702	UK	HX-305
8/9/44	*Pinto*	1,346	UK	HX-305

Total tonnage sunk – 32,621 tons

V

PINTO – THE RESCUE SHIP

A so-called rescue ship is generally attached to every convoy, a special ship of up to 3000 gross registered tons, which is intended for the picking up of survivors after U-boat attacks ... In view of the desired destruction of ships' crews, their sinking is of great value.

Admiral Dönitz

When she was called upon to attend the sinking of *Empire Heritage* in convoy HX-305 in September 1944, the rescue ship *Pinto* was actually taking part in her first rescue mission since being requisitioned for rescue service by the Ministry of War Transport in 1942. She had taken part in nine previous convoys and this, her tenth, was the return leg that would mark her fifth return voyage, all without incident. The outward leg of the voyage from the Clyde with the westbound convoy ON 247 had begun on 2 August 1944 and had arrived in Halifax, Nova Scotia on 13 August.

Pinto was built in Glasgow by Harland & Wolff and launched in February 1927 as the fourth of five steamers ordered by MacAndrews & Co Ltd. She had been designed as a cargo ship destined for the Spanish fruit trade. She was 1,346 gross tonnes, powered by Harland-built Burmeister & Wain 4 stroke 6 cylinder diesel engines giving her a speed of around 12 knots.

Prior to her engagement as a rescue ship she had already sailed in several smaller convoys as a merchant vessel, mostly between Britain and the Mediterranean helping to carry much needed fruit to the British people. Having already been involved in the fruit trade, she simply continued in this role after the outbreak of war, though by early 1940 it was necessary to sail under the cover of the convoys.

Pinto joined convoy HG-14F on 5 January 1940 in Gibraltar and sailed along with fourteen other ships, mostly British, for Britain. They arrived in Liverpool ten days later on the 15th. *Pinto* was listed as carrying 'general' cargo but the other cargoes in the convoy included wheat, fuel oil, diesel and fruit. In total there were seven escort ships attached to the convoy at various stages and durations throughout the trip, with only one ship remaining with them for the entire voyage. The convoy included the ill-fated *Clan Macarthur*, which was lost in August 1943 as part of convoy DN-55. The 10,528-ton steam merchant ship was stopped by a two-torpedo spread from U-*181* some 350 miles east of Madagascar and sank just eight minutes after being hit; 53 men were lost. U-*181* was under the command of Kapitänleutnant Wolfgang Lüth, the second most successful U-boat commander of the war and the captain who had already torpedoed James Peterson on the *New Sevilla* in October 1940. Convoy HG-14F in contrast sailed without incident in January 1940 and arrived safely in Britain. *Pinto* had completed her first wartime trip.

On Valentine's Day 1940, *Pinto* had already returned to the Iberian Peninsula and once more left Gibraltar along with the 24 other ships that made up convoy HGF-19. This relatively small group of ships carried various cargoes including fruit, meat, iron ore, diesel and furnace oil, and though they were primarily British ships, there was also a Norwegian and an Egyptian vessel amongst them. The HGF prefix stood for 'Homeward from Gibraltar Fast' (homeward being Britain), and the convoy departed at 1400 hours on the 14th, and reached Britain on the 23rd, the convoy finally splitting up for several British ports. They had made the voyage at an average speed of 8.3 knots.

She travelled in convoy again on 28 June 1940, once again from Gibraltar to Liverpool in HG-36, a small group of just twelve ships. This was again a diverse group of cargoes – fuel, cereals, linseed, ore – and even passengers in a fleet made up of British, Greek, French, Dutch, Egyptian and Norwegian ships. They arrived in Liverpool on 8 July.

Her next convoy was HG-43 leaving from Gibraltar on 4 September. She was supposed to have sailed in HG-42 on 19 August but for some reason was rescheduled for HG-43. On this occasion, the Master of *Pinto* also acted as Vice-Commodore for the convoy of 21 ships, which included Polish, Swedish, Belgian and Yugoslavian vessels alongside the British ships.

She continued to sail the Mediterranean run, and the following year was still making trips to the fruit-supplying ports around the Iberian Peninsula. On one of these trips *Pinto* landed in Gibraltar and once laden returned to Britain with 23 other ships in convoy HG-58, destined for Liverpool. They left Gibraltar on 3 April 1941 at 1730 hours, formed into an 8-column convoy. They sailed at an average of

7 knots and arrived in Britain on the 21st. Although the convoy made the journey without loss, it was an eventful trip north. On 7 April one of the ships reported a possible submarine contact and dropped depth charges accordingly but no debris was seen and no other contact was made despite a search being carried out while the convoy made an emergency turn. Then on 18 April, as they were passing Ireland, the convoy came under attack from a Focke-Wulf which approached from astern and dropped four bombs close to one of the ships; the Panamanian *Csikos*, though all missed their target. The escort ships opened fire but the aircraft turned away and escaped after jettisoning its remaining bombs, though there were claims that the plane had been damaged and smoke was seen from one of the engines. The *Csikos* was also machine-gunned by the German aircraft during the attack and three of her crew were hit, one of them later dying from his injuries. A second Focke-Wulf attacked soon after but was forced to abandon the assault because of the heavy anti-aircraft fire put up from the escorts. It later transpired that the *Csikos* had taken some damage from the attack and was leaking. As a result she had to break away from the convoy and head to Moville for repair soon after. The convoy went on to arrive safely in Britain, splitting up into smaller groups to proceed to various ports including Belfast, Liverpool and the Clyde, amongst others. This convoy was the first time *Pinto* experienced the growing danger that all merchant shipping now faced in their travels around the world. It would not be the last.

Pinto returned again to the Mediterranean and once again was prepared to return to Britain with a cargo listed as fruit and mail. On this occasion she joined Convoy HG-65, a modest group of just fourteen ships, not including escorts, and this time *Pinto* was acting as Commodore. They departed from Gibraltar on the morning of 14 June 1941 and formed up into five columns. They had an escort of five ships plus the submarine *Olympus*, but even that did not prevent them becoming the target of an enemy attack just a day after leaving port.

At 0650 on 15 June the convoy came under attack from a Focke-Wulf Condor that dived out of the sun and bombed the convoy, dropping a series of bombs close to a Belgian vessel while machine-gunning her decks. Though no direct hits were scored, the convoy was then subjected to several other attacks as more aircraft joined the assault – another two Condors and a Junkers 88. The escort ships closed around the convoy and began defensive firing as the aircraft made pass after pass, coming down as low as 200 feet and moving between the columns of ships, which had also begun firing. After more than an hour of attacking, the aircraft had scored no direct bomb hits and had all taken damage from the barrage of anti-aircraft fire from the ships below. At 0805 they broke off their attack and turned to the northeast. The enemy planes disappeared from view but reports later came in of four aircraft that had crashed off Lisbon after being involved in an attack against shipping near Gibraltar. They were believed to have been damaged by a Catalina aircraft but may well have been the planes that had attacked Convoy HG-65. Although the enemy bombs had failed to score a direct hit, four of the convoy ships were damaged by gunfire and one crewman took a bullet through the thigh, though he recovered from his wound. Once more *Pinto* had escaped unscathed. The convoy carried on north, arriving in Liverpool on 29 June, though on this trip *Pinto* had a final destination of Barry Roads.

On her next trip *Pinto* once again returned to the Mediterranean, and on her return joined convoy HG-71, her final trip as a merchant vessel before her conversion to a rescue ship. HG-71 departed Gibraltar on 18 August 1941 and *Pinto* was one of thirteen merchant ships heading north. Her cargo was cork, and they arrived in Liverpool on 2 September.

The table below shows *Pinto*'s wartime trips as a merchant ship in convoy. She also made several shorter trips independently, which are not listed. These were mainly between coastal ports such as Bristol and Cardiff, or Seville and Gibraltar.

Convoy	From	Departed	Destination	Arrived	Cargo
HG-14F	Gibraltar	5/1/40	Liverpool	15/1/40	general
HG-19F	Gibraltar	14/2/40	Liverpool	23/2/40	
OA-133GF	Southend	20/4/40	At sea	22/4/40	
OG-27F	At sea	22/4/40	Gibraltar	28/4/40	
93KF	Casablanca	2/5/40	Brest	6/5/40	
HG-36	Gibraltar	28/6/40	Liverpool	8/7/40	general
OG-38	Liverpool	17/7/40	Gibraltar	29/7/40	
HG-43	Gibraltar	4/9/40	Liverpool	18/9/40	general
FS-87(3)	Methil	20/9/40	Southend	22/9/40	
FN-99(3)	Southend	4/10/40	Methil	6/10/40	
OA-226	Methil	8/10/40	Rendezvous with OB-226	11/10/40	
OG-46	Liverpool	18/11/40	Gibraltar	5/12/40	
OG-51	Liverpool	26/1/41	Gibraltar	8/2/41	returned to join OG-52
OG-52	Liverpool	5/2/41	Gibraltar	21/2/41	
HG-58	Gibraltar	3/4/41	Liverpool	21/4/41	fruit
OB-319	Liverpool	7/5/41	Dispersed (Pinto to the Clyde)	13/5/41	
OG-62	Liverpool	15/5/41	Gibraltar	29/5/41	
HG-65	Gibraltar	14/6/41	Liverpool	29/6/41	fruit, general, mail

OG–68	Milford Haven	11/7/41	Gibraltar	26/7/41	
HG–71	Gibraltar	18/8/41	Liverpool	2/9/41	cork
BB–69	Belfast Lough	29/8/41	Milford Haven	31/8/41	
OS–8	Liverpool	3/10/41	Freetown	26/10/41	petrol
ST–9	Freetown	22/11/41	Takoradi	27/11/41	
ST–12X	Freetown	8/1/42	Takoradi	13/1/42	
ST–20	Freetown	19/4/42	Dispersed	21/4/42	
LS–5	Takoradi	13/5/42	Freetown	20/5/42	
ST–30	Freetown	5/8/42	Takoradi	Unknown	
TS–21	Takoradi	6/10/42	Freetown	13/10/42	
ST–42	Freetown	13/11/42	Takoradi	18/11/42	
TS–26	Takoradi	29/11/42	Freetown	4/12/42	
ST–49	Freetown	22/12/42	Takoradi	27/12/42	
TS–33	Takoradi	19/3/43	Freetown	26/3/43	
SL–130	Freetown	30/5/43	Rendezvous with MKS–14	11/6/43	
SL–130F	Detached from MKS–14	18/6/43	Liverpool	20/6/43	

As the dangers to merchant shipping increased, there was more need for escort and rescue ships to sail within the convoys and suitable vessels were sought from the merchant fleet for these duties. *Pinto* was one of those identified as a potential rescue ship. She was requisitioned in May 1942, and actually began active service in December 1943. She was ordered back to Glasgow, the city where she was built, but this time to the yards of Barclay Curle & Co. for conversion. She was a unique choice for the Rescue Service being a diesel-powered vessel; the other rescue ships were mainly coal-fired steamships. The alterations required were considerable and included the arming of the ship as well as the installation of medical facilities. Various defensive armaments were installed including a 12-pounder at the foremast, Oerlikons (20mm cannons) both on the bridge and astern of the mainmast and a Bofors 40mm anti-aircraft gun above the aft deckhouse. In addition she was fitted with a hospital and operating theatre and dispensary for the treatment of rescued seamen, plus extra accommodation space to house up to 30 officers and 120 ratings. The new rescue ships were fitted with specially designed rescue boats that could be launched to pick up survivors, initially just one boat but later on with one on each beam. As well as the physical renovation of the vessel, rescue ships were also fitted with detection equipment for locating enemy ships. This included the High Frequency Direction Finding equipment (HF/DF) known as Huff-Duff, which was used to detect enemy radio transmissions.

The charity the British Sailors Society worked hard to ensure that all rescue ships were furnished with a supply of 'survivor's kits', which included clothing, toiletries and other comforts for distribution to rescued seamen, many of whom were taken from the water either naked, or with clothing ruined by fuel oil. A complete 'survivor's kit' cost about £5 and total expenditure exceeded £22,000. The kit consisted of underwear, trousers, shoes and socks, a jersey, a raincoat or oilskin, cap and gloves. Toiletries were provided – razor, blades, soap, toothpaste. The British Sailors Society also provided books, cards, and games for the survivors.

Of course by being so well equipped in the medical department, the rescue ships were often relied upon to treat medical cases within the convoy while on passage, not only in the case of a sinking. Arnold Hague writes in his book *Convoy Rescue Ships 1940–1945*:

> Few if any merchant ships other than liners carried a Medical Officer, the medicine chest in the Master's cabin with a few simple remedies and a pamphlet detailing the most usual ailments and simple injuries was the best one could hope for. The presence of a qualified doctor, operating theatre and pharmacy in the Rescue Ship was soon noted and the naval Surgeon-Lieutenant rapidly found himself GP to a diverse practice of seamen of many nationalities, varying in number from 2,500 to up to 10,000 in the case of the largest convoys. Transfer of patients to, or the doctor from, the Rescue Ship at sea became commonplace.

So after several months of alterations in Glasgow, *Pinto* was finally ready to enter the Rescue Service and her first voyage in her new role began on 8 December 1943 when she left the Clyde to join the combined OS-61/KMS-35G convoy to Gibraltar and Sierra Leone, back on the route she had plied in her fruit-carrying days. The convoy arrived without incident two weeks later on 21 December. After only three days on the Iberian Peninsula she set sail again on the homebound MKS-34G/SL-143 convoy, leaving on 24 December and arriving in Britain on 5 January 1944.

Usually the crews employed on the rescue vessels were handpicked by the ship's master and because of the nature of their work he required the best seamen he could muster. It was highly likely that they would be required to work in difficult and highly dangerous weather conditions, manoeuvring open rescue boats to pick up survivors or carrying out deck work in near or total darkness. For this reason, the crew were often kept on from voyage to voyage, much more so than in other ships where crews could often change. The Rescue Service operation was based on the Clyde, and seamen usually signed on for a complete voyage, sailing from the Clyde and staying with the ship until she returned there, regardless of the duration of the trip. This meant that each crewman saw service in at least two convoys, one outbound and one heading home. It meant that seamen would only be paid if the contract was fulfilled and so to leave the ship before completing the voyage meant that payment could be suspended. An unfortunate outcome of this type of agreement was that some seamen saw their pay stopped in the event of being torpedoed – they were classed as having been 'discharged at sea' and so had not completed their contract, through no fault of their own! For men with families reliant on their wages during those dark years it was a cruel but frequently added blow to shipwrecked seamen.

On her next trip, the *Pinto* took part in her first Atlantic convoy as a rescue ship and she left the Clyde with convoy ON-221 on 24 January 1944. After reaching the east coast of the United States without incident, the convoy dispersed and *Pinto* headed to Halifax, Nova Scotia, arriving on 8 February. The return leg of this voyage was with convoy HX-279, a group of 59 vessels, mostly American, that set sail from New York on 13 February, though the Halifax contingent departed on the 14th and arrived in Liverpool on the 29th. *Pinto* headed once more to the Clyde and this marked her second complete voyage as a rescue ship, all so far without incident.

Her next trip retraced the route of her last, leaving for Halifax on 15 March with convoy ON-228 and arriving there on the 30th. After two weeks in Nova Scotia, she left to join up with HX-287, a larger fleet of 71 ships, again largely American but also including British and Norwegian vessels along with Polish, Panamanian and Dutch. Like all the wartime convoys they carried a variety of cargoes, including fuel, steel, sugar, lumber and refrigerated foodstuffs amongst the various military consignments. They arrived in Britain on 25 April and dispersed to ports all over the country such as Glasgow, Swansea, Belfast, London, Manchester, Hull and Liverpool.

After the completion of these two Atlantic trips, *Pinto* was ordered once more onto her familiar Mediterranean run sailing from the Clyde for Gibraltar on 22 May with convoy OS-78/KMS-52G. They arrived in the Mediterranean on 6 June, D-Day. *Pinto* stayed three days, departing again on 9 June and returning to Britain with convoy MKS-51G/SL-160. They arrived without incident on 20 June. By now she had completed four voyages, escorting eight different convoys, and had yet to be called upon to assist.

Her next trip was not until 2 August when she left the Clyde with ON-228 once more on a westbound trip across the Atlantic. *Pinto* arrived in Halifax on the 13th and remained there until she was ordered to join up with convoy

HX-305 on 27 August before her date with destiny on 8 September. The table below shows all movements of the *Pinto* in her role of rescue ship.

Convoy	From	Departed	Destination	Arrived
OS-61/KMS-35G	Clyde (UK)	8/12/43	Gibraltar	21/12/43
MKS -34G/SL-143	Gibraltar	24/12/43	Clyde	05/01/44
ON-221	Clyde (UK)	24/01/44	Halifax	08/02/44
HX-279	Halifax (NS)	14/02/44	Clyde	29/02/44
ON-228	Clyde (UK)	15/03/44	Halifax	30/03/44
HX-287	Halifax (NS)	14/04/44	Clyde	25/04/44
OS-78/KMS-52G	Clyde (UK)	22/05/44	Gibraltar	06/06/44
MKS-51G/SL-160	Gibraltar	09/06/44	Clyde	20/06/44
ON-247	Clyde (UK)	02/08/44	Halifax	13/08/44
HX-305	Halifax (NS)	27/08/44	Clyde	

The first dedicated rescue ship went into service in January 1941, taking over the role that up to then had been filled by the escorting warships. The advantages of rescue ships were obvious. Over time the use of the warships as rescue vessels was found to be unsatisfactory as it meant they were distracted from defending the convoy or mounting a search for an enemy U-boat following an attack. Dedicated ships were needed to travel in the convoy and be prepared to move into action. They could be properly equipped to deal with injured survivors and would negate the need for other ships in the convoy to stop or alter course, something that they were not supposed to do because of the obvious danger of further attacks. It was a rule often flouted as, quite understandably, their instinct was to try and assist their comrades. The rescue ships began initially on the North Atlantic routes in 1941 but later spread to Britain/Gibraltar and other Mediterranean routes and then onto the notorious PQ convoys travelling to northern Russia.

Normally the convoys sailed in columns and often the rescue ship sailed at the end of a column so it was ready to move forward into action in the event of an attack. By the end of the war the convoy rescue service had taken part in some 797 convoys, rescuing survivors from 119 stricken vessels. A total of 4,194 men were saved; 2,296 were British seamen. These astounding figures highlight just how necessary the Rescue Service became. In making this enormous contribution to the safety of the merchant seamen, six rescue vessels were lost by enemy action, including the *Pinto*. This represented the loss of 231 men; 209 from the Rescue Service crews and a further 22 who had been rescued seamen, picked up from other ships before being lost aboard the rescue vessel. Two of these unfortunate souls were from *Empire Heritage*.

Other rescue ship losses included the *Stockport*, who in her career was the saviour of some 413 men before she disappeared in February 1943 whilst part of convoy ON-166. It was later suspected that she had fallen victim to the U-boat *U-604*. At the time of her loss she was carrying 91 survivors along with her crew of 63. Also lost was the *Walmer Castle*, sunk following a series of air attacks by a Focke-Wulf 200 Condor in September 1941. She was only a week into her first voyage and had already rescued 81 men from three ships in her brief career. In July 1942 the *Zaafaran* was sunk by an air attack during the notorious convoy PQ-17 when 25 of the group of 36 ships were lost en route to Murmansk. Responsible for 220 rescues, *Zaafaran* was sunk with only one fatality when a crewman was struck by debris. The *Beachy* was actually the very first rescue ship, going into service on 9 October 1940 and lost in January 1941 from an air attack whilst she was transferring between convoys with the death of five men. Also with a remarkably brief career but not destroyed by enemy action was the *St Sunniva*, originally owned by the North of Scotland, Orkney and Shetland Steam Co. Ltd. She was sailing as part of the outbound ON-158 convoy and was last seen just two days from Halifax, Nova Scotia. It is believed she probably iced up in the appalling weather and low temperatures and that the weight of the ice caused her to capsize. She was lost with all hands.

There were several ships that served throughout the war from 1941 when the Rescue Service began in earnest until 1945 when hostilities against the convoys ceased. The *Copeland* took part in 36 voyages and rescued 433 men from 11 different vessels; the *Perth* made 30 voyages and rescued 455 men from 14 ships; the *Rathlin*, made 24 voyages and rescued 634 men from 13 ships; and the *Zamalek* sailed in 31 voyages and rescued 665 survivors from 19 ships.

Not all rescue ships were so busy. For example, the *Dewsbury*, another of the veteran rescue ships, sailed on her first convoy on 1 December 1941 and her last, some 22 voyages later, on 11 May 1945. In that time she was only called upon twice, in December 1941 and again in December 1944, picking up two and three survivors respectively.

SHIPS ENGAGED BY THE RESCUE SERVICE

Name	Tonnage	Year built	Year entered Rescue Service	Convoys	Men Rescued	Notes
Aboyne	1020	1937	1943	26	20	
Accrington	1678	1910	1942	36	141	
Beachy	1600	1936	1941	5	–	Sunk by aircraft 11/1/41
Bury	1686	1911	1941	48	237	
Copeland	1526	1923	1941	71	433	
Dewsbury	1686	1910	1941	43	5	
Dundee	1541	1934	1943	24	11	
Eddystone	1500	1927	1943	24	64	
Empire Comfort	1333	1945	1945	8	–	
Empire Lifeguard	1333	1944	1945	6	–	
Empire Peacemaker	1333	1945	1945	8	3	
Empire Rest	1327	1944	1944	11	–	
Empire Shelter	1336	1945	1945	6	–	
Fastnet	1415	1928	1943	25	35	
Goodwin	1569	1917	1943	25	133	
Gothland	1286	1932	1942	41	149	
Hontestroom	1875	1921	1941	11	69	Withdrawn from service May 1941
Melrose Abbey	1908	1929	1942	46	85	
Perth	2258	1915	1941	60	455	
Pinto	1346	1928	1942	10	2	Sunk by U-482 8/9/44
Rathlin	1599	1936	1941	47	634	
St Clair	1636	1937	1944	14	–	
St Sunniva	1368	1931	1942	1	–	Capsized and sank owing to ice 23/1/43
Stockport	1683	1911	1941	16	413	Sunk by U-604 23/2/43
Syrian Prince	1989	1936	1943	19	–	Withdrawn from service December 1941
Tjaldur	1130	1916	1941	3	–	
Toward	1571	1923	1941	45	337	Sunk by U-402 7/2/42
Walmer Castle	906	1936	1941	1	81	Sunk by aircraft 21/9/41
Zaafaran	1567	1921	1941	26	220	Sunk by aircraft 5/7/42
Zamalek	1565	1921	1941	68	665	

VI

NORTHERN WAVE – THE ESCORT SHIP

Minesweeping of course comes almost naturally to the fishermen who man the trawlers. The occupation of handling and towing the minesweepers is almost the same things as their ordinary occupation of handling the trawl.

Rear Admiral H.G. Thursfield

It was HMT *Northern Wave* that became the eventual saviour of the men left floating in the darkness following the double torpedo attacks of U–*482*. After *Empire Heritage* sank, she had begun her anti-submarine duties to try and locate the attacker, but following the sinking of the *Pinto* she had to abandon these duties and become a rescue ship, and not for the first time in her career. Having served throughout the war she had already seen considerable action with convoys all over the world.

The prefix HMT stood for His Majesty's Trawler and *Northern Wave* was exactly that, a Grimsby fishing trawler requisitioned for war service by the Admiralty. She was owned by Northern Trawlers Ltd and was one of fifteen trawlers given the 'Northern' prefix. Several were requisitioned for escort duty including *Northern Sky,* which incidentally was also attached to convoy HX-305 when *Empire Heritage* was attacked.

Northern Wave had been built in 1936 at the Deschimag shipyard in Bremen in yard number 547. 'Deschimag' is an abbreviation of *Deutsche Schiff und Maschinenbau AG*, a major shipbuilder in the German city that had been formed in 1926 when nine smaller shipyards merged, including the AG Weser company that had been prominent in German naval construction during the First World War. *Northern Wave* was 188ft long with a beam of 28ft and weighed 655 gross tonnes. She was built for the Mac Line Ltd, and spent her first year operating out of Fleetwood, but the following year she was transferred to Northern Trawlers Ltd and began operating out of Grimsby. She had the pennant number LO-121, though after her conversion for war service her pennant number was changed to FY-153, which identified her as a converted fishing vessel. After her war service she was registered again at Grimsby and given the number GY-184. In September 1939 Northern Trawlers Ltd sold her to the Admiralty for £33,088.

At the outbreak of war there were around 330 steam trawlers registered in the port of Grimsby, about 250 of which were bought or requisitioned in the weeks leading up to the war. Some of the older ships served for a few months before being returned to their owners but some were destined to serve throughout the conflict, being returned following the German surrender. Only the very oldest vessels were left to carry on as fishing trawlers, though now the available crews were those outside of military age, either too old or too young to serve; every other available seaman ended up in either the Royal or Merchant Navy. Many trawler men were already in the Royal Naval Reserve when war broke out and so were called up almost immediately.

Prior to the outbreak of war, trawler production had been increased to fulfil the expected need for suitable vessels to carry out anti-submarine and minesweeping duties. The size and design of fishing trawlers were considered ideal for these duties and although they could not be particularly heavily armed, it was believed that even a machine gun could make a difference in a battle against a U-boat. At the start of the war, the danger and effectiveness of the U-boats had not been fully realised – and to some extent a machine gun *was* an effective weapon so long as the operator could actually see the U-boat. The gunfire could puncture the submarine's pressure hull forcing her to surface, or force her to dive making her immediately vulnerable to depth charge attacks. The problem was of course, that particularly in the early years, an attacking U-boat would not be seen at all.

Anti-submarine trawlers began to be assigned to groups of five or more ships, with several being attached to larger convoys. Even though they were not very heavily armed, a group of these tough little ships could be a force to be reckoned with if they combined their attacks against a lone U-boat. Because of their diminutive size they were very hard targets to hit with a torpedo, the submerged U-boat's only weapon. Their combined ASDIC could scan a large area for threats and they were ideal for forming defensive perimeters around a convoy while the ships manoeuvred into formation. The trawlers were tough, solid and incredibly seaworthy and with the outstanding seamanship of their crews, they were considered ideal for the escort duties that became increasingly crucial as the war progressed and merchant losses grew. They were also ideal for patrolling the approaches to harbours, because often these were the same harbours that the crews had sailed to and from during peace time and no-one knew the waters or indeed the vessels better than the local fisherman.

In Grimsby the trawler fleet was gradually converted for war service and within a few months of the outbreak of war, the requisitioned ships had been altered for their new roles. The smaller and older boats were fitted out to become minesweepers, boom defence ships or patrol craft. Many of them became contraband control craft and were based around the north and west coasts of Britain where they could observe and even board other ships to search for illegal war materials destined for Germany. The larger and faster vessels were converted for anti-submarine and escort duties. This meant arming them with weapons of some description, whether a large 4-inch gun for the anti-submarine ships or a 12-pounder or smaller for the minesweepers. Regardless of their new roles, they all required some degree of alteration.

Before any deck guns could be installed a considerable amount of work had to be carried out to reinforce the structure of the ship. The frames and deck beams had to be strengthened to bear the extra weight at the forecastle where the heavy guns were positioned. At the aft end there were often purpose-built mountings installed to house machine guns, Oerlikon or Bofors guns, and Lewis guns or Hotchkiss guns were often mounted on the bridge wings. For ships involved in anti-submarine duties, depth charge equipment had to be installed, which included rails for the charges and deck-mounted throwers. They were also fitted with ASDIC equipment. In the beginning the trawlers were fitted out rapidly to get them into service as quickly as possible, which meant that in many cases their only armament was an old and much smaller deck gun that had been relocated from somewhere else. They only received proper armaments as they became available.

As well as the extra armaments, the trawlers were required to carry a much larger crew than they had been designed for, often double the number of men. An average sized trawler that had been converted for anti-submarine duties needed a crew of around 30 men. Therefore all available space had to be put to the best use possible to house the men, supplies and munitions. The fish hold was cleared out and converted into a mess deck for the crew with hammocks hung overhead. Below this, in the very bowels of the ship, the ammunition for the guns was stored in a specially built magazine. So many men living together in such cramped conditions could be immensely uncomfortable, especially in bad weather; though generally the men made the best of it. In fact, the conditions they lived in were probably most comparable to those aboard the U-boats.

The officers aboard ship had quarters just beneath the wheelhouse, also very cramped, though they did at least have the luxury of bunks instead of hammocks and some very simple items of furniture. There was a very small galley where a single cook had the unenviable task of keeping the crew fed and satisfied in all weather and with limited provisions. An officer on *New Westminster*, one of the escort ships sailing with HX-305 at the time of the attack, described the difficulties these ships faced in bad weather.

> It was sheer unmitigated hell. Even getting food from the galley to the forecastle was a tremendous job. The mess-decks were usually a shambles and the wear and tear on the bodies and tempers was something I shall never forget.

The crews aboard the fighting trawlers could be from a varied mixture of backgrounds and ages. The engineers and much of the crew were largely from the fishing industry, either ex-fishermen who had been in the Royal Naval Reserve or older men who had been conscripted. There were also usually some very young men who had joined up when the war broke out but who had little or no previous sea experience, so there could be a curious blend of old hands and inexperienced youngsters who were not even used to the sea under peacetime conditions. In rough seas because of her small size, a trawler would ride on the waves rather than push through them like a more substantial ship, which could make for some uncomfortable journeys. A particularly heavy swell would result in the boat continuously pitching and rolling, making even a simple task near impossible for an inexperienced sailor.

There were several U-boats actually sunk by trawlers, or where they had at least contributed to the attack. There were many more instances where trawlers attacked U-boats unsuccessfully, but their presence would have helped to drive the attackers away from the convoys. On 4 October 1941 U-*111* was sunk by depth charges from the trawler HMS *Lady Shirley* south-west of Tenerife with the loss of eight men. On 10 March 1944 U-*343* was sunk with all hands after a depth charge attack by the trawler HMS *Mull*. On 25 August 1941 U-*452* was sunk with all hands south-east of Iceland by depth charges from the anti-submarine trawler HMS *Vascama* and a British Catalina aircraft. Also south-east of Iceland, U-*551* was sunk by depth charges from the trawler HMT *Visenda* on 23 March 1941. U-*732* was sunk on 23 October 1943 from a depth charge attack by the trawler HMS *Imperialist* and the destroyer HMS *Douglas*; 31 of the 49 crew were lost. On 15 May 1944 U-*731* was sunk with all hands following a combined depth charge attack by the trawler HMS *Blackfly*, the British patrol vessel HMS *Kilmarnock* and two US Catalina aircraft. Of course, there were also many anti-submarine trawlers that were subjected to U-boat attacks, sixteen being sunk and with few survivors.

Northern Wave had been one of 15 ships built for Northern Trawlers Ltd that were purchased by the Admiralty for war service. Three of these were directly attacked during the course of the war. Shortly before midnight on 30 October 1939, *Northern Rover* was on patrol around a hundred miles west of Sumburgh Head in the Shetland Isles. She was hit by a single torpedo from U-*59*, and became the third of 21 ships hit by this U-boat during a career that lasted for the duration. The trawler, based at Kirkwall in Orkney, had been requisitioned for service as an armed boarding vessel on contraband duties. She sank quickly and was lost with all hands. On 8 March 1942 *Northern Princess* was torpedoed off Newfoundland by U-*587*. She had last been seen on the previous evening and then had simply disappeared. There was no wreckage found and no survivors from a crew of 38, and it was assumed she had foundered in thick fog. It was only later that it was discovered she was one of the five ships sunk by U-*587*, who was herself sunk later that same month by depth charges from four British escort destroyers. She was lost with all hands. On 30 August 1942 *Northern Spray* was damaged by an explosion from a suspected torpedo. The ship did not sink and was later repaired but no attacker was ever identified and the source of the explosion remains a mystery.

At the outbreak of war, some 140 newly requisitioned trawlers began to be fitted out for anti-submarine service, and the Royal Navy began establishing groups of these trawlers for use. The 1st Antisubmarine Group of just five trawlers was established at Portsmouth. The 2nd A/S Group of three ships was based in the Western Approaches. The 3rd A/S Group, also of three ships, was formed at Rosyth and the 4th A/S Group of five trawlers was based in the Mediterranean. This was just the beginning however, because by May 1940 anti-submarine trawler strength has increased to 9 at Portsmouth, 23 in the Western Approaches, 65 at Rosyth and 12 in the Mediterranean. In addition there were 19 trawlers based at the Nore, at the mouth of the Thames Estuary, 12 at Dover and 25 for the seas around Orkney and Shetland. They had also stationed five at Gibraltar and had based more in the South Atlantic. The numbers continued to increase over the next few years as the importance of these vessels became clearer.

In May 1944 after nearly five years of war, there were 28 anti-submarine trawlers at Portsmouth, 28 at Plymouth, 33 in the Western Approaches, 10 at Rosyth, 7 in the Thames Estuary and 36 covering Orkney and Shetland. There were another 10 at Gibraltar, 17 in the Central Mediterranean, 13 in the Eastern Mediterranean, 22 in the South Atlantic, 12 in Iceland, 8 in the Azores, 13 in West Africa, 19 in South Africa and 15 in the Indian Ocean.

Northern Wave spent the entire war on active service; she saw her first action in 1940 off the northern coast of Britain. A tanker called *Daghestan* was sunk by a torpedo from U-*57* nine miles from Copinsay in the Orkney Islands. As the damaged ship slid beneath the waves, *Northern Wave* along with another trawler, HMT *Brontes*, moved in to pick up the survivors. Between them they rescued the ship's master and 28 of the crew, leaving two crewmen and a gunner unaccounted for. At this time the *Northern Wave* was under the command of Lieutenant G.P.S. Lowe RNVR. The survivors were later landed at the naval base at Lyness on the island of Hoy, also in Orkney. U-*57* sank a total of fifteen ships over her eleven patrols and served under five different commanders including two Knight's Cross winners: Claus Korth who sank some 73,000 tonnes of shipping in his career and Erich Topp, the third most successful U-boat commander of all time, who sank a staggering 198,000 tonnes – a total of 36 ships. The most significant proportion of his career was spent in command of U-*552* that followed his time with U-*57* during which he sank six ships. His time with U-*57* came to an end on 3 September 1940 when the U-boat was involved in a collision with a Norwegian steamship called the *Rona*. The U-boat was badly damaged and sank quickly resulting in the loss of six of his crew. Topp remained in active service throughout the war, and was still in command of U-*2513* in May 1945 when Germany surrendered. Despite his incredibly long career, Topp never forgot the *Rona* incident and later described it as his worst experience of the war, because of the loss of his men.

The next survivors that *Northern Wave* carried were from an HX convoy in 1941 that she was not actually escorting. Convoy HX-133 was a group of 51 ships that left Halifax on 16 June 1941 and arrived in Liverpool on 3 July. The first section of the convoy had sailed up from Bermuda as convoy BHX-133 and two other sections joined up, one from Halifax and one from Sydney, Nova Scotia. The convoy experienced several days of fog early on resulting in several collisions that damaged some of the ships. In the early hours of 24 June the convoy was attacked and one ship, the SS *Soloy*, was torpedoed by U-*203*. The ship sank fifteen minutes later but all the crew managed to abandon ship with no loss of life. In the evening of the same day the convoy was attacked again, this time by U-*651* and another ship, SS *Brockley Hill* was torpedoed and sunk, again with no loss of life. A third attack came two days later in the evening of the 26th. Two ships were torpedoed and damaged and two others were torpedoed and sunk; SS *Malaya II* and SS *Maasdam* were both torpedoed by U-*564* – SS *Malaya* was carrying a cargo that included dynamite and she exploded killing 41 of her crew; SS *Maasdam* lost just two from her crew of 80. On 29 June the convoy was attacked yet again, and again by U-*651*. The *Grayburn*, a 6,342-ton steam merchant carrying a cargo of steel and scrap was torpedoed just after midnight and sank with the loss of 35 men from her crew of 53. The survivors were initially picked up by HMS *Violet* and then transferred to the rescue ship *Zaafaran* and then later transferred again to the *Northern Wave* who landed them at Gourock on her way to the Clyde. The two ships that U-*651* sunk from this convoy proved to be her only successes; after the torpedoing of *Grayburn*, five convoy escorts hunted down the attacking U-boat and launched depth charges. HMS *Malcolm* hit the submarine and sank her, forcing the crew to abandon ship and surrender to the Royal Navy. The entire crew survived.

In March 1942 *Northern Wave* was assigned to convoy PQ-14, one of the grim Britain-Russia voyages that sailed from Britain to Archangel and later Murmansk. At 1600 hours they departed from Oban in the west of Scotland on 26 March and sailed north to Iceland, arriving in Reykjavik five days later. The first leg passed without incident and after a week they set off on the final stretch east to Murmansk. They departed at 1430 on 8 April and began the dangerous voyage over the top of Scandinavia to northern Russia. They sailed for a week without incident, but on 16 April, three days away from Murmansk, there was an explosion amidst the convoy as the British merchant ship *Empire Howard* (6,985 gross tonnes) which was also acting as the Commodore ship, was struck by a torpedo from U-*403* to the northwest of North Cape. It exploded in the boiler room and at least one more torpedo struck the ship, hitting the engine room and causing a blast that along with the first torpedo killed everyone below decks. There was then a huge explosion from the hold where the ammunition was stored, possibly from a third torpedo, and the resulting blast cut the ship in two. As the *Empire Howard* foundered, her cargo of army trucks slid from the decks into the sea; her total cargo was some 2,000 tonnes, listed simply as 'war materials'. Of her crew of 54, about 40 survived and managed to scramble overboard before their vessel disappeared beneath them – the ship sank in 57 seconds. The escort ships sprang into action including *Northern Wave*, who moved in to fend off the attacker and look for survivors. By this time, the trawler was under the command of Lieutenant W.G. Pardoe-Matthews RNR.

What happened next was to be one of the most unfortunate episodes in the war career of HMT *Northern Wave*. In the desperate scramble to protect the rest of the convoy from the attacking U-boat, *Northern Wave* began dropping depth charges in an attempt to blast the enemy submarine. But they had not realised the men abandoning the sinking merchant ship were already in the water and so close. The explosives detonated beneath them sending powerful shock waves through the water. Several of the men in the water were killed by the blast and many others suffered broken bones and ruptured organs. Eighteen survivors were eventually rescued from the water though many were unconscious and nine died soon after. This was later attributed to post-immersion collapse and Captain John M. Downie of *Empire Howard* later stated, 'Everyone was conscious when taken out of the water but many lost consciousness when taken into the warmth of the trawler.' After a crewman had been rescued from the freezing water there was still a danger of death through cardiac arrest from a collapse of arterial blood, or from the cold blood from frozen limbs reaching the body core.

Following the attack on *Empire Howard*, the convoy continued east and finally landed in Murmansk on 19 April 1942. Incidentally U-*403* was finally sunk herself over a year later on 18 August 1943 when she was attacked with depth charges from a French Wellington aircraft in the Mid-Atlantic off the coast of Dakar. She was sunk with all hands.

In January 1943 *Northern Wave* found herself assigned to convoy RA-52, one of the westbound convoys from Russia to Iceland and later to Britain. The small group of ten merchant vessels plus escorts left Kola Inlet in Russia on 29 January, but before they were halfway through the voyage they came under attack. The escort force for the small group of ships consisted of seven destroyers, two sweepers, three corvettes and four trawlers – an enormous protective screen. Despite this the convoy came under attack from U-*255,* lying in wait in the Norwegian Sea. The American ship *Greylock* (7,460 gross tonnes) was hit by a torpedo that caused considerable damage, though she remained afloat. With no hope of repair the crew were picked up and transferred to other ships in the convoy. Four of these were taken by the *Northern Wave*. The stricken American ship was then sunk by gunfire from one of the escort ships rather than being left for the enemy. It carried a cargo of 1,200 tonnes of calcium phosphate.

The remaining ships finally arrived in Loch Ewe, Scotland on 9 February. U-*255* went on to survive the war with an impressive record of twelve ships sunk over her fifteen patrols and she was still operational when Germany surrendered. After the war she was taken over by the Allies and was sunk as part of Operation *Deadlight* on 13 December 1945.

In May 1943 *Northern Wave* was transferred to the newly established ONS (Outward North Slow) convoys, which had begun on 15 March with ONS-1 sailing from Liverpool for Halifax, Nova Scotia. It was a convoy system that would continue sailing right up until the end of the war; the last, ONS-51, left Liverpool on 21 May 1945, two weeks after the German surrender. Over the 51 convoys that sailed on this route, a total of sixteen ships were lost, and all of them within the first seven months. Eleven were lost from ONS-5, one of the most infamous convoys of the Second World War, although the remaining 31 ships fought back and managed to destroy six of the attacking U-boats with a combination of new technology and much improved anti-submarine tactics. As mentioned earlier, this level of exchange had never been seen before – eleven merchant ships sunk at a cost of six U-boats. Because of this, convoy ONS-5 is regarded as a major turning point in the Battle of the Atlantic.

The factory ship *Tafelberg* showing the stern ramp used for winching aboard whales. The enormous tanks designed to carry whale oil were ideal for transporting fuel in wartime and the factory decks could carry trucks, tanks and even aircraft.

Tafelberg in two halves near Barry after hitting a mine in the Bristol Channel.

The bow section of *Tafelberg*. The figures in the foreground help to give a sense of scale to the enormous ship.

The stern section of *Tafelberg* showing the massive damage caused by the mine.

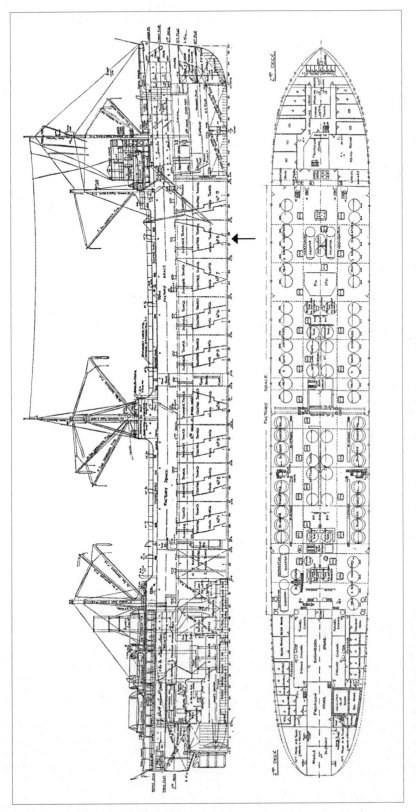

A deck plan of *Tafelberg* showing the approximate position where the torpedo struck (see arrow).

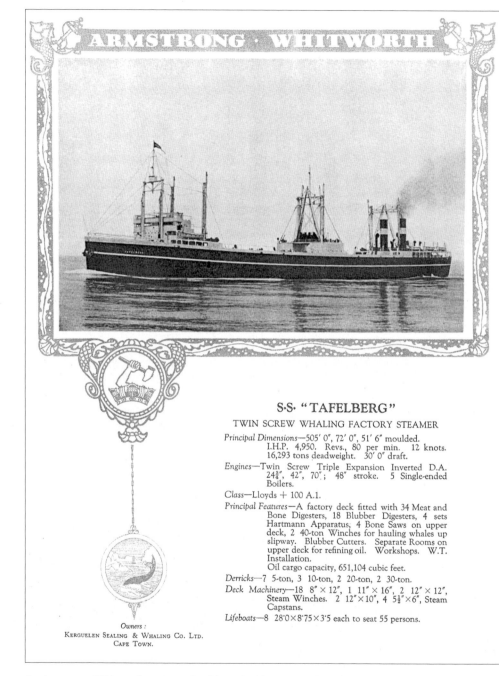

S·S· "TAFELBERG"

TWIN SCREW WHALING FACTORY STEAMER

Principal Dimensions—505′ 0″, 72′ 0″, 51′ 6″ moulded. I.H.P. 4,950. Revs., 80 per min. 12 knots. 16,293 tons deadweight. 30′ 0″ draft.

Engines—Twin Screw Triple Expansion Inverted D.A. 24¾″, 42″, 70″; 48″ stroke. 5 Single-ended Boilers.

Class—Lloyds + 100 A.1.

Principal Features—A factory deck fitted with 34 Meat and Bone Digesters, 18 Blubber Digesters, 4 sets Hartmann Apparatus, 4 Bone Saws on upper deck, 2 40-ton Winches for hauling whales up slipway. Blubber Cutters. Separate Rooms on upper deck for refining oil. Workshops. W.T. Installation.
Oil cargo capacity, 651,104 cubic feet.

Derricks—7 5-ton, 3 10-ton, 2 20-ton, 2 30-ton.

Deck Machinery—18 8″ × 12″, 1 11″ × 16″, 2 12″ × 12″, Steam Winches. 2 12″×10″, 4 5¼″×6″, Steam Capstans.

Lifeboats—8 28·0×8·75×3·5 each to seat 55 persons.

Owners :
KERGUELEN SEALING & WHALING CO. LTD.
CAPE TOWN.

An Armstrong Whitworth & Co. Ltd publicity brochure for *Tafelberg*.

Rejoined, repainted and renamed – *Empire Heritage* in port. At 15,702 GRT she was one of the largest U-boat victims of the war.

Empire Heritage. Length 512 ft, beam 72 ft.

Above left: Merchant Seaman James Peterson.

Above right: James Peterson wearing the Merchant Navy lapel badge.

Left: Kapitänleutnant Graf von Hartmut Matuschka, commander of U-482.

Below: U-482's emblem. Hundreds of U-boat crews adopted their own personal insignia.

Left: The crew of U-*482* at her commissioning in December 1943, Matuschka front and centre.

Below: A Type VIIC U-boat similar to U-*482*.

A T2-SE-A1 steam tanker similar to the *Jacksonville*, U-*482*'s first victim.

The *Jacksonville* burning on the horizon. This photograph was taken from the USS *Peterson* – one of the convoy escort ships hunting for the attacker – by Gunner's Mate Bob Miller.

HMS *Hurst Castle,* which was sunk whilst searching for U-*482.*

The Norwegian ship *Fjordheim,* was sunk while heading westbound from Britain to Halifax, Nova Scotia.

The rescue ship *Pinto.* She had only picked up two survivors from *Empire Heritage* when she was herself torpedoed.

Two views of the escort ship HMT *Northern Wave*, the Grimsby fishing trawler that became a convoy escort ship and the eventual saviour of the survivors from *Empire Heritage* and *Pinto*.

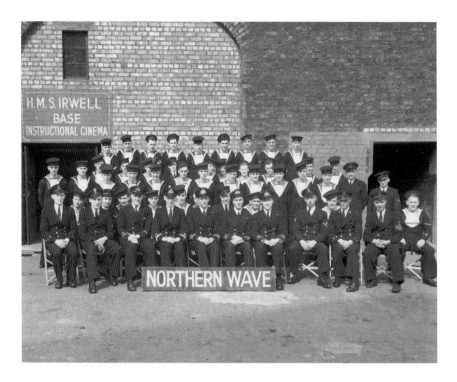

The crew of *Northern Wave* at HMS *Irwell* – a trawler base at Birkenhead. Lt Frederick J.R. Storey sits fourth from left, front row.

Type VIIC U-97 enters port while in the Mediterranean in June 1943. She was sunk on the 16th of that month by depth charges dropped by a Hudson IIIA of 459 (RAAF) Squadron.

3.

2. 4.
    5.   1.

●Glasgow

North
Channel

Londonderry

Belfast

Approximate
positions of ships
attacked by
U-482

1. Jacksonville
2. Hurst Castle
3. Fjordheim
4. Empire Heritage
5. Pinto

Liverpool●

The approximate attack sites of U-482.

Above left: Kapitänleutnant Matuschka on leave after his first extraordinary patrol. He had been awarded the Iron Cross 1st Class and German Cross in Gold.

Above right: James Peterson, Antarctic whaling (right) – he worked for Christian Salvesen in South Georgia in the years before and after the war and was bo'sun on *Empire Heritage* at the time of her sinking.

James Peterson's discharge book showing his discharge 'at sea' on 8 September 1944.

Two of the huge Scotch boilers amongst the wreckage of *Empire Heritage*. The Scotch marine boiler attained near-universal use in the age of steam at sea. The *Titanic* required 29 of them.

The remains of twin derricks still tower above the wreck. The same derricks can be clearly seen in the earlier photographs of the ship.

Part of the cargo of new military trucks lying scattered on the seabed. Their tyres are still intact. *Empire Heritage* was carrying nearly 2,000 tonnes of deck cargo.

Sherman tanks piled up after spilling out of the factory deck of the ship.

A newly built Sherman tank destined for the war in Europe, lying on the rocky seabed of the Atlantic Ocean.

One of the enormous bronze propellers lying at the stern of the wreck of *Empire Heritage*.

Both ONS-5 and ONS-6 were still at sea en route to Halifax when *Northern Wave* joined ONS-7 in Liverpool, and the convoy of 40 ships departed across the Atlantic. They left Britain on 7 May 1943, with *Northern Wave* under the command of Lieutenant J.P. Kilbee. The voyage was to take 18 days and when the convoy finally arrived in Halifax they were a ship down. On the 17th as they were halfway across the Atlantic, convoy ONS-7 ran into U-boat U-657 and the British merchant ship *Aymeric* (5,196 gross tonnes) was torpedoed whilst in ballast. *Northern Wave* proceeded to the wreck site along with the rescue ship *Copeland* and began picking up survivors while attempts were made to locate the attacker. Between them the two vessels rescued 25 men including the ship's master, eighteen crewmen and six gunners. The U-boat was located at the scene and was successfully attacked by the Royal Navy frigate HMS *Swale*. U-657 was depth charged and sunk with all hands.

In June 1944 *Northern Wave* was one of 30 ASDIC-fitted trawlers assigned to take part in Operation *Neptune*, the codename for the naval part of Operation *Overlord*. On 23 May she began convoy escort duties in British waters as the fleet began to amass for the invasion, and on 5 June she was in the Solent as an escort to Force S Assault convoy S10. They crossed the English Channel on 6 June and *Northern Wave* arrived at Sword Beach. She remained on duty with the Allied invasion until 3 July, acting as escort to the sections of Mulberry Harbour as they crossed the Channel, and later on anti-submarine duty. After this she returned to duty as a convoy escort and within a couple of months was to play the vital role of rescue ship to the men of *Empire Heritage* and *Pinto* in September 1944.

On Wednesday 1 November 1944, seven weeks after the losses of convoy HX-305, *Northern Wave* was en route to Falmouth. There was a large convoy just a few miles away but headed in her direction so the trawler altered her course so as to stay clear of its path as it approached. It was broad daylight with good visibility and a calm sea. Then at 1355, something was picked up by her ASDIC, and *Northern Wave* immediately suspected a submerged U-boat, lying in wait for the convoy to move within range. The trawler signalled a warning to the convoy allowing them time to take evasive action. The U-boat assessment committee later decided that it probably had been a U-boat they had picked up, and that it was probably U-978, a Type VIIC snorkel-fitted vessel commanded by Oberleutnant Günther Pulst, who they knew had been operational in that area. The evasive action proved effective and the convoy made it through without incident, but if they had not received the warning from *Northern Wave*, there could have been a very different outcome. Incidentally, Pulst and U-978 carried out the longest snorkel patrol of the entire war; they spent 68 days fully submerged, leaving Bergen on 9 October 1944 and arriving back on 16 December.

September 8 1944 marked the last rescue of *Northern Wave*'s war service. By then she was under the command of Lieutenant Frederick J.R. Storey RNVR. This was perhaps the crowning moment in a distinguished naval career that spanned the war and indeed spanned the world. Of course the actions described above were only the more notable experiences in a constant line of duty, from convoy to convoy and port to port, right across the Battle of the Atlantic theatre. It is a formidable list of achievements for a small fishing trawler from Grimsby.

In September 1945 with the war over, *Northern Wave* was allowed to go home. She was demobilised and returned to her owners. In the months following the end of hostilities, the remains of the old fishing fleet gradually returned to Grimsby, a little different after the wartime conversions but still ready to take up their original role as trawlers. *Northern Wave* would later become one of the very first trawlers to experiment with the technique of freezing fish whilst still at sea. In 1964 she was sold and scrapped at Dunston, Tyne and Wear after a busy and varied career.

NORTHERN WAVE SPECIFICATIONS

Type	Anti-Submarine Trawler
Built at	Deschimag, Bremerhaven
Completed	1936
Requisitioned	1939 (sold to the Admiralty)
Length	188.1 ft
Beam	28.1 ft
Draught	15.5 ft
Gross Tonnage	655
Net Tonnage	254
Pennant	FY-153 (previously LO-121)

VII

ANATOMY OF A U-BOAT ATTACK

The U-boat was the sole instrument which, with a few men aboard, could make a wholly disproportionate contribution to success in war by sinking, for instance, just one ship laden with munitions, tanks or other war material.

Admiral Dönitz

The Atlantic crossing had been uneventful for convoy HX–305 in the days leading up to the early hours of 8 September, as they passed the coast of County Donegal. The massive convoy sailed eastwards through the darkness, oblivious to the danger that lay just ahead of them. According to the Chief Officer of *Empire Heritage*, James C. Gibson, there were approximately 107 ships altogether, formed into fifteen columns with his ship being the fourth ship in the fifth column, with four ships astern of her. On the voyage she shifted position twice but was still inside the body of the convoy. It must be said that this differs from the position stated in the later inquiry. The columns were spread around 7 miles wide at a depth of 3 miles and so covered an extensive area of water. Gibson noted 'the weather was fine and clear, moonlight, with very good visibility; there was a moderate N.W'ly sea and swell, and N.W. wind, force 4.'

The Commodore, Sir A.L. Owens RNR was in the Norwegian ship *Abraham Lincoln* and the Vice Commodore F. Ratsey RN was aboard the British ship *Umgeni*. The 5,740-ton *Abraham Lincoln* was built in 1929 and was owned and managed by Fred Olson & Co. She served safely right throughout the war; her first voyage sailing independently from Vancouver to Seattle on 17 March 1940 and her last was from New York to Liverpool, arriving on 3 June 1945 as part of convoy HX–357, the penultimate convoy of the entire HX series.

The main convoy was surrounded by a significant escort group with several ASDIC-equipped vessels ahead of them, and they had been forewarned of the recent U-boat attacks in the area. To the rear of the convoy was the rescue ship *Pinto* and to the rear starboard side of the escort were the two armed trawlers *Northern Wave* and *Northern Sky*. Crucially, neither of these two vessels was fitted with radar, which left a significant gap in the coverage. Chief Officer Gibson stated that they convoy was sailing at 9.5 knots.

With two hours left until sunrise the convoy sailed east about 15 miles off the coast of Malin Head. Nearby the commander of U-*482* was keeping watch. The U-boat had already had a productive and successful patrol having taken three Allied ships without reprisal. Kapitänleutnant Matuschka noted in the war diary that they had unsuccessfully fired on a destroyer three days before, on the 27th. He believed that they had 'probably' been observed on this occasion but clearly no counterattack was made. He went on to write that they were 'definitely seen during convoy attack on 30/8', which was the attack on convoy CU-36 that resulted in the loss of the *Jacksonville*. From Allied reports we know that in fact they were never detected. After the attack on the *Jacksonville* he noted a definite change in the Allied defence as patrols were increased and convoy protection was tightened up. He noted that before the attack, 'Destroyers patrol singly and in groups, especially in AM52 and 53' and he wrote that in certain areas there were no patrols at all and no sign of aircraft. But after his first successful attack he noted that there were 'more searches, ASDIC impulses and heavy air surveillance'.

This increase in Allied patrols limited the U-boat's ability to snorkel during daylight hours as there was a serious risk of the snorkel head being spotted above the water. As one of the first commanders to use a snorkel-fitted U-boat, Matuschka was able to offer a valuable assessment on the feasibility of using the technology in the North Channel. He wrote in the war diary, 'Various possibilities of using snorkelling boats in the North Channel. The area was not occupied for a fair amount of time, firstly quite easy with relatively harmless surveillance.' As defences tightened up this possibility became slightly more limited and snorkelling had to be confined to the hours of darkness.

After being seen and putting into place a strong defence we could keep boat in the escort's path and main traffic areas for eight days. Night snorkelling was almost always possible, sometimes interrupted … Advantageous for our boat was the bad Gamma rays under the coast, moderate depth of water, which allow us to crawl and lay on the bottom near Inishtrahull.

By staying submerged in the shallower coastal waters, the U-boat was able to remain out of the way of the patrolling convoy support ships. She could lie in wait for passing convoys to come within range, virtually guaranteeing themselves potential targets. Matuschka later wrote of this technique in the war diary:

> A sure way to success is, whenever defence strategies allow, to stay near traffic-intense area ... if defence does not become stronger as observed lately, and if they are not using new methods or improve the existing one vastly, we shall be able to use further boats near the coast.

According to the log of U-482, they had been tracking the convoy for the last couple of hours after detecting a sonobuoy. Matuschka's first record of convoy HX-305 was at 0155 on 8 September when he noted having detected a 'Sound Buoy 130 Degrees.' At this point U-482 was deep underwater but the crew were listening intently to the wall of ocean outside. They were in quadrant AM 5387 on the Kriegsmarine grid map.

It should be noted that all U-boats kept Central European Time to be the same as Berlin wherever they were. The convoy was on British Summer Time. All times recorded here are shown as Greenwich Mean Time for the sake of continuity and to help the various accounts flow. There are also occasional inconsistencies in the exact minute-by-minute timings according to the U-boat log and the accounts and reports from the other ships, but that is to be expected and they are recorded here as in the original documents.

At 0158 they heard a destroyer for the first time at 50 degrees, but it became quieter and disappeared two minutes later. In the darkness below the waves, ships could be identified by the sound of their propellers; large merchant vessels generally had large, slow propellers whereas a sleek destroyer would have high speed ones that became a recognisable danger sign to a U-boat hydrophone operator. At 0226 they detected another sonobuoy at 110 degrees that also went quiet before disappearing some fifteen minutes later, though at 0230 they picked up a hydrophone at 230 degrees that became louder. At 0250 it was at 260 degrees and then loud at 275 degrees. They noted that it was 'probably a destroyer with a sound buoy'. As *Empire Heritage* was the fourth or fifth ship in her column according to differing accounts, and the U-boat was relatively stationary, it can be assumed that this commotion was the convoy moving past on either side of the U-boat, and that she was positioned between the columns. With the ships spread over such a vast stretch of sea it was perfectly possible for U-boats to position themselves in this way and simply lie in wait for an opportunity to attack.

At 0325 the hydrophone had become quieter as it had moved around the U-boat to 130 degrees, and then also disappeared. At 0327 a new sonobuoy appeared, loud at 335 degrees and becoming steadily louder. Then at 0330 it was noted in the log 'A roaring sound strikes the ear, similar to that on 3.9 when the convoy passed.' The convoy referred to was in fact ON-251, the convoy from which U-*482* had torpedoed the Norwegian steam ship *Fjordheim* on 3 September five days before. The log goes on to note 'Several hydrophones aft and at 30, 50, 80 degrees. Steamer sounds.'

There was now no doubt that the crew of U-*482* had found themselves amidst another convoy and were surrounded by ships that they could add to their growing list of successes. From their dormant position in the deep, the U-boat sprang into life.

0330 – To combat stations, to periscope depth. From the attack periscope only outline shapes can be detected. Now level with the central periscope. There is sufficient brightness for an underwater attack. The boat is actually in the middle of a convoy again, following the same course. Nearby steamers are easy to detect. A quick look shows their formation and strength. The convoy should not be taken yet.

Air was slowly pumped from the compressors aboard the Type-VIIC into her ballast tanks, forcing out the water and gently bringing her towards the surface. The U-boat levelled off beneath the surface and Matuschka put up the periscope giving him the first glimpse of the early morning sky and of the vessels moving steadily eastwards. At 0351 he noted the conditions overhead. 'Overcast, moon glimmers through the clouds, slight swell, grey dawn.'

At periscope depth the Commander and the hydrophone operator were the only ones with contact with the outside world. The rest of the crew had to rely on what information could be gleaned from their leader and the orders he gave out. Men had to simply go about their duties and could only guess at what was occurring around them.

Matuschka selected a target from the ships moving past. *Empire Heritage* was heavily laden and lying low in the water; in her huge tanks designed for carrying whale oil there was 16,000 tons of fuel oil and her factory deck, the enormous open space used for the processing of whales, was packed with 1,947 tons of trucks and Sherman tanks. In addition she had ample crew accommodation from her days as a whaling factory ship. She was listed as carrying 85 crew including four army personnel, seven naval gunners and two signalmen, along with 73 passengers – mostly seamen who were returning to Britain after the loss of their ships on other voyages. Her sheer size would have made her stand out as a perfect target as U-482 surfaced along her starboard side. Despite this it was still difficult to determine her full size in the darkness and initially she was logged as a freighter of around 5,000 tonnes.

As a Type-VIIC U-boat, U-482 had five torpedo tubes, four in the bow and one in the stern and they generally set out on patrol with fourteen torpedoes aboard. By this stage of course, U-482 had already used several. With the torpedo tubes loaded and ready, Matuschka used the attack periscope to track his target as the U-boat turned smoothly through the water to line up the shot. The maximum submerged speed of the U-boat was 7.6 knots while the convoy was moving at over 9 knots. The distance between the two vessels would have to be accurately calculated to ensure a direct hit.

In the German Navy a torpedo was known as an 'aal' (eel) and they were very different from other types of weapon in that they were self-propelled rather than fired and so except for their initial launch from the torpedo tube, they travelled through the water by their own propulsion system. Within the outer body of the torpedo were a number of highly complex components including the electrically powered propulsion system, a guidance system and depth controls, a pistol device to detonate the torpedo, and of course a warhead containing 280kg of hexanite. Depth control systems allowed crews to set the depth that the torpedo would run at so that they could approach the target without surfacing, reducing the chance of being detected, and also it allowed the torpedo to run right under the hull of a ship to blast the keel, breaking her back and destroying the ship with just a single torpedo. Electrical propulsion systems featured two counter-rotating propellers that ran off an enormous battery system that made up around a third of the torpedo's total mass. They replaced an earlier steam-driven version and had the advantage of being almost entirely silent and leaving no bubble trail that could act as a warning to a vigilant enemy. At the front of the torpedo was the warhead and pistol firing device. There were two types of pistol – magnetic and contact. Magnetic pistols were designed to detonate the warhead when triggered by the magnetic field of the enemy ship and they would explode right under the hull. Contact pistols situated at the nose of the torpedo were designed to detonate the warhead when the torpedo struck against the side of a ship. Most torpedoes were fitted with both pistol systems allowing the commander to select the best device for the situation.

By this time, the crew of U-482 had experienced how unreliable torpedoes could be. In his war diary at the end of the patrol Matuschka noted that 'two T5s set properly did not get to the target' estimating that one had possibly hit a foxer decoy device being towed behind a ship, and that one had lacked the power to reach the target. He also noted that a T3 had failed during the attack on

Jacksonville on 30 August, though it had later detonated. However, most of their torpedoes worked without any problems.

Matuschka lined up the bow of U-482 to the required position ahead of *Empire Heritage* as the tanker and the rest of the convoy continued eastwards along the Donegal coast. Within the U-boat everything had been set; the torpedo battery had been warmed up to around 30°C ready for firing and the torpedo tube had been flooded and the pressure equalised with that of the ambient sea pressure outside. The muzzle door at the front of the submarine had been opened and with the depth and speed of the torpedo calculated and set, everything was ready. The launch of a torpedo resulted in a sudden and significant change in the buoyancy of a submarine and this had to be accounted for by adjusting the trim of the ship. This was done by the flooding and draining of ballast tanks in different parts of the boat to maintain even distribution and so keep her level. This had to be adjusted constantly in a U-boat when even the movement of crew or supplies within the vessel could quickly alter its trim.

With everything ready Kapitänleutnant Matuschka gave the order to begin the attack, and the first torpedo was fired. '0351 – Shot from Tube 3 at freighter 5000 BRT'. BRT stands for '*bruttoregistertonnen*', the German equivalent to GRT or Gross Registered Tonnage. This figure was merely an initial estimate by Matuschka of the type and size of ship he was attacking. With the torpedo away, the crew of U-482 waited tensely, ticking away the seconds as the 100hp electric motor propelled the seven metres of torpedo towards the target. It ran at a maximum speed of around 30 knots.

The torpedo had of course to be fired ahead of the target to allow for the travelling time of both the ship and the torpedo. The torpedo cut through the water between the two vessels in just over 40 seconds and rendezvoused perfectly with *Empire Heritage*; the tip of the torpedo struck the hull of the tanker on her starboard side and in a millisecond the contact pistol detonated the warhead, throwing an enormous blast forward into the ship and tearing a massive hole through her steel skin.

The tanker shuddered violently as a second explosion echoed from the number 8 tank on the starboard side just behind the bridge. The listening U-boat crew noted it in the U-boat log, 'Direct hit 0 minutes 42 seconds. Hit not observed.'

Empire Heritage had nine large hold compartments and each compartment contained three tanks left over from her whaling days. Tank 8 like all the other tanks was full of fuel oil. According to Chief Officer Gibson 'A high column of water was thrown up on the starboard side, which flooded the fore part of the vessel, and there was a bright flash. The vessel immediately took a heavy list to starboard, and settled rapidly by the bows.'

The tank was torn open by the blast and almost immediately the fuel oil ignited causing a huge secondary explosion as the ship began to flood. Lookouts aboard HMCS *Dunver*, the ship carrying the senior officer of the escort reported sighting red flashes within the convoy, rising to a height of 70 feet.

As the tanker listed to starboard the flooding worsened and the factory deck, which was little more than a foot above the waterline, began to slip beneath the surface. The crew had only seconds to react to the sudden attack and with the ship already beginning to founder, they prepared to abandon ship, donning lifejackets and heading onto the deck to release life rafts. For those asleep or below decks there was precious little chance of escape. Chief Officer Gibson was asleep in his cabin when the first explosion woke him. 'I jumped out of bed, slipped on some clothes and my lifejacket, and hurried on deck, arriving there approximately two minutes after the explosion. I noticed that the fore deck was completely awash.'

While seawater rapidly flooded into the hold of *Empire Heritage* and the heavily loaded factory deck sank below the surface, Kapitänleutnant Matuschka was already manoeuvring U-*482* to deliver a coup de grace. A second torpedo was fired. '0355 – Shot from Tube 1 (T3) at Freighter 5000 BRT.'

While this second shot began its journey towards the sinking tanker, James Gibson was trying to make his way along the deck with the bow of the ship already covered by the sea. However a sudden wave halted his progress.

> I was lifted off my feet and washed overboard. I did not have time to fasten the tapes of my lifejacket before taking to the water and on surfacing I grabbed a buoyancy tank which had broken away from a lifeboat. I was just in time to see the funnel of the ship disappearing, approximately three minutes after the explosion.

The tanker slipped under the water before any flares could be fired or any emergency signals sent. Those who had made it onto the deck were mostly washed overboard and the fortunate ones made it to rafts or boats that had broken free as the ship went down. But many more had never made it out of the ship at all, and were trapped below as the cold, oily seawater flooded in.

By sheer coincidence the torpedo had struck the ship very close to the spot where it had previously been torn open after hitting a mine in the Bristol Channel in January 1941. On that occasion the hull had been damaged to the point that it was eventually torn in two and although it had been entirely repaired and the ship returned to service, it is always possible that some weakness remained. Her enormous weight, full tanks and laden factory deck were doubtless the reason she went down so fast once her hull was breached, but a lasting structural weakness could certainly have broken her apart and hastened her extraordinarily rapid demise.

Among the men that made it off the sinking tanker was Bo'sun James Peterson who went into the water unable to swim despite a life spent at sea. As previously mentioned, he had already survived a U-boat attack just a few years before in 1940 when he escaped from the torpedoed *New Sevilla* just a few miles east of where *Empire Heritage* had now sunk.

At 0356 SS *Jamaica Planter* sent the first radio message informing the convoy of the attack:

> SSSS *Empire Heritage* 2 explosions – Capsized

The second torpedo fired by U-*482* did not explode and apparently missed the target – Matuschka noted in the log at 0356 that it missed because he had made a miscalculation of the torpedo speed but it may simply have been the fact that the tanker had already sunk and was no longer there to hit. *Empire Heritage* had gone down so fast that even her attackers had not realised she had sunk.

With the ship gone the sea was left churned up in the darkness, covered in oil and strewn with debris and survivors desperately trying to find something buoyant to cling to. Men and wreckage were sucked down in the partial vacuum created by the sinking tanker and many survivors came back up bleeding from the eyes and ears from the immense pressure created underwater. The leaked fuel oil in the water caused terrible burning to their skin, eyes and throats, and the after-effects of swallowing quantities of it could be deadly. For those unfortunate souls who did not escape it was the unimaginable end suffered by mariners throughout history; they were dragged to the seabed inside the sinking ship, trapped in the freezing darkness, waiting for the coming flood or the steel to crumple under the immense pressure.

Elsewhere in the convoy, the rescue ship *Pinto* began making her way to the attack site. She was positioned at the very rear of the fifth column, which meant she was in the same column as *Empire Heritage* with just three ships between them if the position given by Chief Officer James Gibson was correct. The armed trawler *Northern Wave* also headed towards the point of attack; she had been positioned in the middle of three escort ships sailing astern of the convoy and was also close to the column that had been attacked. Both ships increased speed and readied themselves for action; *Pinto* preparing to begin rescue duty for the first time in her career and *Northern Wave* preparing to search for the attacker.

Meanwhile aboard U-*482* the crew could hear the sound of the tanker slipping away. '0355 – Sound of the first steamer sinking audible throughout the boat for 1-2 minutes. The crack of shots and other sounds.' James Gibson later stated that he believed that

… the explosion was fairly shallow and that the hole caused by the torpedo opened the factory deck, which extended the full length of the ship. This deck, which was filled with Sherman tanks and motor transport vehicles, was only 12/18 inches above the water line, and must have flooded very rapidly.

With Matuschka believing that *Empire Heritage* was still afloat and that his second torpedo had merely missed her due to a miscalculation, U-*482* prepared to fire a third shot. Calculations were made and the bow torpedo tubes were lined up once more. Another torpedo was launched leaving three empty tubes and just one more loaded in the bow, plus one in the stern tube. '0359 – Shot from Tube 4 (T5) at Freighter 5000 BRT'. This shot was a more advanced T5 or GNAT torpedo, an acoustic torpedo designed to home in on the sound of turning propeller blades. Designed for attacking faster escort ships, this was used to try and ensure another precious torpedo would not be wasted by missing the target, which by now they could no longer see. Of course the target was no longer there and the hydrophone device in the torpedo found no propellers to attack. On U-*482* they recorded 'Blast 2 minutes 7 seconds, hit not observed.'

No other ship in the convoy was damaged at this time and there is no other evidence of what this torpedo actually hit. The most likely explanation is that the torpedo came to the end of its run and merely detonated itself. However, aboard U-*482* they believed that they had in fact scored another kill.

Despite the fact that a ship had been sunk nearby, the rest of the convoy had to carry on and although alterations were made within the convoy, the ships left rescue work and the task of locating the attacker entirely to the escort group. For other ships to slow down or approach the area of the attack was simply too dangerous.

By now Kapitänleutnant Matuschka was turning his U-boat sharply around to try and line up an attack using the stern torpedo tube but by the time he had completed the manoeuvre he found that there were no targets. 'Turned towards Bb for a stern attack. Once turned I lose my firing position and the last ships of the convoy.'

As U-*482* turned away from the wreck site, the Senior Officer broadcast the code word 'pineapple' to all ships of the convoy; it was a signal that ordered an increase in speed and for there to be no lights. Meanwhile *Pinto* and *Northern Wave* were speeding towards the wreck site. At 0411 Matuschka recorded hearing a loud blast nearby. 'Either a depth charge or another boat in the convoy'. There is no record of any depth charge attacks made at this time so this may have been a secondary explosion from the sunken tanker. He goes on to record two other explosions at 0423 and 0425 though these were clearly farther away, 'blast less loud'.

Soon after the first of these explosions *Pinto* arrived at the wreck site approaching on the port side. The site was strewn with bits of wreckage, rafts and men, all covered in the thick oil which had leaked from the tanks of *Empire Heritage* as she sank. By the time the rescue ship arrived there was no sign of the tanker but the sea was dotted with the small lights from lifejackets bobbing up and down like fireflies in the waves. James Gibson was one of the men in the water:

> I eventually drifted alongside a raft, which had floated clear, and scrambled on to it. There were already five men on it, all of whom had been in the water and were covered in fuel oil. After being on the raft about half an hour, the Rescue Ship *Pinto* came along, stopped amongst the wreckage and commenced picking up survivors.

Jimmy Reeves was aboard *Pinto*:

> I then went out in a dinghy and we picked up two survivors from *Empire Heritage*. We brought them back to the ship and they were taken on deck for medical attention. After that we took the boat in. The second boat which went out with us could not get back to the ship because it had got a rope around its propeller. The Second Mate was in this boat.

Scrambling nets and booms had been deployed over the side of *Pinto* to help the men get aboard. Survivors were moving slowly through the debris towards the rescue ship, some on rafts and others with lifejackets or clinging to floating wreckage and swimming slowly through the oily Atlantic.

At 0416 *Northern Wave* arrived on the scene to find the *Pinto* already present and the rescue operation under way. The trawler broadcast the message 'closed wreck' to the Senior Officer of the escort. He responded by asking which side *Empire Heritage* had been torpedoed to try and help determine the position of the submarine, but of course the tanker was already long gone. The trawler then began a square search of the area but was immediately hampered by the number of men in the water and was forced to cut her speed to avoid causing further injuries to the survivors.

Meanwhile U-*482* had circled and was heading back towards the wreck site with *Pinto* at a standstill among the wreckage and *Northern Wave* close approaching. Through his periscope Kapitänleutnant Matuschka saw the rescue ship and the available evidence indicates that he mistakenly identified it as a sinking ship. He knew by now that the first ship had sunk because they had heard it, so he thought this was a second ship – the one that he believed he had hit with the acoustic torpedo fired from torpedo tube 4 at 0359. This torpedo had actually hit nothing. He thought the men and boats in the water were abandoning the ship, not making their way towards it. He was unaware that he was in fact looking at the rescue ship *Pinto*. Matuschka recorded in the log:

> Turn back to an east course, since a steamer is clearly sinking up ahead. Quickly draw near to GF, it's a stricken tanker. I miscalculate and pass very close to its bow and to liferafts a few metres away where flashlights are being deployed, as on the tanker itself.

At periscope depth, Matuschka passed right through the wreckage and between the men in the water, sailing past the bow of the rescue ship. His protruding periscope did not go unnoticed as it sailed right through the scattered survivors from *Empire Heritage*. Shouts broke out of a submarine in the vicinity, and someone on the bridge of *Pinto* shouted out 'Periscope – starboard bow'.

The gun crew on the *Pinto* manned the 12-pounder deck gun but it was immediately clear there was little they could do without further endangering the men floating in the water. The periscope moved through the wreckage and rafts and was reported to have been just six yards from *Pinto* at one point. Chief Officer Gibson was watching from his raft, one of around 15 witnesses who later reported seeing the enemy submarine.

> … I saw about 8 feet of the periscope of a submarine passing close to the *Pinto*'s bows from starboard to port, and also heard her engines. This submarine came from the direction of the land, steering approximately N.N.W. at roughly 10 knots. A few seconds later the periscope disappeared.

Pinto was stationary in the water, with rafts of survivors from *Empire Heritage* pulling alongside and trying to secure themselves to the boom nets. There were still only two survivors so far that had actually been brought onboard. Through his periscope Matuschka spotted the armed trawler *Northern Wave* which was continuing to search nearby, just three cables or three-tenths of a nautical mile off the port beam of *Pinto*. At 0431 the rescue ship sent the signal 'periscope port' upon which Lieutenant Fred Storey on *Northern Wave* turned his ship hard to port and increased to full speed in an attempt to ram the U-boat. Because of the relative fragility of a U-boat hull, ramming could be very effective, the collision could cause catastrophic damage to the submarine by damaging the pressure hull or crucial apparatus like the hydroplanes, rudder or propellers. This could be achieved with minimal damage to the much tougher hull of the surface ship, and if it did not completely destroy the U-boat, it could at least force it to the surface where it would be defenceless against the superior deck guns of the enemy.

The periscope seemed to disappear from view as the trawler sped to port. As word of the periscope sighting spread amongst the survivors, Jimmy Reeves was back aboard *Pinto* after picking up two survivors in the ship's dinghy.

> I was soaking after being in the boat and told the Bo'sun, a Shetland Islander, that I was on my way down to change my clothes. He called me back at first because a submarine had been sighted but we did not believe that we would be attacked because the Rescue Flag was up and all the gunners had their guns pointing in the air.

The ship may have been flying the rescue flag, but Matuschka did not see it through the periscope of U-*482*. He manoeuvred his U-boat through the field of debris and survivors and past the rescue ship, into the darkness on her port side. As the armed trawler gunned her engines and went in pursuit of U-*482*, Matuschka was lining up the stern torpedo tube once more. '0437 - Shot from Tube 5 (T5) at the stricken tanker straight ahead, about 6000 BRT'.

It is worth taking a moment to consider how the survivors of *Empire Heritage* must have felt at that moment. Their ship had been torpedoed in the dead of night, had broken beneath them and had sunk in just two minutes. Dozens of men had never even made it on deck before the tanker went under and now the lucky ones were floating helpless in the freezing water. They were coated in the thick fuel oil that had spewed from their ship as it sank; it filled their mouths and burned their throats and eyes. Many were not even fully dressed and had been given no time to prepare for abandoning ship. They knew already that many of their comrades were gone, sucked down inside the vessel or in the enormous vacuum that was created by her sinking. Finally the rescue ship arrived and there was a glimmer of hope that they might survive. The fear must have been immense, floating in the freezing, oily darkness or clinging to a raft or wreckage, moving slowly towards the rescue ship, their only hope of salvation. The minutes must have seemed like an eternity as each man waited to be picked up, hoping he would get aboard before he froze or drowned, or was suffocated by the thick oil filling his mouth as he struggled to stay afloat. But then there was shouting, and the sight of a periscope and the panic that their only chance of rescue could be cruelly denied them.

The *Pinto's* rescue boat was around two ship-lengths astern of the ship with the 2nd Officer and two able seamen aboard when they suddenly spotted something in the water. They shouted across to the *Pinto*: 'torpedo track approaching from starboard'.

After disappearing off the port side of *Pinto*, U-*482* may have turned about and headed back to starboard as this is where the torpedo approached from, though this manoeuvre is not mentioned in the U-boat log. This led to later confusion as to how a single U-boat could have been spotted off the port side and yet soon after attacked from starboard. It was suggested that a second U-boat may have been present but there is no evidence to support this and the torpedo attack was detailed in Matuschka's log, meaning it was certainly fired from his vessel. The most likely explanation is that the U-boat changed direction immediately after it disappeared from view, and that as the T5 was an acoustic torpedo it may not have necessarily fired along on a straight track but rather turned towards the noise of the rescue ship.

By now *Northern Wave* was on the port side of the *Pinto* and according to Lieutenant Storey several rafts had made it to the rescue ship and were secured alongside. As the torpedo was rapidly approaching, a crewman was being lowered over the side of *Pinto* in a rescue basket to help get survivors aboard. Jimmy Reeves was stopped again by the Bo'sun as he tried to go below decks. 'As I was going back down to change my clothes for the second time he stopped me again because a torpedo had been sighted heading for us.'

Just over half a minute after it was fired from the stern tube of U-*482* the acoustic torpedo reached the hull of the rescue ship and detonated on the starboard side, tearing open a hole just below the bridge. The blast shook the ship violently and sent black plumes of smoke skywards. The impact was recorded in the log of U-*482*. 'Hit after 37 seconds, midship. The explosion creates black mast-high columns and a small fire.'

At 0434 *Northern Wave* signalled the Senior Officer of the escort 'Rescue ship torpedoed'. At 0436 this message was passed on to the escort ships. The massive explosion from the torpedo tore through the hull of *Pinto* with fatal consequences for the men on the rafts that had been secured alongside. Lieutenant Fred Storey on *Northern Wave* later wrote in his report that 'a large number of survivors must have been killed when rescue ship was torpedoed as several rafts were secured alongside at the time. According to reports a number were killed on board by the explosion.'

The unfortunate crewman who had been in the process of being lowered over the side in the rescue basket was never seen again.

The explosion caused massive internal damage to the *Pinto*, which caused one of the bulkheads in the engine room to collapse, flooding a large section of the ship in seconds. Chief Officer Thomson was standing on deck when the torpedo struck and the force of the blast threw him upwards as an enormous column of water shot up and broke over the starboard side. The mainmast collapsed along with other parts of the ship's superstructure and the ship rapidly began to sink. Jimmy Reeves was trying to escape the ship, which was already foundering.

I then ran to the port side and tried to launch a raft by knocking out the release pin. The pin refused to budge so I jumped overboard. I had no life-jacket on and as the ship was going down I was drawn under the ship.

The medical officer on board *Pinto* was Temporary Surgeon Lieutenant Philip Noel Holmes, M.B. Ch.B., RNVR. As the torpedo struck he was on deck treating the two survivors who had just been brought aboard. They were near the coal locker was positioned just beside the operating theatre when the explosion rocked the ship and threw Holmes against the rails, bringing a wave of water and debris – including lumps of galley coal – down on top of him. The crew of the 12-pounder, still manning the deck gun though they had been unable to use it, were washed overboard by the enormous wave of water that broke over the ship after the blast. Only one of these men was seen to surface.

The ship's master Captain Lawrence Boggs was on the bridge at the moment of impact and was thrown on his back by the blast. He was helped to his feet by the helmsman whom he then instructed to get to safety before leaving the bridge onto the deck on the port side, giving similar instructions to other crew that he met. It was immediately obvious that the ship would not survive.

As *Pinto* began to go down by the stern, Temporary Surgeon Lieutenant Holmes went to search for the sickbay attendant and to check that the hospital was clear before reporting to Captain Boggs. He found the Captain on the port side. He too was instructed by the Master to get himself to safety. Then the ship seemed to drop with a lurch, and Holmes was left standing on the deck up to his waist in water.

Chief Officer Thomson began collecting other crew and getting them into lifeboats. They released no.5 lifeboat, then the jolly boat and then the no.6 lifeboat positioned on the foredeck, which had received some damage in the blast. They also released one of the rafts from the forward rigging.

Suddenly, the rescue ship plunged beneath the waves and in a matter of seconds had disappeared completely. Philip Holmes became tangled in the rigging as the ship lurched and he was carried down with it as it fell away into the dark abyss. As the remaining superstructure of the ship slipped beneath the waves, four other life rafts came loose and floated clear of the wreck along with all the other debris. The ship went down by the stern, sucking wreckage, rafts and men down with it as it plunged. It took a minute and a half for the ship to disappear completely. Lieutenant Storey on *Northern Wave* noted: 'At 0434 *Pinto* was torpedoed and sank in 90 seconds but managed to exhibit the prescribed red light before sinking.' Her loss position was given as 55.27N 08.01W.

Meanwhile U-*482* had turned once more towards the wreck site. Kapitänleutnant Matuschka scanned the area with his periscope and spotted *Northern Wave*.

A check of the area shows up an outpost fishing steamer nearby. Clearly audible now and straight ahead are the sounds of sinking.

Swung the periscope back. Nothing more of the tanker to be seen.

Jimmy Reeves from *Pinto* who had jumped overboard without a lifejacket and been pulled under the ship as she went down, finally surfaced and made it to one of the boats that had been released.

Suddenly I found myself pushed up to the surface near a dinghy with seven men in it. After getting into the dinghy a squall came and the boat turned turtle and flooded. There were other squalls, during which the boat turned over again, finally leaving only two of us holding on to the flooded dinghy.

Despite being trapped in the rigging when *Pinto* sank, Temporary Surgeon Lieutenant Philip Holmes also somehow managed to get free and came floating back up to the surface as the ship continued down towards the seabed. He had suffered serious lacerations to one hand and to one of his legs, but still managed to cling onto some wreckage to keep afloat until help could arrive. The survivors grasped at anything they could to try and stay afloat, including the rafts and wreckage from the first ship that went down. Chief Officer Gibson from *Empire Heritage* recalled, 'Many survivors from the *Pinto* climbed on board our rafts.'

Chief Officer Thomson from *Pinto* was in the water for around half an hour before finally getting onto one of the rafts and by now several of them had been manoeuvred together and tied to each other. The oily sea was littered with debris and men – living and dead – from both ships, in the freezing darkness of the early morning. The hope of rescue was dwindling with every minute; the only other ship nearby was *Northern Wave* and somewhere there was still a prowling U-boat.

The crew of the armed trawler had witnessed *Pinto* disappear as they continued their search for the U-boat. They were still struggling to move across the attack site without running through the survivors and at 0445 found themselves approximately 7 cables from where the ship went down. Lieutenant Storey noted in his report, 'I was continuing Operation Observant round wreck still hampered by survivors.' Despite the number of casualties in the water it was impossible for *Northern Wave* to stop or even slow down to pick up survivors because of the significant risk of further attack. The other ships in the convoy had all turned off their running lights as ordered for fear of becoming a target so there was no illumination aside from the tiny dots of light coming from the lifejacket lamps.

What happened next is not entirely clear because the accounts given by the U-boat log, the witnesses in the water and the crew of *Northern Wave* are very different. After the *Pinto* went down, Kapitänleutnant Matuschka broke off his attack and began to manoeuvre U-*482* away from the debris and the nearby armed trawler. He recorded in the U-boat log: 'I retreat from the area and set a west course.'

Having fired four torpedoes Matuschka had only one bow torpedo tube that could potentially still be fired although there is no record of him firing again after making his retreat. However there was sudden alarm aboard *Northern Wave* as a suspected torpedo was reported closing on the trawler's position. Fearing it could be an acoustic torpedo homing in on his propellers, Lieutenant Storey took evasive action turning *Northern Wave* hard to port while reducing his speed down to 8 knots in an attempt to elude the deadly warhead that may or may not have been in the water. But then he actually saw something himself moving through the water. 'Almost simultaneously I sighted something approaching through the water at Red 40 close. Suspected torpedo.'

The forward gun crew suddenly shouted 'submarine' and the suspected torpedo was believed to pass right under the ship, reportedly striking the port bow. Afterwards there was no further sign of the object but Lieutenant Storey was still not convinced that he had seen the attacking U-boat and was not willing to risk a counterattack. 'Suspected submarine on port bow but I was not definitely sure as I had not been able to distinguish what object was. This uncertainty and the fact that anything up to 100 men were in the water in the near vicinity decided me against firing a pattern.'

To have launched a depth charge attack into the water would have been to put the survivors floating there at incalculable risk because they would have been unavoidably caught up in the blast from the explosive canisters. *Northern Wave* had previously been involved in a situation where survivors had been killed in such an attack and Lieutenant Storey was not willing to take any chances on this occasion.

Witnesses on the trawler later claimed that the object that struck the port bow was actually the submarine, and claimed to have seen periscopes, the swirl from propellers and even 'the outline of [a] submarine passing under the bow in a steep dive', though the last of these seems hardly plausible in the darkness. If this really had been a collision between *Northern Wave* and U-*482*, it is difficult to believe that such a collision would not have left the U-boat with some damage. The U-boat log made no record or mention of such a collision, and there is no record of such damage upon her return to port.

Seaman J. Richmond from *Northern Wave* who had been monitoring the trawler's ASDIC wrote a report on the incident.

Rescue ship *Pinto* torpedoed on our starboard beam ... a few minutes later, through transmission reverbs, torpedo effect was heard faintly bearing Red 30.

Transmissions were switched off, torpedo approaching confirmed and bridge immediately notified. Bearing moved slowly left to Red 40 growing louder, and at ship going to port, Hydrophone effect remained steady, gaining in volume until it faded, torpedo passing across bow. No submarine contact obtained.

Despite the shouts of 'submarine' from the gun crew, there was no actual ASDIC contact obtained. U-482 slid away quietly beneath the waves as at 0446 the Senior Officer of the escort ordered the two escort ships Huntsville and Hespeller, which had been at the front of the convoy, to turn back and move astern to support Northern Wave. Lieutenant Storey signalled 'submarine in my vicinity' to the Senior Officer aboard HMCS Dunver. This message was broadcast at the time of the submarine sighting but was not actually received by the Senior Officer until around twenty minutes later at 0505 because of the massive amount of radio congestion following the attacks. Meanwhile Northern Wave continued her search of the area for the suspected U-boat, now using the position of the 'collision' as their focus point. Because they were searching around the attack site, the trawler had to move slowly through the field of debris and survivors left from both ships. No further submarine contacts were obtained.

The convoy of ships was stretched over an area of around three miles from front to back so it had taken some time for the support ships to turn back and make their way astern to assist in the search and rescue. In the meantime the men in the water struggled to stay alive as the first glimmers of sunrise were beginning to show in the overcast morning sky. While some men had made it onto rafts and so had the extra protection of weather screens, many more were continuing to cling to pieces of wreckage in the water, many with a range of injuries. In his report, Chief Officer James Gibson wrote that in his opinion all the crew and gunners 'behaved well throughout' and he went on to praise in particular the Fourth Officer from Empire Heritage, R.P. Tweedy. 'Whilst on a raft he speedily rigged the weather screens, and then jumped on to another raft and did the same, thus protecting the occupants of the rafts from exposure.'

At 0512, more than 25 minutes after being ordered to the attack site, the escort ship HMCS Hespeler – a Castle-class corvette – finally arrived and broadcast to the Senior Officer. 'Astern of convoy. Report situation.' It was now almost 40 minutes since the attack on Pinto, and over 70 minutes since Empire Heritage went down.

HMCS Huntsville, also a Castle-class corvette, arrived shortly after and was ordered, along with HMCS Hespeler, to head to the attack site. A signal was sent to Hespeler from the Senior Officer of the escort. 'Take Huntsville astern where trawler is. U-boat is there.'

Northern Wave had seen the support ships approaching and prepared to hand over the search to them so that she could finally begin rescue operations. The escorts arrived and *Northern Wave* passed all available information over to them including the details of the suspected ramming or collision. Lieutenant Storey reported, 'Escorts closed, commenced search, gradually extending.' The trawler then manoeuvred back towards the debris and prepared to begin picking up survivors.

Unfortunately just as the sky was lightening and the rescue operation got under way, the weather conditions began to deteriorate. The wind, which had been blowing around force 4, increased to a strong north-north-westerly force 6 increasing with daylight to force 7. Also there was 'a heavy short sea making rescue work difficult'.

By this point Matuschka had put some distance between his U-boat and the convoy despite being limited to a maximum submerged speed of 7.6 knots on electric motors or just 6 knots running her diesels through the snorkel. There was no question of surfacing because of the approaching daylight and their close proximity to the escort ships. On *U-482* they could hear the movements of the other shipping in the convoy, and the escorts moving towards the attack site, but it was some time before any type of counter-attack was noted. Lieutenant Storey on *Northern Wave* believed that the U-boat had submerged beneath the survivors to evade the searching Allied forces. The fact that it could not be detected in the surrounding waters reinforced this theory and he later wrote that '[the] technique employed by U-boat appears to have been to remain submerged beneath survivors, ultimately probably bottoming.'

Aboard *Northern Wave* scramble nets had been distributed over the side of the ship to help survivors climb aboard from the rafts. Attempts were made to lower the ship's whaler to help collect men from the water but failed; this was blamed on the spacing of davits that held the small boat. So all rescue work was carried out from the trawler itself. Lieutenant Storey noted that 'Boat work under prevailing conditions was considered useless ... In my opinion no further success would have been gained by using [the] boat which would have endangered the boat's crew and added to difficulties.'

The weather and sea conditions had deteriorated and continued to remain unsettled as the morning wore on. The wind moved around to a westerly and brought squalls that led to variable visibility. The conditions began to spread the oil over a larger area as the swell increased. The trawler had already made preparations for the rescue operation; the sick bay was prepared, clothing and blankets were organised, and food, cocoa and soup were made ready to serve to the survivors as they came on board.

Because both ships had gone down in approximately the same position, the survivors were relatively close together in the water to begin with, though they had begun to be spread downwind. Though the rescue operation had taken considerable time to get underway, before too long many of the survivors had been taken aboard. Lieutenant Storey wrote in his report that of the men that were picked up 'most … were taken from rafts, spars, floats, wreckage and a number from the water. Only two boats and one dinghy appeared to have got away, all of which were damaged.' The fact that a total of just three damaged lifeboats had managed to be launched from the two sunken ships, and in fact had all come from *Pinto*, further emphasises the astonishing speed at which both vessels had foundered.

There were now several ships involved in the hunt for the U-boat and the search was steadily moving outwards from the attack site. Meanwhile the rest of the convoy had carried on eastwards as the sun rose and was moving steadily along the Irish coast towards the North Channel.

Aboard *Northern Wave* the survivors were treated for their injuries, clothed and fed, and rum was issued to each man. They had begun the rescue operation at 0515 when the other ships arrived to take over the hunt for the U-boat, and the search for survivors went on for several hours. Temporary Surgeon Lieutenant Philip Holmes, the medical officer from *Pinto*, was one of the survivors taken onboard the trawler and despite having been injured himself, he immediately set about treating the men who had been picked up. Chief Officer James Gibson mentioned him in his report:

> The Doctor of the *Pinto* also did extremely fine work. Although soaked through, he did not even stop to change his clothes until he had attended to all the injured in the *Northern Wave* and, assisted by his Sick Bay Attendant, worked unceasingly throughout. He set a magnificent example by his cool and efficient conduct.

At 0546 the Senior Officer of the escort sent a message to *Northern Wave* asking them to interview the survivors in an attempt to gather more information about the attacker, but the trawler crew were still involved in the rescue operation. Then at 0606 he asked for a report regarding the suspected collision with the U-boat and Lieutenant Storey eventually replied that they believed they had rammed the submarine at 0425. The search for the U-boat had not obtained any contacts and the Senior Officer was looking for any information or witness reports that could help determine her likely whereabouts.

The task of bringing the survivors of the two ships aboard was difficult and dangerous in the deteriorating weather conditions and many of the crew from *Northern Wave* put their own lives at risk to get the survivors aboard. After several attempts to get one injured man aboard, Seaman Harry Pashby and Telegraph

Operator Jack Ashe bravely volunteered to go into the water, as the casualty was too weak to climb up the scramble nets. In the process of the rescue, the line attached to Harry Pashby broke and he was quickly swept away by the sea, leaving Jack Ashe working alone to secure the man. Then he too was forced underwater by the waves, and was at considerable risk of being smashed against the side of his own ship. By the time he was taken back on board, he had swallowed a considerable amount of oil and was in little better condition than the other survivors. Meanwhile Harry Pashby had managed to get a hold of a float that had been thrown to him from *Northern Wave*, and after some fifteen minutes floating in the oily water he too was brought back on board, unconscious.

Fourth Engineer Galbraith from *Pinto* later told of how he had escaped the sinking rescue ship but was then left struggling in the water unable to get himself onto a raft. He said that he owed his life to Ordinary Seaman Skelton, another of the crew aged just seventeen who was on a raft with some others when he spotted the Engineer in difficulty. According to Galbraith the young Skelton stripped off his lifejacket, dived in and helped the heavier man get to the raft and get himself aboard.

Meanwhile Kapitänleutnant Matuschka had continued to try and put distance between U-482 and the ships that were scouring the sea in search of him, though with their significantly higher speeds they had already circled round in front of him. From beneath the waves Matuschka could hear the sounds of the hunt.

0600 – Sound buoys and destroyer sounds straight ahead and at diagonals – ASDIC – Impulse

The escort ships had been carefully sweeping through the water using ASDIC and having started around the attack site, their net was gradually widening. All they needed was to obtain a contact, for just one of their sonar 'pings' to reach and bounce off the U-boat hull, and the Allied ships would rapidly form a ring around the target and bombard it with depth charges until they could be sure of its destruction. U-482 continued her passage away from the Irish coast but the hunting ships were still dangerously close. It was not until 0618 that one of the ships fired the first depth charges, either against a suspicious contact or else in an attempt to flush out the enemy by shattering their nerves and forcing them to surface. If they had obtained a contact it was a false reading such as a wreck, and was certainly not U-482. But the extensive depth charge attack went on for nearly an hour and a half, and the crew of U-482 could hear the massive explosions echoing through the waves.

0618 – The first depth charges, then 44 in total at various intervals until 0742 hours, some far off, others close by but none dangerous.

Matuschka gave no sign of being concerned by the depth charge attack, and described them as 'bombs which could be flying depth charges with the aircraft being steered blindly … Releasing depth charges precisely is similar to dropping bombs from a great height in heavy cloud cover.' Matuchka had not personally experienced the destructive potential of the Allies' anti-submarine arsenal, and his reaction to these distant attacks showed a lack of respect for what could be a dangerous and devastating weapon. The day would come when he would experience first-hand just how accurate they could be.

At around 0745 *Northern Wave* took onboard their last survivor, though they did not know it at the time and the rescue operation went on for several more hours. There were still a large number of men unaccounted for. At this stage it was around two and a half hours since the trawler had begun picking up survivors, and though it is not known which ship this last survivor came from, he must have been in the water for a minimum of three hours and possibly nearly four. Several other ships joined the search along with some air support.

Chief Officer Gibson, Bo'sun James Peterson and the other survivors from *Empire Heritage* had been taken on board along with Chief Officer Thomson, Surgeon Philip Holmes and the other survivors from *Pinto*. Meanwhile Jimmy Reeves from *Pinto* who had been left clinging to a dinghy with another man had drifted some way from the attack site but was eventually spotted in the water by an RAF Short Sunderland flying boat. The aircraft acknowledged it had seen them by dipping its wings and then dropping some flares. The pilot must have radioed their position because they were picked up a while later by a destroyer which had been heading west with an outbound convoy. They were eventually landed in Londonderry several days later.

Kenilworth Castle joined in the search at around 0800 and HMS *Helmsdale* came to assist at around 0905. When the *Helmsdale* arrived on the scene, she signalled to *Northern Wave* that she was 'coming alongside to shout'. Lieutenant Storey passed to her Commanding Officer all the available information on the attack, including the position of the two wrecks, the suspected ramming incident, and also the initial reports and statements that had been obtained from the survivors. In his later report Lieutenant Storey wrote 'It is estimated from reports from survivors that a great number went down with *Empire Heritage*, reported to have broken in half and sunk in two minutes. Passengers probably suffered heaviest loss.'

The River-class frigate HMS *Helmsdale*, which had been commissioned in October 1943, would be involved in another U-boat hunt the very next day. On 9 September she, along with the Corvette HMS *Portchester Castle*, attacked and sank U-*484* with depth charges to the north-west of Ireland. U-*484*, commanded by Korvettenkapitän Wolf-Axel Schaefer, was a sister ship of U-*482*, one of the six U-boats ordered together from Deutsche Werke AG in Kiel.

At 0855 Lieutenant Storey signalled the Senior Officer of the escort, estimating the results of the rescue operation up to that point. It was the first indication that there had been significant loss of life. 'About 80 survivors including Doctor and Chief Officer from *Pinto*. Still searching'. At 0927 *Northern Wave* received a signal asking whether she needed further assistance in the search for the survivors and Lieutenant Storey immediately replied that she did, though no other survivors were located. The signal was broadcast 'Please help Trawler find survivors.'

U-*482* had continued moving steadily away from the attack site and at 1000 Matuschka logged that they were sailing submerged and had their LF or low frequency antenna deployed above the water. LF transmitters and receivers were primarily used for sending and receiving beacon signals from aircraft and other U-boats. By then they had moved out of Kriegsmarine grid quadrant AM5387 and were in AM5375, slightly to the northwest. They could still hear the sounds of the support ships moving back and forth trying to hunt them down, and they could hear 'pings' from the sonobuoys that had been lowered into the water to try and detect them. Like the earlier depth charges, Matuschka thought that these buoys had been deployed from aircraft though it is more likely they had been lowered from ships. '1000 – Spent the day navigating our way through a corridor of sound buoys which seemed again to be the work of aircraft. Pursued different courses.'

While U-*482* continued to make her retreat, there were some adjustments being made within the convoy. With *Northern Wave* heavily involved in the rescue operation and no longer able to be part of the close escort for HX-305, the Senior Officer of the escort was forced to reorganise his ships to maintain protection around the convoy from all sides. He shifted the Flower-class corvette HMCS *Algoma* to the position the trawler had been covering and ordered it to 'replace *Northern Wave* as escort for Liverpool section to K.1 Buoy.' It had been planned that once the convoy made it to Britain and dispersed, *Northern Wave* would sail with the portion of the convoy heading to Liverpool, so HMCS *Algoma* took over this role.

At 1030 *Northern Wave* sent a signal to the Senior Officer aboard HMCS *Dunver*, and to the Commander-in-Chief, Western Approaches.

Empire Heritage and *Pinto*, torpedoed and sunk 55°27'N. 0801'W. at 0400 and 0434. Following survivors on board – *Pinto* 41, *Empire Heritage* 46. Unaccounted for 21 and 110 respectively. Rammed submarine whilst taking avoiding action from torpedo. Damage unknown. Still searching. Intend proceeding to Londonderry on completion.

Finally at 1200, more than eight hours after the attack began on *Empire Heritage*, the search was abandoned and HMT *Northern Wave* set a course for Londonderry so she could land her passengers. At 1225 Lieutenant Storey signalled the Commander-in-Chief, Western Approaches: 'Abandoning search. Proceeding to Moville in company with *Ambuscade*.'

The trawler left the attack site and, under escort by the Royal Navy Destroyer HMS *Ambuscade*, sailed east along the Donegal coast from Malin Head down to the mouth of Lough Foyle. *Northern Wave* anchored briefly at Moville for her ASDIC dome to be removed from under her hull and so a pilot could be arranged to take them up the river. They then proceeded to Lishally where the trawler docked so the survivors could be disembarked and transferred to Londonderry. They finally arrived at around 1730. It is hard to imagine the immense sense of relief that must have been felt by these men as they felt solid ground under their feet for the first time in two weeks, coupled with the sense of loss for their many comrades who did not make it. Lieutenant Storey listed the injured in a signal to the Commander-in-Chief, Western Approaches as '5 Cot, 4 walking, remaining 77 superficial'. The '5 Cot' were cot cases – men who had been totally incapacitated by their injuries.

The survivors mentioned in this signal totalled just 86 though Lieutenant Storey wrote in his later report: 'Total survivors picked up – 88. 'Pinto' 41 saved, 21 unaccounted for. 'Empire Heritage' 47 saved, 109 unaccounted for.' This gives a total of 156 men aboard *Empire Heritage* at the time of her loss. However, the final casualty figures for *Empire Heritage* recorded in the Shipping Casualties Section Report on 21 September 1944, list a total of 158 men aboard her and 110 men unaccounted for, 56 of her crew and 54 of her passengers.

From *Empire Heritage* the *Northern Wave* rescued 25 crewmen, 20 passengers, two gunners and a signalman. Amongst the 110 missing men were the ship's master James Campbell Jamieson, the 3rd Officer, the 2nd, 3rd, 4th, 5th, 6th and 7th Engineers, the 2nd and 3rd Radio Officers, all four Army Gunners, five of the seven naval gunners, one of the signalmen and 54 of the 73 passengers. The youngest men lost were only seventeen years old: Radio Officer Charles Thomson from Aberdeen; Cadet William Easton; Galley Boy John Gallagher from North Shields; and Galley Boy George Gillian from Greenock. The oldest man lost was Greaser William Stant who was 67 years old. Also amongst the dead were brothers Henry and Stanley Colebourne, aged 30 and 26 respectively. They both worked as firemen aboard *Empire Heritage* and their deaths must have been an unimaginable blow to their family. 2nd Radio Officer Edward Douglas Anderson survived the sinking and was one of the men eventually rescued by *Northern Wave* but he later died of his injuries and was returned home to be buried at Warriston Cemetery in Edinburgh.

From *Pinto*, the trawler had picked up 41 men from a total complement of 59. The fact that the crew were already at action stations when the torpedo hit was why so many escaped before the ship went down. The survivors were made up of 29 crew, eight gunners, two sickbay attendants, a signalman, and Temporary Surgeon Lieutenant Philip Holmes. Amongst the missing were six crew, eight distressed seamen, a signalman and the master, Captain Lawrence Boggs MBE, who had last been seen ordering his men to safety on the port side of *Pinto* as the ship went down. Donkeyman Michael Hillan and Chief Engineer Officer Alexander Thomson were both rescued from the water but later died, both being buried at Pennyfuir Cemetery in Oban.

At 1400 Kapitänleutnant Matuschka noted in the U-boat log that they were in position AM5296 on the Kriegsmarine grid, meaning they were still travelling west. They could still hear sonobuoys searching for them.

By 1800 they were further west in position AM5292 showing that they had turned slightly and were now travelling in a north-westerly direction. Then at 1934 and 1937 Matuschka recorded hearing '2 bombs distant' as the Allied ships began depth charging another suspected target. They had travelled a significant distance and for a considerable number of hours on their electric motors and had not been running their diesel engines since some time before they began stalking the convoy. Their batteries were largely depleted and could only be charged by running the engines, either by surfacing the boat or by engaging the snorkel. Despite the fading light of the early evening, surfacing would have been far too risky with the number of ships still patrolling nearby and U-482 could have easily been picked up by radar so Matuschka decided to begin snor-, kelling. This also meant that by charging up their batteries through the hours of darkness the U-boat would be able to travel fully submerged on her electric motors during daylight. Matuschka took the U-boat to snorkel depth and prepared to start the engines despite the fact they could still hear sonobuoys in the distance.

> 2048 – Begin snorkelling. 3 sound buoys at 100, 205 and 240 degrees, the latter with ASDIC transmission.

At 2200 hours Matuschka noted that they were in quadrant AM5259, which meant they were still travelling in a north-westerly direction. At 2223 the hydrophone operator reported the sounds of a destroyer at 290 degrees followed just two minutes later by a sonobuoy at 310 degrees. Matuschka notes in the log that they sound 'loud in the boat'. The noises persisted until 2245 when 'the sound of the destroyer [was] lost at 280 degrees.'

U-482 continued snorkelling through the darkness for several hours and at 0200 it moved into quadrant AM5256; they had turned farther towards the north and were travelling approximately north-north-west. At 0433 they disengaged the snorkel and with their batteries charged they restarted the electric motors so they could remain submerged. They continued moving farther north on their passage, which would eventually take them around the north of Scotland and across to the North Sea. The sounds of shipping nearby were still detectable and though the U-boat remained submerged, she was never far from the danger of being detected.

Sound buoys day and night, surfacing out of the front sector, occasional propeller sounds, distant explosions now and then, only a few nearby. I think I am still near a convoy route.

They passed the daylight hours submerged and then began snorkelling again at 2118, running on their diesels until 0240 on the morning of 10 September, nearly two days since the attack on *Empire Heritage*.

Then at 0248, under the cover of darkness, U-482 finally surfaced. Compressed air was pumped into her buoyancy tanks, pushing out the ballast water and allowing her to float up to the surface. They had been underwater for several days and even now it was not safe to remain on the surface for long.

Even surfacing briefly was very useful for a U-boat. It allowed radio transmissions to be sent and received, and it gave the navigator a rare opportunity to use celestial navigation to fix the U-boat's position instead of relying on dead reckoning. The diesel engines could be run allowing the U-boat to travel at more than twice the speed that it could submerged and it allowed them to charge the batteries of the electric motors. It also meant the crew were able to get out of the hatch onto the conning tower for much needed fresh air, and it allowed fresh air into the boat, helping to clear out the odour of food and unwashed bodies that had been trapped there.

On the surface they were at risk of being detected by Allied radar technology, even in the darkness. So at 0340 after less than an hour U-482 submerged once more. They carried on in a north-westerly direction to take them clear of the Western Isles of Scotland before turning east. At 1400 Matuschka logged hearing 'Several distant explosions' but again there seemed to be nothing close to the U-boat and they were likely related to some other incident involving another convoy. They carried on in much the same pattern of sailing mainly submerged, snorkelling by night and running on electric motors by day, and very occasionally surfacing when conditions allowed. Matuschka noted that they travelled underwater almost the whole way between the Faroe Islands and Shetland, surfacing only once, and they did not hear or locate any enemy patrols.

The crew effectively turned night into day during this time with meals being taken while the U-boat was snorkelling during the night, and many of the crew having their rest time during the day. Matuschka noted that this system worked well once they were used to it and that the crew health was good. 'The drive to and from the operational area was not especially demanding and the crew was peaceful.' They finally completed their 2,729-mile patrol on 26 September when they arrived back in Bergen to great acclaim.

By the time the sun had gone down over the coast of County Donegal on 8 September 1944, there was little sign of the tragedy that had occurred there just a few hours before. The two torpedoed ships had long since come to rest on the seabed where they remain to this day. The floating wreckage had been spread far and wide by the heavy sea and the massive slick of leaked fuel oil had gradually begun to disperse. The survivors had been taken ashore in Londonderry for medical treatment while the rest of the convoy had passed through the North Channel where it split into smaller groups that sailed to different ports all across Britain. The support ships that had been hunting the enemy U-boat were gone from the scene having found no trace of the assailant, and the attacking U-boat was now far to the north on the long return voyage to Norway. The devastating attack had taken the convoy completely by surprise, left a trail of loss and destruction, and delivered a huge blow to the Allies' system of convoy protection. Now they had to try and unravel exactly what had happened to convoy HX-305, and they had to try and work out how they could prevent it from ever happening again.

VIII

REPORTS AND INQUIRIES

With the last of the survivors picked up and the rest of the convoy making it to port shortly afterwards, the process began of interviewing witnesses and gathering reports from the other ships involved to attempt to piece together the events leading up to and following the attack. While the assailant had escaped unharmed and remained unidentified, there were questions to be answered about what had actually occurred in all the confusion and what could have been done to prevent it. Two ships had been lost with a terrible loss of life and the enormous *Empire Heritage* had gone down with cargo of great value. Of course the Allies did not have the advantage of seeing the U-boat's log, and so only had a one-sided view of the events, but there are two very significant documents that shed further light on the attack on HX-305; the findings of the Official Inquiry held on 15 September 1944, and the Report of Proceedings from *Northern Wave*, the only other ship that was actually at the scene of the attack.

THE OFFICIAL INQUIRY

In the days following the attack on HX-305, an investigation was begun which resulted in an inquiry held a week later. At 0930 on 15 September 1944, a group assembled on board HMCS *Dunver*, a Canadian ship that had sailed in the convoy, acting as a Board of Inquiry 'to hold a full and careful investigation into the circumstances attending the loss of SS *Empire Heritage* and R.F.A. *Pinto*'.

In the week between the attack and the inquiry a certain amount of information had already been gathered from survivors and other witnesses, and the Board had also collected several other documents including:

Sailing Telegram for Convoy HX-305 from the Port Director, New York

Group orders from the Senior Officer of C5 group

Senior Officer of C5 group's communication memo (dated 28 August 1944)

Report of proceedings by HX-305 Convoy Commodore Sir A.L. Owens RNR

Report of proceedings by Surgeon Lieutenant Philip Holmes (*Pinto*)

Operation report by P. Herd (*Pinto*)

EVIDENCE

The Board begin by considering the contact obtained by the *Pinto* the night before the attack when at 2259 a bearing was picked up by HF/DF that indicated a U-boat in the vicinity. It was reported as being a submarine drying out her aerials and was estimated to be over 30 miles away based on the signal. No other ship in the convoy heard the transmission but *Pinto* did report it to the Senior Officer of C5 Group, though there was no trace of it having then been passed on to Force 33 or to the shore authorities. The Senior Officer stated that it had certainly been passed to SOEG5 by TBY. Ultimately however, it was agreed that this piece of intelligence was too small and vague to have influenced any orders from the Senior Officer of C5 and also that even if it was a U-boat that had been detected, it was unlikely to have been the one that went on to attack the convoy the following morning.

TACTICAL DISPOSITION OF CONVOY HX-305 AND SUPPORT FORCES

The Board decided that at the time of the attack, the area covered by the main convoy was approximately 7 miles wide by 3 miles deep, and was formed in fourteen columns, with the number of ships in each column ranging from six to nine ships. They record that *Empire Heritage* was in the ninth column, and was the fifth of eight ships in that column. This is at odds with the account given by the Chief Officer of *Empire Heritage*, James C. Gibson who stated the convoy was formed into fifteen columns, with his ship being the fourth of eight vessels in the fifth column. Presumably they believed the layout they used in the inquiry was the correct one. The escort vessels were distributed around the convoy at a distance of approximately 5,000 yards. The Senior Officer of the Canadian Escort Group C5, was Commander George Hay Stephen RCNR, who was aboard HMCS *Dunver*, sailing to the port side at the rear of the convoy.

The Board found that at the time of the attack, the wind was blowing north-north-west force 2 to 3, with moderate visibility. The moon had risen at 2140 and had occasionally been obscured by cloud while sunrise was at 0549. ASDIC

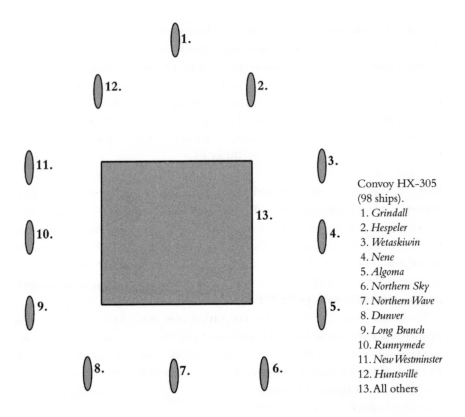

Convoy HX-305
(98 ships).
1. *Grindall*
2. *Hespeler*
3. *Wetaskiwin*
4. *Nene*
5. *Algoma*
6. *Northern Sky*
7. *Northern Wave*
8. *Dunver*
9. *Long Branch*
10. *Runnymede*
11. *New Westminster*
12. *Huntsville*
13. All others

conditions were described as good. It was the opinion of the Board that at the time of the attack the escort forces should have been better positioned around the convoy so as to offer the most effective defence, and was of the opinion that they were arranged in a manner 'more suited to mid-ocean escorting than to escorting in the shallow coastal waters of the North Western Approaches'.

They also believed that Commander Stephen had too few ships positioned ahead of the convoy, and that there were sufficient escort ships to have formed a tight ASDIC screen that should have been two miles in front. They were of the opinion that a better disposition would have been to have Commander Stephen's Escort Group 5 supplement the Close Escort Group, which would then have provided sixteen ships for a close escort to form the ASDIC screen with the rest of the ships in the group being distributed astern and down both sides of the convoy.

The Board was also critical of the positioning of *Northern Wave* and *Northern Sky*, two armed trawlers that were of limited speed and had limited radar capabilities, placed together at the rear of the convoy. They believed this 'unnecessarily weakened the starboard quarter'.

It was decided that Commander Stephen should have better positioned the escorting vessels to defend against a submerged attack, and it was thought 'most unlikely that a U-boat would approach on the surface' owing to the large number of aircraft and surface ships that had been performing ASDIC sweeps on the surrounding area for several days following the recent U-boat attacks in the vicinity – carried out by U-482. Having investigated the positioning of the convoy preceding the attack, the Board of Inquiry then moved on to what took place immediately after the first torpedo struck.

It was noted that at 0355 two lookouts aboard HMCS *Dunver* sighted red flashes in the convoy, which they described as rising to a height of 70 feet. This was reported immediately to the Officer of the Watch, Lieutenant Macmillan, who then reported it to the Second Officer of the Watch, Lieutenant Pearce, but it was not forwarded on to any senior officer at that time. It was then noted that no distress signals were received from the attacked ship, and no flares were fired. The first signal regarding the incident was made by SS *Jamaica Planter* at 0356 when they broadcast the radio message 'SSSS *Empire Heritage* 2 explosions – Capsized'.

The Board found that *Empire Heritage* sank almost immediately and SS *Jamaica Planter* was commended for her 'prompt reporting of the torpedoing'. The message was broadcast on 2410 kilocycles and received by *Hespeler* and *New Westminster* and was partially received by *Dunver*, *Huntsville* and *Algoma*.

Then at 0358 *Jamaica Planter* broadcast 'SSSS' – the distress signal to report a submarine attack – which was received by *Dunver* and *Runnymede*. The CO of HMCS *Runnymede*, Lieutenant Richard Chenoweth RCNVR, was criticised by the Board for failing to pass this information on to the Senior Officer of C5 Group, despite the fact that they were responsible for monitoring signals broadcast on that frequency. The SOC5 responded 'Which side ship torpedoed' addressing the signal to *Northern Wave* though it was received by all ships of the escort group. It was reported at this point that prior to her sinking, Commander Stephen had not been aware that *Empire Heritage* was carrying passengers in addition to her crew, and it was discovered that this information, though very important, had not been recorded in the Sailing Telegram from the Port Director, New York, or in the A.1 form – the form which recorded for each convoy the cruising order, the layout of the ships within the convoy, as well as other pertinent information such as where each ship was heading, its height above the waterline, where the Commodore ships were, their service speed, and in most cases which ships were carrying passengers.

The Board found that following the sinking of *Empire Heritage*, Commander Stephen had not ordered any alterations in the tactical disposition of the convoy, leaving the ships ploughing on in the same course at the same speed, despite the fact that an unidentified enemy was in the vicinity.

It was not until seven minutes after the first explosion on *Empire Heritage*, at 0402, that Senior Officer C5 ordered Operation *Pineapple*, a pre-arranged anti-submarine operation that convoys and escort ships could adopt in the event of an attack. There were a range of different tactics that could be used depending on the situation, and these were largely created by Captain Gilbert Roberts RN at the Western Approaches Tactical Unit (WATU) in Liverpool. Other operations had names like *Raspberry, Banana, Gooseberry, Beta Search* and *Step Aside*, and involved different combinations of speed and illumination for the convoy and hunting tactics for the escorts. For example, during *Raspberry* some of the escorts would fire star-shell rockets to light up the area while others began triangular sweeps of the surrounding waters to try and locate the U-boat via radar. *Pineapple* was designed particularly for use during a night attack from a U-boat positioned ahead of the convoy, and normally involved the escort ships increasing speed towards the U-boat, often whilst firing star-shells to illuminate the surrounding area and scare the U-boat into diving while the convoy made it away safely. Then the escorts would turn back to rejoin the convoy, performing an ASDIC sweep as they did so. The U-boat would be forced under as the ships passed overhead, where it would be caught in the ASDIC sweep, and then attacked with depth charges.

On this occasion the Board found that Operation *Pineapple* was correctly interpreted by the ships of the convoy and the escorts to mean no illumination, and it was found that the order was satisfactorily carried out by the convoy. However, they also noted that in the circumstances, *Banana* would have been a more suitable operation because of the fact that this procedure 'provides a more efficient asdic sweep to detect a U-boat which has attacked'.

While *Pinto* began the search for survivors, *Northern Wave* began searching for the attacking U-boat. Both these manoeuvres were carried out in accordance with the group orders of the Senior Officer C5 Group; a set of orders issued prior to the convoy's departure. It was decided that the actions of the two ships was found to be satisfactory, and that they had closed to the area 'with promptitude'.

Just as the rescue was getting underway aboard *Pinto*, a second torpedo slammed into the rescue ship. At 0434 *Northern Wave* broadcast the message 'Rescue ship torpedoed' which was picked up by all ships of the escort group. At 0436 the SOC5 sent a message to all ships in the group giving the pennant number of the torpedoed ship so that they could identify the position of the attack. It was incorrectly given as Pennant 74 though shortly afterwards the Convoy Commodore sent another signal correcting the position as Pennant 95.

The Board note that prior to the attack, *New Westminster* was the only ship in the entire group to have the bridge radio telephone loudspeaker switched on.

By that point *Northern Wave* was alone with the attacking U-boat, and the surrounding water was strewn with men and debris. It would be a considerable time before other resources arrived to support the armed trawler.

At 0446, 51 minutes after the attack on *Empire Heritage* and twelve minutes after the sinking of *Pinto*, Commander Stephen made the decision to alter the tactical disposition of the convoy. Two of the escort ships, *Hespeler* and *Huntsville*, which had been sailing ahead of the convoy, were re-routed and ordered to move astern of the convoy. This order was initially met with confusion from the two ships who did not know why they had been ordered to change position and *Hespeler* requested further instructions having not been kept informed of what had occurred elsewhere in the convoy. The previous day it had been agreed that in the event of any attack or any U-boat contact being obtained, these two ships – the only two squid-fitted ships in the group – would be put at the disposal of the escort group. Therefore they had already begun moving towards the scene of the attacks when they received the orders of the Senior Officer of the escort group.

Then at 0510, *Long Branch*, which had been sailing off the port side towards the rear of the convoy, was ordered to proceed up the port side and to take station ahead of the considerable Loch Ewe portion of the convoy, a large group of ships that were grouped together so they could break off easily to head to Loch Ewe in Scotland once HX-305 reached Britain. At 0533, *Nene* and *Wetaskiwin*, which had been to the front and starboard side of the convoy, were also ordered to proceed towards the Loch Ewe portion. Between 0520 and 0630, the ASDIC screen was reorganised in an attempt to better protect the convoy from further attack.

The Board found that all ships of C5 Group were correctly on station at the time of the attack, and it was found that all orders subsequently issued were satisfactorily implemented. It was also noted however that no witnesses had been questioned from the two escort ships *Northern Sky* and *Northern Wave*.

It was usual in an inquiry of this kind to attempt to ascertain 'probable tactics of the U-boat before, between and after the attacks'. In this case the Board of Inquiry noted that they were unable to put forward any findings on the probable tactics of the attacking U-boat at any time surrounding the attacks because they had not been able to interrogate any actual witnesses from *Empire Heritage*, *Pinto*, *Northern Wave*, *Northern Sky* or the 5th Escort Group. Also the witnesses from C5 group that had been interviewed had produced no evidence to indicate what the movements of the U-boat might have been. This lack of eyewitness evidence seems unusual when there were so many potential witnesses who could have been interviewed, and when the later report from *Northern Wave* contained so much information regarding the attacking U-boat. Had there been more time between the attack and the inquiry, more evidence would have been available.

FINDINGS

It was found that the after the sinking of *Pinto*, the response made by the Senior Officer of the escort group was not rapid or decisive enough to deal with the aftermath of the attack. There were not enough resources committed to either the locating of the attacker, or the rescue of the survivors and they noted that 'the action taken was insufficient because no force in a position to give undivided attention to locating and destroying the U-boat was on the scene for at least one hour after the first attack.'

Following the attack on *Pinto*, *Northern Wave* was left unsupported at the scene with a prowling U-boat and many survivors scattered across the sea. It was estimated that there could have been as many as 218 men in the seas around the attack site between 0434 and 0500, and there were no other ships in a position to rescue them. These survivors also restricted the trawler's speed and ability to defend itself, meaning it was a potentially easy third target for the U-boat.

The Board found that after *Pinto* went down, no additional rescue measures were taken, and it was not until 0500 that other ships of the escort group arrived on the scene, thereby allowing *Northern Wave* to finally begin rescue work. The trawler had initially arrived at the attack site to begin searching for the enemy U-boat so that *Pinto* could concentrate on picking up survivors. But once the rescue ship was lost the trawler could not stop to pick anyone up because of the risk of becoming a target herself. And so it was not until other ships arrived at 0500 that the rescue operation began, more than an hour after the torpedoing of *Empire Heritage*, and some 25 minutes after *Pinto* went down.

Many of the problems in organising the rescue operation seemed to stem from communications issues within the convoy. 'We consider that communications in C5 Escort Group left much to be desired.' To back up this judgement, the Board cited several examples of what they believed were failings within the group. It was found that once the Senior Officer had decided to order Operation *Pineapple*, the signal took approximately five minutes to be passed to the convoy and that three repetitions of the signal were required before it was implemented. It was also noted that no 'authenticity' word was broadcast with the original order which made the signal 'ambiguous' and made the receiving ships initially unclear as to the intention of the order.

The Senior Officer had stated in evidence, with the backing of other witnesses, that there had been considerable interference on the radio telephone from the ships of the support group, and offered this as a possible reason for the inefficiency of the communications within the convoy. But this argument was disregarded by the Board of Inquiry after careful examination of the radio telephone operators' logs for the period between 0400 and 0500 on the date of the attack. In addition it was found that there had been no use of the 'clear the air' signal by the Senior Officer of the escort group – the obvious procedure to clear any radio traffic that was causing interference within the convoy.

The Board found that until approximately 0443, some three-quarters of an hour after *Empire Heritage* had been sunk, only two of the escort ships of C5 Group had received definite information that she had even been attacked. Then at 0915, more than five hours after the attack on *Empire Heritage*, another trawler in the convoy *Northern Sky* had signalled asking the name of the ship that had been sunk; incredibly some ships in the escort were still not aware which ship had gone down. This lack of communication almost certainly slowed down any rescue operation; a quicker response would have meant a much more efficient rescue and U-boat hunt, and could well have prevented the second attack from ever taking place. It may also have led to the attacking U-boat being detected and counter-attacked instead of being allowed to escape unhindered.

CONCLUSIONS

The Board believed that all relevant ships' ASDIC systems were 'efficiently in action' throughout, but that no potential contacts had been obtained at any time before, during or after the attacks. However it was also noted that although all ships' radars were working, the arrangement of the radar-fitted escort ships left large parts of the surrounding area totally unswept. This meant that there was a sufficient gap for a U-boat to have gone undetected as the convoy entered the area. At 0418 the escort vessel *Huntsville* which was positioned in front of the convoy, did obtain an ASDIC contact but it was not believed to have been a U-boat and could certainly not have been the attacking U-boat, which must have been positioned on the starboard side and would have been in the process of turning after the attack on *Empire Heritage*.

The Board also concluded that the initial report from *Northern Wave* that claimed *Pinto* had been torpedoed on her port side was obviously incorrect; a simple and understandable mistake in the darkness and in the confusion of the attack. They also went on to note that they 'have no evidence as to whether the U-boat or U-boats fired submerged or on the surface'. This highlights how little information the Board had at the time of the inquiry; they could not even be sure of how many enemy vessels had been involved in the attack. In fact, it would be many years before any accurate picture of the night's events could be drawn; most of the survivors probably never knew who their enemy had been that night or what had really happened.

At the time of the inquiry, just days after the event, there was very little to be learned from the attack. Nothing was clear and the inquiry was one-sided; they did not have the advantage of German U-boat records showing vessel movements and attack reports. Despite all the evidence pointing to a U-boat attack, nobody could be sure of what had actually attacked the convoy, nor of how many attackers there had been. It is only many years later that it is possible to piece together what actually happened, and who had been responsible. All the Board of Inquiry could do was point out the obvious factors that could have prevented it based on the evidence they had. They found that in the attack on convoy HX-305, there were five counts of failure, and that blame could be attributed to two individuals.

Lieutenant Richard Cassils Chenoweth RCNVR, Commanding Officer of HMCS *Runnymede* was held responsible for failing to pass on to the Senior Officer of Escort Group C5 the 'SSSS' distress signal made by SS *Jamaica Planter*, despite the fact that his ship was supposed to be monitoring signals on this frequency. They found this to be 'due to inexperience' rather than negligence.

Commander George H. Stephen RCNR, Senior Officer of Escort Group C5 was found to be responsible on four counts and 'for not using his forces to the best advantage and for not making greater efforts to have the situation after *Empire Heritage* was torpedoed clarified.' The Board noted that the disposition of the escort forces left the starboard quarter weakened to a submerged U-boat attack, and particularly in the area where there were just two armed trawlers (*Northern Wave* and *Northern Sky*) without any radar. This also was found to be 'due to inexperience'.

The significant amount of time taken to reorganise the ASDIC screen after the attacks and the time taken before a search began for the attacker was found to be unacceptable, and the Board decided that this had been 'due to negligence' on the part of the Senior Officer. The equally significant length of time it took before support arrived for *Northern Wave* to allow the trawler to begin rescue work was found to be 'negligence of a lesser degree'. There can be no doubt that the length of time the men were left helpless in the sea would have had a direct effect on the number of survivors.

Finally, it was found that the numerous communications failures between the Senior Officer's ship and the other ships of the escort were 'due to negligence'. They were not informed quickly enough of what had happened, they were not given enough information to respond effectively and this would have had a direct effect on the success of both the rescue operation and the subsequent hunt for the attacker.

Therefore Commander Stephen was held largely responsible for the failings within the convoy for two principal reasons. Firstly for not ensuring the convoy was as well-protected as it could have been with the resources at his disposal, and secondly for not making better use of communications within the convoy to have the situation after the attack clarified and to better organise the necessary rescue operation.

The fact was that the escort knew there were U-boats operating in the area, and that in the preceding week there had been significant losses to merchant shipping, so it seems strange that the Commander was not more vigilant when passing through such a potentially dangerous area. Perhaps the fact that prior to this recent spate, U-boat attacks had tailed off considerably against the HX convoys – there had not been a loss from a U-boat attack since April 1943 – had lulled them into a false sense of security.

> We have formed the impression that by the night of the 7th/8th September, 1944, the general alertness of the group had deteriorated in spite of the Admiralty U-boat Reports and Senior Officer C.5's General Signal.

NORTHERN WAVE – REPORT OF PROCEEDINGS

The *Report of Proceedings for period 0400 till 1730 Friday, 8th September* was sent from the Commanding Officer of *Northern Wave* to the Commanding Officer of HMS *Irwell* on 11 September 1944, three days after the attack and four days before the inquiry.

Northern Wave's Commanding Officer Lieutenant Frederick J.R. Storey began his report by stating that the passage from St John's was 'without incident' up to the time of the attack, except for some fog experienced in the earlier stages of the convoy. He noted that it was known that U-boats were in the area.

> Signals were received from Admiralty on two occasions to the effect that submarines were in vicinity of convoy. Senior Officer made general signal to effect that the convoy was entering area of German submarines, as sinking of ship from ONS-251 proved re-opening of U-boat warfare. He requested ship's companies might be informed, I immediately ordered 1st degree readiness.

That readiness was to be tested and Lieutenant Storey noted that after the signal regarding *Empire Heritage* having been torpedoed, *Northern Wave* proceeded to the wreck site and found *Pinto* already present. With the rescue ship attempting to pick up survivors, and the trawler crew finding themselves amongst many survivors in the water, they reduced speed and began to carry out 'observant' to the windward side of the wreck site. Storey goes on to note that at 0425 '*Dunver* closed from astern' and he assumed that it was joining in the search for the attacker. Then just minutes later at 0431, *Pinto* was 3 cables from the trawler when she signalled 'periscope port' upon which Lieutenant Storey turned hard to port and increased to full speed in an attempt to hunt down the attacking U-boat. Three minutes later the torpedo hit the *Pinto*. Storey notes that although the rescue ship went down in just 90 seconds, she still managed to 'exhibit the prescribed red light before sinking'.

The *Northern Wave* continued 'observant' on the wreck site though their movement was hampered by the number of men in the water until they were some 7 cables away from where the *Pinto* went down. At around 0445 they received a report of a torpedo in the water with the members of the forward gun crew shouting 'submarine' and Storey himself sighting something moving through the water towards them. Lieutenant Storey turned the trawler hard to port again, and reduced his revs to slow the ship to 8 knots, in case a GNAT acoustic torpedo had been fired. Seaman J. Richmond of *Northern Wave*:

> Rescue ship '*Pinto*' torpedoed on our starboard beam, approximate time 0433. A few minutes later, through transmission reverbs, torpedo effect was heard faintly bearing Red 30. Transmissions were switched off, torpedo approaching confirmed and bridge immediately notified. Bearing moved slowly left to Red 40 growing louder, and at ship going hard to port, Hydrophone effect remained steady, gaining in volume until it faded, torpedo passing across bow. No Submarine contact obtained.

Lieutenant Storey then claimed to have personally spotted something approaching in the water which he suspected to be a torpedo but the forward gun crew shouted that it was the submarine. Meanwhile ASDIC reported the torpedo passing under the bow of the trawler just as something struck the port bow. The signal then faded and disappeared and although Lieutenant Storey suspected he had collided with a submarine, he wrote 'I was not definitely sure as I had not been able to distinguish what the object was.'

The uncertainty about what had passed underneath them meant that Storey was not confident about counter-attacking, and he wrote 'this uncertainty and the fact that anything up to 100 men were in the water in the near vicinity decided me against firing a pattern.' But clearly he later believed that he had in fact collided with the attacking submarine, writing that it was 'later confirmed' by evidence given from four different witnesses from his crew:

1) Sub. Lt. Meads, RNVR saw and reported feather in water.

2) Leading Seaman Watson, PSGL 4 Gun layer saw two Periscopes about 2 ½ ft up and about 6 ft apart, close by port rigging, on converging course, coming from approximate direction Red 120.

3) Signalman W.T. Rogers saw feather in water on same bearing as above.

4) Seaman Hughes saw swirl of water from propellers and outline of submarine passing under the bow in a steep dive.

Northern Wave sent a signal 'submarine in my vicinity', and Lieutenant Storey noted in his report that although the despatch time of the signal was recorded as 0505, it was actually sent before this time but was delayed due to the congestion of radio traffic. This backs up the point made by the Board of Inquiry that there should have been use of the 'clear the air' signal by the Senior Officer, so that important signals such as this could get through much sooner. At this point, *Northern Wave* carried out 'observant' using the position of the collision as datum point, though no contacts were obtained.

At 0515 *Northern Wave* abandoned the search for the attacker, leaving the duty to the other ships that had finally arrived at the scene, and began rescue work. Most of the survivors were picked up from 'rafts, spars, floats, wreckage and a number from the water'. With so little time for the survivors to don lifejackets, debris from the ship became their only hope of buoyancy. He also noted that from the two torpedoed ships, only two boats and a single dinghy had managed to get away, and that these had all been damaged to some extent in the process.

By this point the weather had begun to deteriorate, and Lieutenant Storey observed that there was a strong north-north-westerly blowing around force 6, that continued to strengthen towards force 7 as daylight approached. The survivors of the two ships were quite close together in the water, though they had been spread downwind in the worsening conditions. The heavy seas made the rescue work difficult though he writes that it 'progressed speedily and was not long before the majority had been picked up'.

In his report, Lieutenant Storey stated that the rescue work began at 0515, and that they brought the last man aboard at 0745. He wrote that all rescue work was carried out from the ship itself, and that using the ship's boat under the prevailing conditions was 'considered useless'. Two attempts were made on *Northern Wave* to launch the whaler boat but these failed and it was abandoned.

The *Kenilworth Castle* joined in the search for more survivors around 0800, and the *Helmsdale* arrived on the scene at 0905. Lieutenant Storey brought *Northern Wave* alongside this ship and passed all available information on the wreck positions, and the ramming of the suspected U-boat along with some initial survivors reports. The search was officially abandoned at 1200, when *Northern Wave*, escorted by *Ambuscade* headed for port. He totalled the survivors as follows: 'Total Survivors picked up – 88. *Pinto* 41 saved, 21 unaccounted for. *Empire Heritage* 47 saved, 109 unaccounted for.'

This is slightly different from the radio message sent from *Northern Wave* to the Commander in Chief, Western Approaches which was recorded as transmitted at 1030. 'Following survivors on board – *Pinto* 41, *Empire Heritage* 46. Unaccounted for 21 and 110 respectively. Rammed S/M whilst taking avoiding action from torpedo. Damage unknown. Still searching. Intend proceeding Londonderry on completion.' At 1045 *Northern Wave* signalled *Helmsdale* after talking to survivors, 'Survivors from *Pinto* report sighting two subs in vicinity of wreck.'

Lieutenant Storey revealed that at the time that *Pinto* was torpedoed, several rafts were secured alongside with the survivors waiting to be taken onboard and that 'a large number of survivors must have been killed.' Also according to reports he had received from the survivors that had been interviewed, 'a number [of the *Pinto*'s crew] were killed on board by the explosion.' He also estimated from interviewing survivors that 'a great number went down with *Empire Heritage*' as it was reported to have broken in half and sunk in just two minutes. Fuel oil from the ex-whaling ship was 'most prevalent' around the wreck site.

Lieutenant Storey went on to report on the conduct of his own crew throughout the ordeal which he describes as 'exemplary … Survivors were picked up speedily and without injury. Sick Bay was ready on arrival and Ambulance Party had clothing, soup, cocoa and food ready to serve. Rum was issued to each man.'

At 1225, more than eight hours after the torpedo struck *Empire Heritage*, *Northern Wave* signalled to Western Approaches, 'Abandoning search. Proceeding to Moville in company with *Ambuscade*.'

Finally he stated that he believed that there were two submarines in the vicinity of the wreck and that the attacker appeared to remain submerged beneath the survivors in the water and probably lay on the seabed. He added that survivors remarked on the unusually high speed of the submerged submarine as being around 15 knots; this was gauged by the 4 feet of periscope that was believed to be seen moving through the water.

Lieutenant Storey also recommended that when trawlers were attached to escort groups for ocean escorting of this type, an additional officer could be of the 'utmost value in increasing fighting efficiency'. During the action when all three officers were engaged in other duties it meant there was no officer on the bridge to supervise communications or direct the action.

This report was sent from *Northern Wave* to HMS *Irwell* on 11 September and then forwarded on to the Flag Officer in Charge, Liverpool, on 14 September. It was accompanied by additional remarks including a recommendation that TBY radio sets be made available to all ships working with escort groups in ocean convoys so that information was not missed in the event that it had not been duplicated by the Senior Officer through the radio telephone. The Flag Officer in Charge concurred with this recommendation.

A recommendation was made in relation to Lieutenant Storey's comment regarding an additional officer being made available; an additional junior officer or midshipman would be desirable to attend to communications and to keep a record of times and proceedings. This was concurred with but it was ultimately noted, 'This is desirable but I doubt if it is worth raising at this stage of the war in the present manpower situation.'

In addition the problems *Northern Wave* experienced in launching her 27-foot whaler to aid in the rescue operation were investigated with the crew placing the blame on the davits that held the boat and claiming they were wrongly positioned. This was found to be an unacceptable excuse and it was noted that this should have been 'found out and corrected' long before the boat was needed in an emergency situation. 'The efficiency of the boat's gear should have been checked before the ship sailed on operation.' It was decided that this situation needed further investigation and a change made in the way rescue boats were stored in future.

It is considered that the whaler in a Rescue Trawler should normally be secured for sea 'turned out' and only kept 'turned in' in heavy weather. It is requested that this matter may be investigated and measures taken to ensure that this is the standard practice in all Rescue Trawlers in future.

At the end of this document it was noted, 'This report was not available to the Board of Inquiry and details of rescue work by *Northern Wave* were therefore not investigated.' This was dated 27 October. Ultimately these reports were filed alongside the Report of Proceedings of the convoy.

On 9 November the Commander in Chief, Western Approaches sent a memo to the Flag Officer in Charge, Liverpool with the recommendations made about the storage of whalers aboard rescue trawlers and that four sets of TBY radios should be allocated for use in escort trawlers as required. The Flag Officer responded with the argument that in the case of *Northern Wave*, it was a case of 'defective equipment' and that one davit had had to be repositioned on the ship's return to harbour.

NOTE ON SENIOR OFFICER GEORGE H. STEPHEN RCNR

George Hay Stephen was born in Aberdeen, Scotland though eventually settled in Montreal, Canada. He served in the Merchant Navy prior to the war but joined the Royal Canadian Naval Reserve in November 1939. He was promoted to Acting Lieutenant Commander of HMCS *St Laurent* in July 1940 and became First Commanding Officer of HMCS *Mayflower* on 28 November that year, serving until May 1942. In that time he was awarded the Distinguished Service Cross for the salvage of the merchant ship SS *Imperial Transport*.

This Officer has displayed great devotion to duty and given invaluable service in connection with the escort of convoys during exceptionally severe winter months. Lieutenant-Commander Stephen has consistently shown himself capable of carrying responsibility and by his exemplary conduct, has set an example to others and thus improved the efficiency of others under his command.

On 14 May 1942 he became Commanding Officer of HMCS *Columbia* and during the ten months he spent with this ship he was awarded the OBE for the salvaging of a second ship and her 'valuable cargo'.

Under the determined handling by Lieutenant-Commander G.H. Stephen, HMCS *Columbia* performed an exceptional service in connection with the salvaging of SS *Matthew Luckenbach* ... this ship had been abandoned twice and it was entirely due to the prompt and strenuous efforts of HMCS *Columbia* that the ship was brought safely back to harbour.

He was also awarded a Mention in Despatches for having 'displayed outstanding seamanship in taking one of His Majesty's Ships in tow and under most difficult circumstances, bringing it safely into harbour.'

In March 1943 he returned to the destroyer HMCS *St Laurent*, this time as Commanding Officer. He stayed with her until April 1944 and in this time he was awarded a Bar to his DSC for his part in the destruction of *U-845* on 10 March 1944. HMCS *St Laurent* was one of four ships that launched a depth charge attack on the U-boat and eventually destroyed it. It was awarded for 'good service in destruction of a submarine'. This award was published in the *London Gazette* on 13 August 1944 and in the *Canada Gazette* on 9 September, the day after the sinking of *Empire Heritage*.

In May 1944 Stephen joined HMCS *Dunver* where he served as Escort Commander and was in this position when they sailed across the Atlantic in convoy HX-305. Despite the achievements of his long and distinguished naval career, the failings that the Board of Inquiry found had contributed to the devastating attacks on convoy HX-305 were largely placed at his door, and it was not for the first time.

A couple of months before on 8 July 1944, the westbound convoy ON-243 was south-east of Greenland. They had departed from Liverpool on 3 July and eventually arrived in New York on 18 July. There were 89 ships in the convoy not including escorts, and it included two MAC ships or Merchant Aircraft Carriers, *Empire MacCallum* and *Empire MacColl*.

In the vicinity of the convoy was the Free French submarine *La Perle*, en route from Nova Scotia to Britain after refitting in Connecticut. Her course had been planned so that she would avoid areas where U-boats were operating, and so she would avoid any convoys that might detect her and mistake her for an enemy vessel. All shipping was informed of her presence and warned to check for identification signals before attacking should they find themselves nearby. As her voyage progressed and was charted by the Newfoundland Force, it was noted that ON-243 had been rerouted and was now moving very close to the submarine. This led to concerns for *La Perle*'s safety for obvious reasons, and so she was also rerouted to move her out of range of the convoy, but unfortunately not far enough to be out of range of the aircraft of the two MAC ships. There were bombing restrictions of 50 miles ahead and astern of the submarine, and 20 miles off either beam.

A Swordfish aircraft piloted by Lieutenant Otterveanger from the *Empire MacCallum* was flying ahead of the convoy doing a routine sweep when the pilot, a Lieutenant of the Royal Netherlands Navy, spotted a submarine in the water nearby, moving on a north-easterly course. It was 1253 hours. He assumed it was a German U-boat and reported it to the Senior Officer of the escort, George Stephen aboard HMCS *Dunver*. Commander Stephen shared the pilot's concern and he immediately ordered the two aircraft carriers to launch all available aircraft, reportedly instructing them to 'sink the bastard'. The submarine was *La Perle*.

The Swordfish continued circling while the other aircraft – four from *Empire MacCallum* and two from *Empire MacColl* – formed up and began circling clockwise over the submarine to prepare for their attack. By now it was just before 1400. At this point, it seems that Commander Stephen realised he may have acted somewhat recklessly, and he sent a message to the two MAC ships by radio telephone, 'Have aircraft been informed that submarine *La Perle* might be in our vicinity?' This warning was decidedly late, especially as the aircraft were beginning their attack run. The MAC ships had been told nothing of the French submarine and the air staff officer aboard *Empire MacCallum* was somewhat confused by this message. He decided to try and warn the aircraft, ordering them to 'look out for recognition signals in case the sub is friendly. If not, attack.'

But the airwaves were cluttered up with radio traffic and only one aircraft heard the signal, and even then asked for it to be repeated because it was still not clear. By that point the first aircraft had already begun to attack; the same Swordfish that had first sighted the submarine nearly 75 minutes before. As he approached the submarine he noticed it flashing a series of 'L's from the conning tower, the correct identification signal for that day. This should have immediately confirmed that it was a friendly vessel, and the fact that it had taken no evasive action since clearly having been spotted and was making no attempt to attack should also have suggested this was the case. But the pilot had not heard the warning about *La Perle* and decided the signal was a ruse. Ignoring it, he decided to attack and fired four pairs of rockets at the submarine. In desperation, the submarine began firing back with her deck gun as the other aircraft flew in, with even more rockets and finally a couple of depth charges. The whole attack only lasted for a minute and the submarine could not possibly defend against such a relentless assault from so many attackers. The damage proved to be too much and *La Perle* sank in under four minutes. Commander Stephen informed the Commander-In-Chief, Western Approaches of the sinking who immediately feared it may have been the French submarine. But it was too late to do anything for them and only one man was rescued from a crew of 60.

George Stephen was an experienced officer who had been escorting convoys since 1941 with an unblemished record. He was an OBE, had been awarded the Distinguished Service Cross for past services and he was highly regarded by his superiors, and yet had carelessly ordered this horrendous act of friendly fire. There had been countless signals regarding *La Perle*, and Stephen should have known she was in the area. He later claimed in his defence that his hasty order to attack had been influenced by recent reports of U-boat activity in the vicinity, and to some extent this was accepted as being a likely influence on his actions.

At the inquiry following the incident, it became clear that the air staff in the two MAC ships had not been kept informed of *La Perle's* movements, and were unaware that she was so nearby. It later transpired that Stephen was warned by the leading signalman on the bridge of the *Dunver* that it may have been *La Perle* and was allegedly ignored with what was described as a 'non-committal grunt'. The same signalman later had appendicitis and was unable to give evidence at the inquiry but later said that Stephen often refused to sign or even acknowledge signals as they were brought to him, and often ignored them altogether, showing 'disinterest to the point of rudeness'. This led to a great deal of confusion amongst the ships of the convoy because they were simply not kept informed, similar to the confusion amongst the escort following the attack on *Empire Heritage*. The responsibility of keeping the convoy up-to-date with naval signals certainly lay with the Senior Officer of the escort because the merchant ships did not have the capability to do this for themselves. Stephen tried to claim that he had passed on all relevant signals but had received no acknowledgements from the other ships. Also no transmissions had been logged by the ship's communication department, something which Stephen should have been overseeing. Because of this there was no way to prove what signals had been sent or received by HMCS *Dunver* or the MAC ships.

The inquiry found the communications department on HMCS *Dunver* to be at the heart of the problems stating that it 'appears to be run in a most irregular manner'. But Stephen himself was largely given the benefit of the doubt, particularly because of his past record and the fact that he claimed he had acted in light of the recent reports of U-boat activity. The ratings of the communication staff were not blamed because 'their supervision had been inadequate and unsatisfactory.' Blame was also put on the Commander In Chief, Western Approaches for not taking sufficient action in rerouting the submarine so that it would avoid the convoy. 'The diversion of *La Perle*, when made, was not sufficiently drastic to increase her separation from the convoy to a sufficient extent.'

The inquiry also investigated the action of the Swordfish pilot who first sighted the submarine, first attacked and who had ordered the depth charge attack. He was totally exonerated as it was clear that he had not been informed about the presence of *La Perle*. The Captain of HMCS *Dunver* and the Group Signals Officer were reprimanded for 'not exercising closer supervision over the signals of this group'. The decision to reprimand these officers instead of Stephen was not popular amongst the staff officers at St John's and they recommended the Naval Service Headquarters to revise their decision. Ultimately, two actions were ordered. Firstly, Acting Commander George Stephen was to be informed that 'He had incurred the severe displeasure of the Department for failure to exercise complete control over the escorts of his Command.' Secondly, the original order to inform the Commanding Officer of *Dunver* and the Group Signals Officer that they had 'incurred the severe displeasure of the Department' was cancelled. Stephen was reprimanded and was considered very lucky not to have ended up facing a court martial over his actions or lack of them – 59 men were dead and a submarine was lost because of inefficiency and a lack of competent supervision, and ultimately the responsibility lay with Stephen. If it had not been for his outstanding war record, and had the leading signalman not been in hospital with appendicitis and had been able to give proper evidence at the inquiry, it is very likely that Stephen would have faced a much more serious outcome.

It can be argued that he repeated the same kinds of mistakes just a few weeks later when once again communications issues and a lack of clear control over the escorts under his command would be blamed in part for the confusion that followed the sinking of *Empire Heritage* and *Pinto*. Following the inquiry Stephen joined HMCS *Runnymede* as Escort Commander but not actually in command of the ship. In April 1945 he joined HMCS *St Laurent* for a third time as Commanding Officer. He was demobilised on 31 August 1946 with the war long over. George Hay Stephen died at the age of 90 on 22 March 1994 in St Petersburg, Florida.

IX

AFTERMATH

'Never think that war, no matter how necessary, nor how justified, is not a crime.'

Ernest Hemingway

Empire Heritage now lies close to where she sank, on the ocean floor about 15 miles north-west of Malin Head in County Donegal. *Pinto* lies barely half a mile to the southwest, both ships lying at a depth of around 65 metres on a white sand and gravel seabed. Their wrecks were discovered in the late 1990s, having sat undisturbed for half a century. The wreck of the *Pinto* is complete though largely collapsed now, the hull having come apart and fallen outwards, and the deck and bulkheads are all lying flat on the seabed. But the *Empire Heritage* has become widely regarded as one of the most striking discoveries in wreck history.

The hull of the ship lies twisted and partially upside down with the stern facing upwards, an enormous but intact four-bladed bronze propeller still fixed to the stern gear. There are six exposed boilers and two large engines before the wreck begins to deteriorate revealing the incredible cargo that the ship was carrying on her factory deck when the fatal torpedo struck. A number of Sherman tanks and dump trucks lie scattered across the ocean floor, some piled up or lying upside down, like abandoned toys. They lie in all positions, as though they had been simply tipped over by unseen hands, still waiting for the action they were built for, their guns never fired; many still have their tracks and tyres intact. The dump trucks are loaded with tyres and they stand ready to go, as though they could start up and set off across the seabed. More tanks lie abandoned in the hold along with other supplies. Lying so exposed to the currents and tide of the Atlantic, much of the wreck has deteriorated and is in a worse state than expected for a ship that took just a single torpedo. The bow section is in the worst condition and lies flat to the seabed, smashed apart and badly damaged.

Diver and underwater photographer Leigh Bishop has dived wrecks all over the world and puts the wreck of *Empire Heritage* in his top ten.

Interestingly enough for a vessel that took a single torpedo she now lies in quite a broken and unusual manner. The wreck lies 17 miles North of Lough Swilly 55.27N 8.01W over a gravel rock seabed in a position just off NW/SE and practically across the tide. The position in which she is exposed to the Atlantic Ocean possibly accounts for her condition. The very stern end of the wreck lies at the Northern position. There is a huge four-bladed bronze propeller here still attached to the wreck that is enough to dwarf a diver and although the prop rises high above the seabed the stern section itself is virtually upside down. The wreck then appears to twist back on itself before the diver meets an exposed and very large six-cylinder triple expansion engine and then six huge scotch boilers that tower high above the seabed. From the boilers themselves the diver is able to see in the distance two high derricks that rise 15m from the deck to a depth of some 50m. On the deck level adjacent to these derricks are sections of deck winch machinery and it is here that you are able to stand high on the wreck and view all the Sherman tanks and trucks across the seabed. Many of the military trucks amazingly still have their tyres attached and are totally intact whilst bucket dump trucks become obvious in the clear distance. In one corner close to the starboard side of the wreck there lies quite literally a pile of tanks on top of one another. Many of the tanks themselves still have their tracks attached, some lie on their side, some upside down while others that lie upright and fully intact make for great silhouette images. From amidships the diver swims in a direction forward where he or she will cross a cargo hold with its hatch combing still very much intact, the hold appears empty quite possibly at one time where some of the 16000-tons of oil was stored. Today the hold is home, as is the entire wreck, to an abundance of wrasse and ocean pout, so many fish in fact that inside the hold on occasions it becomes virtually impossible to see! Visibility in general over the wreck site is always around 30m/100ft and on days with the sun high in the sky possibly more. The bow section of the wreck is in a poor state compared to the remaining wreckage and lies very flat to the seabed and fairly smashed over an even area.

Empire Heritage was the 18th largest ship to be sunk during the Second World War and one of only 21 ships to be lost above 15,000 tonnes. Another two of these were also whaling factory ships: the *Kosmos II* (16,966 tonnes) and the enormous *Terje Viken* (20,638 tonnes).

After the attack on HX-305 *Empire Heritage* and *Pinto* sank fast, settled unheard on the ocean floor and became graves to the men still trapped within them as the rest of the convoy continued on and the U-boat slid silently away. The survivors of both ships were taken to Londonderry before eventually returning to mainland Britain. The rest of the convoy completed the voyage through the North Channel to Liverpool before dispersing to their various ports, arriving two days later on 10 September. Those who had survived the devastating loss of their ships were faced with the grim prospect of returning to sea, joining a new ship and carrying on as before. Once again they would have to face the risk of attack from an unseen enemy. Many would be back at sea within a matter of weeks.

If we go back to the discharge book of Bo'sun James Peterson for example, we see that following his discharge 'at sea' on 8 September, he was next engaged on the steamship *Sevilla*, a much smaller vessel registered in Stanley in the Falkland Islands. He joined the ship at Greenock on 20 November 1944, ten weeks after surviving the *Empire Heritage* sinking. He served on the *Sevilla* for the remainder of the war, until he was discharged at Greenock on 30 April 1945, the day of Hitler's suicide in Berlin. With the Führer gone, the mantle of power passed to Admiral Karl Dönitz who had been Commander of the U-boats throughout the war, and was now appointed Reich President. James served once more on the *Sevilla* for a trip between 1–24 July before the recommencement of the whaling in South Georgia with Christian Salvesen and Co, Ltd. Finally, after these terrible years of conflict he returned to his pre-war occupation.

Salvesens had lost all of her whaling factory ships in the war, *Empire Heritage* being one of them. But in the autumn of 1945 they took delivery of a brand-new vessel, the *Southern Venturer*, construction of which had begun towards the end of the war. She was specifically intended for post-war whaling. Of course, the industry demanded many more, but the massive rebuilding programme that began to replace the huge losses incurred during the war meant that yard space was extremely limited. *Southern Venturer* was delivered in time for the 1945/46 season and James Peterson joined her on 17 September 1945 to spend the British winter in South Georgia.

When he returned to Britain on 21 May 1946, it not only marked the end of the whaling season, but also the official termination of his war service, and on the 25th he was discharged from the Merchant Navy. In six years of war he had served on five different ships, all over the world, sailing from Britain to South Georgia, America, Canada, the Mediterranean and the Caribbean. He had been torpedoed twice and lost two of his ships and many friends and crewmates. And yet his story is not exceptional but merely representative of those of so many brave Allied merchant seamen.

Following the inquiry into the attack on HX-305, the outstanding conduct of certain members of the crews involved saw them considered for awards, and on 24 October 1944 Admiral Sir Max Horton, Commander-in-Chief of the Western Approaches put forward the recommendations to the Secretary of the Admiralty. They were listed in an order of merit, as recommended by the Admiral:

Recommended for Decoration
Officer
Temporary Surgeon Lieutenant Philip Noel Holmes, M.B. Ch.B., R.N.V.R. (*Pinto*)

Recommended for Mention in Despatches
Officer
Temporary Lieutenant Frederick John Robb Storey, R.N.V.R. (*Northern Wave*)

Recommended for Mention in Despatches
Ratings
Harry Holman Pashby, Seaman (*Northern Wave*)
Jack Ashe, Telegraphist (*Northern Wave*)

Medical Officer Holmes was recognised for his part in the treatment of the survivors from both ships, both while on the rafts and continuing on board the *Northern Wave*, and this despite injuries sustained himself when his own ship was torpedoed. The recommendation form stated:

Recommended for the award of a decoration for courage, great coolness, efficiency and devotion to duty in emergency ... Both the Principal Sea Transport Officer, Clyde and Scottish Ports and the Medical Transport Officer, Glasgow, were much impressed by the modest way in which Surgeon Lieutenant Holmes gave his account of what transpired at the sinking.

Admiral Sir Max Horton remarked that he fully concurred with the recommendation, adding, 'This Officer displayed outstanding devotion to duty.'

Commanding Officer Fred Storey of the *Northern Wave* was recommended for his part in the rescue operations that commenced following the sinking of both *Empire Heritage* and *Pinto*. He was mentioned in despatches, 'For coolness and resourcefulness and skilled handling of *Northern Wave* in the dark and in wind force 6, in rescuing 88 survivors'. Once again Sir Max Horton concurred.

Seaman Harry Pashby and Telegraphist Jack Ashe were put forward for reward for 'outstanding devotion to duty whilst engaged in rescuing survivors from tanker

Empire Heritage and rescue ship *Pinto*'. As detailed earlier, they worked over the side of *Northern Wave* and while in the water, Pashby was swept away in the process of bringing a survivor on board and was left in the water for some time before finally being rescued himself. It was noted: 'This rating acted in an exemplary manner showing courage, resourcefulness and disregard for his own life under bad weather conditions (wind force 6) during dark hours when water was covered with thick oil.' Jack Ashe had endured similar conditions during the rescue:

> The water was coated with oil fuel. Ashe was forced to work almost continually submerged causing him to swallow a considerable amount of oil. In the dark he was in great danger in the existing weather (wind force 6) of being washed away or killed against ship's side.

Horton agreed that both men should be put forward for an award and on 20 November 1944, The Honours and Awards Committee put all four of these men forward for consideration by the King. All four were awarded a Mention in Despatches, after approval of the First Lord and His Majesty King George VI on 25 November.

A Mention in Despatches is an award for gallantry or other commendable service, which has not been deemed to qualify for a medal or higher award. Despatches are simply published reports by an officer, which detail the conduct on military operations, and in Britain these were published in the *London Gazette*. The Mention in Despatches was the lowest form of award published. Those awarded received no medal, but a certificate was issued detailing the despatch in which the recipient was mentioned. During the First World War it was decided that anyone who had been mentioned could wear an oak leaf emblem to signify the award. The awards received by the four men from convoy HX-305 were published in the *London Gazette* (no.36825) on 5 December 1944, and they were listed as being awarded 'For good services to survivors from a Merchant Vessel which was sunk by enemy action'.

By the time the awards to the men of the *Northern Wave* and *Pinto* had been published in the *London Gazette*, James Peterson was back at sea. He joined the 7,022–ton steamship *Sevilla* on 20 November 1944 at Greenock. Built in 1900 by Priestman's shipbuilders in Sunderland, the *Sevilla* was one of Salvesen's old whaling transports that were not considered reliable enough for convoy duty owing to age and condition. Instead, she spent most of the war in the Clyde, operating as a depot ship.

During this time on the *Sevilla*, James had two significant changes in his home life. His father John died on 26 January 1945 back home in Shetland; his mother had died in May 1939. The following month he went to Edinburgh and married Betsy at Palmerston Place Church Edinburgh on 17 February 1945. Shortly afterwards he returned to the Clyde, and was back at sea to continue his service on the *Sevilla*.

After the war, James Peterson was invited to St James's Palace where he was awarded the British Empire Medal (Civil Division) in the King's Birthday honours list. It was awarded to him personally by King George VI on 14 June 1945. It was printed in the fourth supplement to the *London Gazette* of Friday 8 June, 1945 which was published the following week.

> The King has been graciously pleased, on the occasion of the Celebration of His Majesty's Birthday, to approve the award of the British Empire Medal (Civil Division) to the undermentioned:-
>
> James Peterson, Boatswain, SS '*Sevilla*,' Chr. Salvesen & Company

In addition to the British Empire Medal, he also received the 1939–1945 Star and the War Medal for service throughout the war, the Atlantic Star for service during the Battle of the Atlantic, and the Italy Star for service in the Mediterranean.

Eventually James and Betsy returned to Shetland, and by the early 1950s had settled back in Braewick where James had grown up. They had two children, Annette and John. Following the war James continued to work as a whaler with Salvesens, spending each winter in South Georgia before returning home to Shetland each May to his family and their home, which he had named *Heritage* in memory of his experiences on that ship. It was an experience that he would rarely talk about in the years to come, but that he would never forget. His last season with the company was in 1962/63 working aboard their very last factory ship, *Southern Harvester*. This ship was sold later that year, marking the end of Salvesen's Antarctic whaling operations, and the end of James's life at sea.

After pulling away from convoy HX-305 and making her escape unscathed and barely even detected, U-*482* headed north. On 10 September 1944, BdU noted under 'Current Operations' in their *Kriegstagebucher* (KTB) or war diary:

> U-*482* has commenced return passage from North Channel, all torpedoes expended. Boat sank one destroyer from anti-submarine patrol on 1.9 in AM5612, a tanker of 7,000 GRT from convoy entering port on 30.8 in AM5397, on 8.9 in AM5387 freighter of 5,000 GRT and tanker of 6,000 GRT. T5 hit on freighter of 5,000 GRT after 2 mins 47 secs, presumed sunk.

For that same date under 'Reports of Success' they recorded:

U-482   4 ships   1 destroyer   23000GRT

By 11 September U-482 had moved out of quadrant AM53 into AM29 and Matuschka made a transmission to BdU, to which they responded by informing him that he had been awarded the Iron Cross First Class. He confirmed details of his successes, and gave a situation report recorded in the war diary for that date under 'current operations'.

Situation North Channel (U482)
In 10 days sighted 3 large convoys with destroyer and air escort. Convoy route over AM5282 – 5387 – 5397. Noise buoys concealed convoys. During night while at depth of 40 meters 2 convoys were picked for first time as they passed overhead. Diving attack. Strong defence by sea and air. Over 300 depth charges dropped, none dangerous, no destroyer came near. Hydrophone and location conditions very bad. Mobile noise buoys. Depth charge attacks by night undisturbed.

With no torpedoes remaining U-482 headed north and made her way back to Bergen. She remained mostly submerged as she moved up the west coast of Scotland and around the north of Britain, between the Faroe Islands and Shetland, and out into the North Sea. In the BdU war diary of 23 September there is a record of an air attack on U-482 at 0625 in position AF7687, and a further note that U-482 had been spotted at 0700 in position AF7923 by the 18th Escort Group. But these incidents may have been unconfirmed intelligence reports that were merely attributed to U-482, or maybe they were accurate sightings. Whatever the case, they were evidently of no consequence because U-482 sailed on unhindered and oblivious. There had been a significant strengthening of air patrols following U-482's successful attacks in the North Channel but by clever use of the snorkel Matuschka managed to remain safe on the voyage home.

Over sixteen days they slid silently and steadily back to their Norwegian base, and arrived triumphantly in Bergen on 26 September. They had completed their first patrol with extraordinary success, and without any damage or loss, and 29-year-old Hartmut von Matuschka had gained the German Cross in Gold.

The intensive losses suffered in the North Channel badly shook up the Allies who had begun to feel relatively safe from attack so close to their own shores. Captain S. W. Roskill, the naval historian wrote in his epic The War at Sea (Part III Volume 2):

The loss of large ships such as fell to this single U-boat almost on our front door-step and at our most sensitive spot – for comparatively few ships were as yet coming in through the South Western Approaches – was an unpleasant shock, the more so because all the victims were sailing in convoy.

Of course U-482 was not the only vessel ordered to the North Channel at this time, and following the success of Matuschka's patrol, Dönitz immediately ordered more U-boats to the North Channel to see if this seemingly fertile hunting ground could be further exploited. Expectations were high and the ships, all despatched from Norway, were hopeful of achieving a similar success. But it was not to be.

Of the eight other U-boats sent out to the North Channel during this stage of the war, only one other submarine managed to damage an enemy vessel. U-483, a sister ship of Matuschka's U-482 built at the same time in Kiel, set out for the North Channel under the command of Hans-Joachim von Morstein. On 1 November she torpedoed the 1,300-ton frigate HMS *Whitaker*, fatally damaging the ship near Loch Swilly. She was the only other success alongside U-482. The other vessels that headed for the North Channel in the autumn of 1944 met little success and sometimes a swift end.

U-484 was another Type VII from the same batch as U-482, built at Kiel in 1943. They started their first patrol on 1 August 1944, under Korvettenkapitän Wolf-Axel Schaefer, setting off from Horten and sailing up past the Faroes and down towards the North Channel. They were detected and attacked to the west of Northern Ireland by depth charges from HMS *Portchester Castle* and HMS *Helmsdale* without achieving a single success against the enemy. In early September U-743 under command of Helmut Kandzior was lost to an unknown cause, possibly a collision. U-1200 under Hinrich Mangels left port on 7 October but had to abort her patrol shortly after following a failure of her telemotor pumps. U-248, U-1003 and U-1004 all went on patrol as ordered but did not achieve any success and returned to port with nothing to celebrate apart from their own survival. U-248 would later be sunk with all hands after a depth charge attack in January 1945. U-1003 was scuttled in March 1945 after being severely damaged in a collision with HMCS *Glasgow*. The commander and 16 of her crew were killed. U-1004 had more success on her second patrol, sinking two ships to the east of Falmouth on 22 February 1945 from convoy BTC-76. Following the war she was transferred from Bergen to Loch Ryan and sunk as part of Operation *Deadlight*.

Other U-boats set sail still hoping for success but not one seemed able to get a foothold amongst the convoys sailing into Britain. Some were lost, some survived, and some were forced to abort through mechanical failures. But not one returned to port with the triumph of Count Matuschka and his men. In fact over the next few months it became clear that this new chapter in the U-boat war was not going to change the end of the story for the Kriegsmarine. The new coastal operations became more and more dangerous and by April 1945 they had been abandoned completely, U-boats were once more operating some 300 miles out to sea. Kapitänleutnant Peter Cremer of U-*333* wrote of the experience in his log:

> Getting close to the convoys is impossible. We spent most of the time on the sea bed, carefully monitoring signals. All lights are out to save power and avoid taxing accumulators. The men are lying on their bunks to save oxygen. This feeling of hopelessness saps our strength. Without let up, the U-boat resonates from the 'ping ping' of aircraft bombs, the shock waves of the depth charges and the dull hammering of destroyer propellers.

At the time, the failure experienced by these other U-boats in the wake of U-*482* only further highlighted her extraordinary success. At a time when the crews were struggling just to survive, they managed to pull off a series of devastating attacks, evade an extensive hunt and make it back to Bergen without ever coming close to serious danger. It is understandable that Admiral Dönitz was keen to reward the young commander upon his return, and equally understandable that similar achievements were expected from him on his future patrols.

On 18 November Kapitänleutnant Matuschka and the crew of U-*482* had returned to active duty and were once again preparing to leave port. During the period between the two patrols, the U-boat crew had been on leave and Count Matuschka had returned home to Germany. But now they were back in Norway, the U-boat was fuelled and armed, and the crew were refreshed after several weeks ashore. They left port and headed west to try and repeat the good hunting of their first extraordinary patrol. The story of the U-*482* was to continue (see next chapter).

Even as Berlin crumbled, the Battle of the Atlantic continued. The very last casualty of the entire campaign was the *Avondale Park*, sunk on 7 May 1945 by U-*2336*, one of the new Type XXIII vessels. This loss, at the very closure of the conflict marked the end of the longest campaign in naval history. In that final year of war, more than 100 U-boats had been sent out against a now much stronger and technologically superior enemy, and were lost with all men. The crews had died for little strategic benefit to their steadily disintegrating homeland. But they had kept up a relentless and courageous campaign in some of the most dangerous conditions imaginable.

A U-boat was always a very fragile machine. Of the 1,174 U-boats that went into service during the war, 784 were lost. Out of the 39,000 U-boat men that went to sea, 32,000 were killed or captured, more than three-quarters of the total. In the final year of the war, only a Kamikaze pilot stood less chance of survival. After the turnaround of May 1943, the life expectancy of a German submariner was estimated to have fallen to around 50 days. Most of them were lost very early on in their service and the German U-boat historian Dr Axel Niestle estimated in his book *German U-boat Losses During World War Two* that a third of U-boat crews were lost on their first active patrol.

In their ceaseless bravery and devotion to duty the U-boat crews outshone all others and no other part of the German naval forces was so well decorated as the men of the U-boat arm. They received 530 German Crosses in Gold, the award between the common Iron Cross and highly-prized Knight's Cross. Overall 318 Knight's Crosses were awarded to the entire Kriegsmarine throughout the war, given for bravery or leadership in the field. Of these, 144 were awarded to men of the U-boat arm, nearly half of the total amount, though the U-boat service only accounted for around five per cent of the men in the Kriegsmarine. In addition, 29 men of the U-boat service were awarded the rarer Knight's Cross with Oak Leaves and a further five received the very rare Knight's Cross with Oak Leaves and Crossed Swords, the second highest award available for acts of bravery; only 150 were ever handed out during the war. The highest level of award available was the Knight's Cross with Oak Leaves, Crossed Swords and Diamonds. Only 27 such medals were ever awarded, the Kriegsmarine received two of them, and both to U-boat commanders.

At the end of the war there were only 45 U-boats still at sea, with another 377 lying up in bases across Northern Europe. All vessels were ordered to proceed on the surface to British anchorages, as designated by the Allies, for surrender. Of those at sea, 23 sailed into British ports, three surrendered in the United States, four in Canada and two in Argentina. The rest returned to Norway or Kiel, apart from two that were scuttled off Lisbon and one that ran aground in Holland. Of the 377 lying in port, 156 obeyed the Allies and sailed to their designated ports for surrender where they were later interned, but a further 221 were scuttled in defiance of the request. Most of the interned ships were later towed to an area 30 miles north of Malin Head and sunk as part of Operation *Deadlight*, close to the site where *Empire Heritage* and *Pinto* were lost.

For all the technological advances in detection such as ASDIC, HF/DF and radar, and the improved air coverage and anti-submarine weapons, the U-boats in the North Atlantic remained right to the end a very real and effective threat. Prime Minister Winston Churchill:

Even after the autumn of 1944, when they were forced to abandon their bases in the Bay of Biscay, they did not despair. The schnorchel-fitted boats now in service, breathing through a tube while charging their batteries submerged, were but an introduction to the new pattern of U-boat warfare which Doenitz had planned … By stupendous efforts and in spite of all losses, about sixty or seventy U-boats remained in action until almost the end … such was the persistence of Germany's effort and the fortitude of the U-boat service.

At the end of the war in May, there were 25 U-boats either operational in UK waters, or on passage to or from there. The consequence of even this meagre presence was that some 400 Allied anti-submarine vessels and around 800 spotter aircraft were still operational against the threat of an attack, an immense amount of men and resources being tied up by the danger of U-boat activity. Admiral Dönitz:

In view of the vast enemy forces our U-boats were tying down, we came again and again to the same conclusion: The U-boat campaign must be continued with the forces available. Losses, which bear no relation to the success achieved, must be accepted, bitter though they are.

It was acknowledged that the U-boats were never entirely conquered, and Captain Stephen W. Roskill, the Royal Navy's official historian from 1949 to 1960 concluded: 'We never gained a firm and final mastery over the U-boats.'

The endless, resolute sense of duty shown by the U-boat crews was comparable only to that shown by their prey: the crews of the allied Merchant Navy. They too sailed on persistently in the face of incredible danger, returning again and again to brave the peril of the sea. The need for food and supplies saw them doggedly navigate the world's oceans from country to country, continent to continent, only remaining in port long enough to load and unload before setting off once more. Never did a crew refuse to sail, never did their tenacity fade, even in the darkest months of 1942. And also like the U-boat arm, the Allied Merchant Navy endured enormous losses. Somewhere in the region of 63,000 Allied and neutral merchant seamen were lost in the 3,500 ships that were sunk, proportionately more casualties than the three main Allied services. There were also some 11,000 civilian passengers lost at sea as a result of enemy action.

In a conflict such as this, there were tremendous acts of heroism and bravery, and in the course of the war, 6,500 awards for gallantry were handed out to Allied merchant seamen who had spent nearly six years under the terrible threat of being lost at sea.

X

THE END OF U-*482*

'My U-boat men! Six years of submarine warfare lie behind us. You have fought like lions! A crushing material superiority has forced us into a narrow area ... Undefeated and unble mished you lay down your arms after a heroic battle without equal. We remember in deep respect our fallen comrades, who have sealed with death their loyalty to Führer and Fatherland!'

Final radio signal sent by Admiral Dönitz, 4 May 1945

The story of Count Matuschka and U-*482* does not end with their triumphant return to Bergen. After the success of their first patrol in the North Channel, Matuschka and his crew were sent out on patrol again to the same hunting ground where they achieved their previous success. They were one of two U-boats (the other was U-*775*) that left Bergen on 18 November 1944 and headed west. They were to sail across the North Sea, through the Shetland Narrows – the area between Shetland and the Faroes – and then down the west coast of Scotland towards the North Channel. On 21 November U-*482* received a message from BdU to say she had been allocated a patrol area off the North Channel, close to the area of her previous successes near Malin Head. Confident that Matuschka could shine once more, BdU recorded in their war diary for 21 November the allocation of patrol areas to the next four submarines approaching Britain through the Shetland Narrows: 'U-*482*, North Channel, on her first trip this boat had great successes close inshore in this area. After temporary stoppage of traffic, U-*483* sank one ship, and probably sank another in this area on 1.11.'

It can be assumed that the crew of U-*482* received these orders and were preparing to carry them out, but this is where the mystery begins, for soon afterwards

U-*482* disappeared. No transmissions were received from the U-boat and she never returned to Bergen; somehow and somewhere she had been lost. At the time however, it was not realised that she was missing as it was common for U-boats to be out of contact for long periods, particularly if submerged. It was usually several weeks or even months before a vessel was accepted as lost.

On 24 November she was recorded as being in area AM32, which was to the west of Shetland and that same day BdU noted an intelligence report of minefields having been laid in the North Channel, in the very area that U-*482* had been ordered to patrol. This point would be important later on in determining the possible fate of U-*482*. The intelligence stated: 'Minelayers *Plover* and *Apollo* laid over 2,000 mines north of Ireland during September. Information was obtained from a member of the crew of an English minelayer.'

When this information was being noted in the war diary, U-*482* was likely already lost, though at the time there was no evidence to suggest that she was anywhere other than where she should have been. On 25 November, when she had certainly been destroyed, BdU was still recording her as operational, estimating her to be in area AM33, noting that 'U-*482* has been given a free hand in North Channel, where she carried out her first operation.'

On 5 December BdU still marked U-*482* as operational despite having had no contact with her for nearly two weeks. BdU received a report from U-*1003* who had just returned from the North Channel stating that there were few opportunities to attack, most likely because of the recent routing of convoys back through the south-west approaches following the German loss of the Biscay bases. Orders were broadcast to the U-boat to change her location for a better hunting ground. 'The possibility arises that chances for attack are not good enough in AM 53–56–61 to 6410. Therefore U-*482*, who was in the area, received orders to push S.E. into the Irish Sea after a survey of the North Channel situation.'

No contact was received from U-*482*, and so even BdU could not be sure of where she was. This could be a common problem when tracking a U-boat and often BdU records only showed a ship's 'assumed' position based on where they were supposed to be judging by their last known position and intended route. This also meant that when intelligence came through of an attack against an enemy ship, they could only assume who the attacker was by working out which operational ships were thought to be in the approximate area at the time. This could only ever be confirmed by communication from the U-boat itself. Of course this system was fraught with variables, and enemy losses were consistently attributed to U-boats that were later proven to be nowhere near the area in question, or in some cases U-boats that had already been lost.

Therefore when BdU received reports of two ships, the British escort carrier HMS *Thane* and the Norwegian tanker *Spinanger* attacked and damaged on 15 January in broad daylight just a mile from the Clyde Lightship, U-*482* was considered to be the only operational U-boat anywhere nearby and was therefore wrongly credited with the attacks. In fact it later transpired that the attacks had been carried out by U-*1772*. U-*1772* was definitely in the area and was not destroyed until several weeks later.

Following this attack it was believed that U-*482* had been hunted down and destroyed on 16 January 1945 by five ships of the 22nd Escort Group to the west of Kintyre after a prolonged chase and attack, but this too proved wrong. HMS *Peacock*, *Hart*, *Loch Craggie*, *Amethyest* and *Starling* got a radar contact with what they suspected to be a U-boat and carried out some 37 attacks, of which 13 were made with the deadly Squid launcher, the more effective incarnation of the Hedgehog. The target seemed to remain intact and no debris appeared; in fact it was reported to be stationary on the seabed throughout the assault. This was not expected of a vessel under such an intensive attack and at the time it was believed they had picked up a non-sub target, something of a similar size and shape that had been picked up by the ASDIC operator. This was a fairly common occurrence and it was likely an old wreck or similar, but later it was a convenient explanation for the loss of U-*482*, even though the oil that had appeared over the site was furnace oil rather than diesel as would be expected. Then in 1993 a reassessment of the evidence discounted this theory and the cause of U-*482*'s loss simply became 'unknown' as there were no other Allied reports from January 1945 of a successful attack against a U-boat in the vicinity of her expected location. This left the most likely causes of loss being either an accident of some kind, or that she had been blown up by a mine.

At the end of the war, a list prepared for the Allies by BdU accounting for all operational U-boats gave the date of U-*482*'s demise as 7 December 1944 though no information was given to explain how they arrived at that seemingly arbitrary date, particularly when they continued estimating her location well into January 1945. It would seem that they too assumed she was lost as a result of mining, as according to their estimations she would have been passing through a known minefield at that time. Since Matuschka's last patrol in the area to the north of Ireland, two fresh anti-sub minefields had been laid at a depth of 150 feet. Ironically it was likely his previous successes in that very area led to these mines being laid. But as it turned out this was also a mistake, and it took a chance discovery of another U-boat in the English Channel to establish an agreed theory on the demise of U-*482*.

Divers filming a U-boat wreck in the English Channel – previously believed to be that of U-772, sunk there on 29 December 1944 – positively identified the boat as U-*322*, a vessel thought to have been sunk by HMS *Ascension* to the west of Shetland in late November. Like U-*482* she was a Type VII, built at the Flender-Werke in Lubeck and commissioned on 5 February 1944. She had been lost with all her 52 crew including her master, Oberleutnant Gerhard Wysk. Also like U-*482*, she had been lost for a long time before it was realised by BdU and they were plotting her estimated position and listing her as operational long after she must have been sunk. All through December 1944 she was assumed to be operational though on the 30th they finally noted: 'According to dead reckoning based on fuel supplies [U-*322*] will have to return.'

This acknowledgement that the U-boat simply did not have enough fuel to still be on patrol meant it was unlikely she was going to return. Similarly, on 12 January 1945, for the first time in over six weeks, U-*482* is recorded as being 'on return' as it was clear she could no longer be operating in a patrol capacity. She was still listed as on return until the BdU records ended on 15 January when she was estimated to be in area AM28. The BdU war diary records were only recovered up to this date by the Allies at the end of the war; later records were presumably destroyed prior to the German surrender. U-*322* had left Horten on 15 November and was ordered to patrol the waters off Cherbourg. Unaware that the U-boat had been lost, BdU assumed that she was patrolling in her designated area or had moved to the Bristol Channel having found the conditions near Cherbourg unfavourable. The BdU assumption that U-*322* was operating in the Channel was more accurate than the Allies' conclusion that she had been lost to the west of Shetland, as the former is where she eventually turned up all those years later. Aiding in the identification of U-*322* was the presence on the wreck of four pressure-proof rubber boat containers fitted on the forward upper deck. These were generally only installed after October 1944, and only to vessels based in German ports. U-*322* was known to have had these containers installed in October 1944, in her home port of Horten, whereas U-*772* based in Trondheim certainly had not.

This revelation about the identification of U-*322* created a ripple effect, and posed two important questions. Firstly, where had U-*772* actually ended up, and secondly, what was the U-boat destroyed by HMS *Ascension* in November 1944 to the west of Shetland? It was known that U-*772* had left Trondheim on 19 November and like U-*322*, had been directed to the area off Cherbourg, or if conditions were not good, to proceed towards Milford Haven. Kapitänleutnant Ewald Rademacher was on his first proper patrol, and like Matuschka in U-*482*, was originally credited with attacking three separate convoys off Cherbourg. These attacks resulted in the loss of four vessels totalling some 21,100 tonnes; the US Liberty ship *Black Hawk*; the British steamer *Slemish* on 23 December; the British freighter *Dumfries* on 29

December; and the British troopship *Empire Javelin* on 28 December. The *Empire Javelin* had 1,500 soldiers on board when she was hit, but owing to a highly successful rescue operation, only six lost their lives. As well as these losses, the 7,200-ton Liberty ship *Arthur Sewall* was damaged on 29 December.

It is now clear that these losses were not caused by Rademacher in U-*772* at all; she had already been lost. Rademacher and his men were sunk by depth charges on 17 December to the south of Cork, nearly two weeks prior to the loss of U-*322*. It seems that *Dumfries*, *Arthur Sewall* and *Black Hawk* were attacked by U-*322*, as her later discovery has proven that she was the only likely vessel in the vicinity at the time. The *Empire Javelin* and *Slemish* were probably not torpedoed at all; with no other U-boats known to have been in a position to attack them it seems most likely that they were lost to mines.

So with U-*322* taking over the position and attack credits of U-*772*, we can assume that she suffered the fate that was recorded for Rademacher's vessel. On 30 December 1944, a Wellington from the Canadian 407 Squadron spotted the U-boat's snorkel in the moonlight and on a calm sea. The pilot C.J.W. Taylor flew over the protruding snorkel and dropped six depth charges right on target, destroying the submarine with all hands. For years this attack had been recorded as U-*772*, but it has finally been proved to be U-*322*.

This leaves the second question regarding the identification of the ship that had been attacked on 25 November much farther north. If U-*322* was confirmed to be the ship lying in the Channel south of Weymouth, then what was the U-boat attacked and sunk off Shetland by the Royal Navy frigate HMS *Ascension*? It had been the only recorded anti-submarine attack in that area at that time, so it was a case of identifying which U-boats could have been in that area and had not been found anywhere else. There was a review of the known U-boat activity in the Shetland area at that time to see what vessels could possibly have been the mysterious victim of HMS *Ascension*. There was only one possible conclusion.

U-*482* was the only unaccounted-for U-boat, the only vessel that fit the puzzle. BdU had plotted her route all the way towards the North Channel, but had not actually received any confirmation from her after crossing the North Sea. It turned out that U-*482* had never made it to the North Channel at all, and had been lost on her outward journey, just six days after leaving Bergen. She had not been sunk to the west of the Clyde by depth charges or fallen victim to minefields in the North Channel. For decades, HMS *Ascension* had been credited with the sinking of the wrong vessel.

On 24 November 1944, six days after leaving Bergen for her second patrol, U-*482* had moved around the top of Shetland and was lying to the west of the islands on her way to the North Channel. Meanwhile a Sunderland Flying-boat from No.330 (Norwegian) Squadron was on patrol at 1,500 feet several miles away. Based at Sullom Voe in the Shetland Islands, the aircraft was on her second patrol of the evening. It was 2157 and it was dark and foggy so visibility was particularly poor. The aircraft, piloted by Lieutenant J. Buer, picked up a radar contact at a range of six miles, and suspecting it could be a U-boat, he swung his plane round and homed in on the contact. As he closed the gap, Buer decreased his altitude in preparation for an attack if necessary but by the time he passed over the position, he could see nothing because of the bad visibility, though he had dropped to less than 300 feet. He came around and began to circle but the fog made it impossible to see and so at 2210 he signalled to base that he had obtained a Grade 1 radar contact, and gave a GEE fixed position, GEE being a navigation system introduced by the RAF in the war, used to improve navigational accuracy.

The Sunderland continued picking up the radar blip and homed in several more times but each time they lost the contact when they came within four miles and the continuing poor visibility meant that they never actually sighted any enemy vessel. Finally after several passes overhead, the blip was lost and not regained.

But the unconfirmed contact was not dismissed, and shortly afterwards other aircraft prepared to home in on the position. Also the Commander-In-Chief, Rosyth who had been notified of the contact, ordered Escort Group 17 to investigate the site, and informed them that other aircraft would be carrying out a homing procedure.

A Liberator aircraft carrying out a box patrol close to Lieutenant Buer's Sunderland obtained a radar contact at a range of 10 miles. The pilot homed in on the blip until the contact disappeared when only about half a mile ahead. He used the powerful Leigh light to search the sea beneath him but the poor visibility diffused the beam of light to the point that nothing could be seen through the haze. At 2245 the Liberator signalled to base 'Have Grade 1 Radar contact in Gee fix position 60° 40' N by 04° 49' W.'

Escort Group 17 sprang into action and set a course to intercept the suspected U-boat. The course of the enemy vessel was assessed as 225° 3 knots, and at 2259 the group set a course of 339° to intercept. The ships of the Escort Group assembled in a line 2,000 yards apart, at a speed of 14 knots. The slow electric motors of U-*482* could not possibly outrun them; her only hope was to hide. It is impossible to know whether the crew of the U-boat had heard the drone of the aircraft circling overhead, but very soon they would be deafened by the propellers of the ships sent to destroy them. They were outnumbered, outgunned and their time was running out.

Midnight came and went, and in the early hours of 25 November, the hunters were getting near. Amongst them was the Colony-class frigate HMS *Ascension*. She had been one of 21 ships built in Providence, Rhode Island for Lend-Lease transfer to the Royal Navy in 1944. She was launched in August 1943 with the name USS *Hargood* but had her name changed upon her transfer to the Royal Navy in November of that year. She served throughout the war with the pendant number K-502, before being returned to the US on 31 May 1946 where she was finally sold to the Hudson Valley Shipwrecking Corporation, New York, in October 1947. She had initially been under the command of Lieutenant Commander Archibald Wilkinson RNR but had recently been taken over by Commander William Jocelyn Moore RNR, who remained in command until the end of the war.

In early November 1944 HMS *Ascension* had been ordered, along with four other frigates, to sweep the waters between Shetland and the Faroes, in order to cover the return of a convoy heading back from Northern Russia. On 10 November they passed through Scapa Flow and headed for Shetland waters to begin their patrol.

In the weeks preceding the detection of U-*482* passing west of Shetland, HMS *Ascension* and the 17th Escort Group had already seen considerable action in this area. Less than two weeks previously the group had carried out an attack on what was believed to be a submerged U-boat. Captain-class frigate HMS *Cranstoun* had obtained a radar contact at a range of 3,000 yards on 13 November, which faded just two minutes later, giving the impression of a submarine that had just dived. After closing on the position, the frigate carried out a Hedgehog attack, which produced an initial explosion after six seconds, followed by several more.

The Hedgehog launcher was a new development in anti-submarine warfare. Also known as the Anti-Submarine Projector, it was an improvement on the depth charge system and got its name from the rows of spigots that launched up to 24 explosives at a time, and which looked like the spines of the hedgehog. Rather than using a fuse that had to be timed to explode when it had reached a certain depth, the Hedgehog projectiles only exploded on contact so it was much easier to tell whether an attack had been successful. Also it was much more effective than a depth charge attack because any resulting explosions were actually in contact with the hull of the U-boat, not just nearby. With a detonating depth charge there was often a 'cushion' of water between the blast and the hull that dissipated much of the force from the blast. With a Hedgehog attack the blast was directed fully against the side of the ship and so a single hit could spell disaster for the fragile hull of a U-boat. The explosives were launched from the Hedgehog in a single barrage and in an arc so as to land in a circular pattern around 100 feet in diameter, giving the best chance of achieving at least a single hit. Once a target was located, the barrage could be fired into the approximate area, often with devastating results. It had the added advantage that any projectiles that did not hit the target simply sank away, exploding later on the seabed. This was important because underwater explosions affected the sonar and could take up to fifteen minutes to resettle, by which time a lucky U-boat could have taken evasive action and moved clear of the attack area. This was another of the advantages of the Hedgehog over the depth charges, which all exploded regardless. In total it was considered that the Hedgehog achieved a kill rate of around 25 per cent whereas depth charges never achieved higher than 7 per cent.

After the Hedgehog attack by HMS *Cranstoun* there was no other movement from the submerged contact but also no evidence of destruction, so she continued to attack along with HMS *Ascension*, using both Hedgehog and depth charges. HMS *Loch Killin* joined in with her Squid, another more modern type of depth charge launcher. Eventually some debris came to the surface including oil, slabs of paraffin wax, pieces of fat and tallow, and surgical rubber gloves. These were recovered and forwarded to the Director, Anti-U-boat Division; the glove was later found to be of American origin but the actual trademark was indecipherable. A sample of oil was recovered and believed to be diesel oil but the samples were broken before they could be chemically tested. It was ultimately decided that in light of the gloves and the lack of other evidence, the attack had most likely been on a wreck lying on the seabed, and not actually an active U-boat despite the initial radar contact.

Two days later in the afternoon of 15 November, the group was involved in another attack, this time on what was considered to be a U-boat. The initial contact was made with ASDIC though initially it could not be confirmed as a submarine because of large quantities of fish in the area. Despite this HMS *Ascension* decided to launch an attack, and at 1524 she made a pass and fired her Hedgehog at the target running at a depth of 100 fathoms. All the ships in the group had difficulty maintaining contact with the U-boat and it became clear that it was taking evasive action, aware of the danger closing in all around it. Nevertheless the Hedgehog pattern produced several explosions just nine seconds after firing, after which all contacts became 'woolly' and at 1546 all contact was lost.

HMS *Ascension* was not fitted with a British echo sounder to search for the submarine, so HMS *Loch Killin* was ordered to move in and take a sounding for her She picked up an object lying on the seabed at a depth of 600 feet. It was approximately 400 feet long by 50 feet high. She remained in contact while the rest of the group spread out to search the surrounding waters in case the enemy vessel had slid away unnoticed. While she was over the contact HMS *Loch Killin* fired a single

Squid attack which produced a white, lard-like substance full of splinters of glass. The other ships picked up no other contacts, and there was no movement from the suspected U-boat for a period of 72 hours after the attack. The sample recovered was forwarded to the Director, Anti U-boat Division for closer examination, and it was later decided that the attack had been against a U-boat because of the evidence recovered, the initial ASDIC contact, and the following movement tracked by both plotting and Doppler sounding. Also the fact that the resulting explosions from the first attack had been well clear of the bottom and so had not merely detonated on the seabed and the fact that the object did not move afterwards led the Senior Officer of the group to decide that a U-boat was present.

And so we come to the fate of U-*482*. On the night of 24/25 November 1944 the line of frigates sped towards the site of the suspected U-boat; at 14 knots they were not long closing. It was 0050 when HMS *Ascension* gained an ASDIC contact bearing 354° at 1,100 yards; she homed in on it and passed the U-boat, losing contact briefly as it moved down the port side but quickly regaining it when it reappeared astern. HMS *Moorsom* altered course and joined the *Ascension* but did not gain a contact herself until 0136. The two ships circled the submarine like hungry sharks. In the darkness beneath them was U-*482*; surely every man aboard her was aware of the dreadful fate that had crept upon them. The *Ascension* had passed overhead twice, her high speed propellers tearing up the water as her powerful engines roared through the waves above them. It must have been terrifying. Kapitänleutnant Peter Cremer of U-*333* wrote in his log of one similar experience: 'Amidst the din, we find ourselves in a weird state of mind; midway between torpor and terror ... I wonder how long the nerves of my seamen will resist this terrifying concert. They are exposed for too long to unbearable tension.'

The target was estimated to be on a course of 220° altering slowly to the west. At 0140 HMS *Moorsom* was in firm and steady contact with the target and HMS *Ascension* decided to launch a Hedgehog attack against it.

According to reports from the two ships, the U-boat did not appear to take any evasive action, and it was suggested that maybe the submarine has been lulled into a false sense of security by the two previous passes made by the searching frigates. What could have been going through the minds of the crew of U-*482* as they sat huddled around their Commander in the silent dimness of their ship? As they listened carefully to the wall of ocean outside and the rattling din above them, were they as Peter Cremer suggested, 'midway between torpor and terror' and waiting for the end to come? Or did they think that the danger had already passed, that any attack would have already come by now? If the crew of U-*482* thought the latter, that they were to escape once more to carry on their patrol, they were mistaken.

At 0147 HMS *Ascension* passed over the U-boat once more and fired her Hedgehog, the pattern of explosives hitting the water and sinking rapidly towards the submerged U-boat. Kapitänleutnant Joachim Matz wrote of his own similar experience in U-70, his Type VIIC U-boat that was lost south-east of Iceland in March 1941 during the same convoy battle that saw the loss of Günther Prien in U-47 and the sinking of the 20,638 ton *Terje Viken*, the largest merchant loss of the war:

> Then they came at us again! The grinding noise of the propellers became louder. The bearing remained static; and that meant the destroyer was coming straight at us. Then with our ears we could clearly hear the rhythmic beat above our heads … twenty seconds of oppressive, absolute silence and then with a roar and a crash down came a pattern of charges helter-skelter all round us. The ship shuddered from stem to stern, shook herself; lockers sprang open, from here and there came the tinkle of splintered glass …

As HMS *Ascension* carried on overhead, the deadly Hedgehog projectiles continued quickly down through the dark water towards U-482. The seconds ticked by. The first explosion was clocked at 19.5 seconds after firing, with a second blast recorded almost immediately after. The remainder were heard exploding on the seabed some time later, at a depth of more that 500 fathoms. But at least one charge had hit the target, with the second explosion being either a second contact or a secondary explosion from the first. Either way, a single explosion right on target was more that enough to puncture the fragile outer hull of a U-boat.

The two frigates remained in contact with the target for the next ten minutes but with a 'very woolly echo' that eventually faded completely and could not be regained. At 0200 HMS *Moorsom* delivered an attack of ten depth charges over the position, but in the early morning darkness, no evidence of destruction could be observed. Still no ASDIC contact could be gained, and the escort group manoeuvred back into formation for a line abreast search, combing the surrounding waters for any sign that the U-boat might have escaped.

Then at 0704 as the sky began to lighten, the group sailed back over the attack site, and observed a large patch of oil spread across the surface of the sea. By daylight the oil slick had broken up in the heavy seas, and isolated streaks reportedly stretched for ten miles across the surface. But the weather had deteriorated rapidly, and the gale-force north-east winds made it impossible to obtain a sample from the heavy seas, which could prove the existence and destruction of a U-boat. Eventually after several failed attempts, a blanket was lowered over the side and dragged through the water. This was then forwarded to the Director, Anti U-boat Division for analysis. No other debris was observed and no other ASDIC contact made, but the presence of such a large quantity of oil, along with the double explosion produced by the initial Hedgehog attack, led to the decision that the target had been a U-boat and that it had been destroyed.

The final assessment was 'that the attack by *Ascension* hit the U-boat with at least two projectiles and probably caused it to sink. The action is assessed "U-boat probably sunk", the credit for success being shared by HMS *Ascension* and Sunderland G/330.' The wreck of U-*482* has never been inspected or even located, and so there is no way of knowing what damage the U-boat suffered in the attack. The ravages of time may well mean that no-one will ever know.

The end for a doomed U-boat generally came in two ways: blindingly fast or painfully slow. Following a successful attack the hull would be burst and water would gush in, the crew killed instantly either by the blast or by drowning soon after. The slower alternative was the U-boat becoming disabled and left unable to move or surface. In this case the submarine would slowly sink to the seabed, with the crew trapped inside what became a steel coffin. As the oxygen slowly diminished, the crew would slip away, forever entombed in their vessel beneath the waves. But with a direct hit from the Hedgehog attack, it is most likely that the explosion tore through U-*482*, ripping the vessel open and causing it to sink quickly.

Of course, because U-*482* has never been located she has never been officially identified. The theory that she was lost to a mine in the North Channel was perfectly possible and would account for the loss of contact, but the facts that U-*482* was known to be alone in the area at the time of HMS *Ascension*'s attack, that no other successful anti-submarine attacks were reported against unidentified U-boats in that vicinity, and that no reports or transmissions were received from her after this date, despite her being ordered to proceed to the North Channel, suggest that this was ultimately her fate. U-*482* was destroyed with all hands at position 60.18N, 04.52W in the heavy seas to the west of Shetland. The final fate of Kapitänleutnant Graf von Hartmut Matuschka and his men was like that of their victims; quick, lethal and delivered with horrible accuracy in the early hours.

After these actions by the 17th Escort Group it was noted that HMS *Ascension* would have benefited greatly by being equipped with her own echo sounding equipment, as in each case she had been unable to take her own records of the seabed and had to order another ship to do this for her. It was recommended that all Colony-class frigates should be fitted with these instruments as soon as possible so that they could search for enemy vessels more effectively. It was also noted that the Hedgehog had been a very satisfactory weapon in the attacks the group had made. It was finally concluded in relation to the 17th Escort Group's patrol in the period 7 November–3 December that 'all ships of the Group performed their duties during this Operation, in which six separate gales were encountered, in a very creditable manner.'

The operation also resulted in several of the men involved being recommended for honours and awards. They were put forward on 3 May 1945 and approved by King George VI on 17 May. They were published in the *London Gazette* (no.37098) on 29 May 1945 and finally awarded on 2 June. In total, there were six men recommended for awards, five from HMS *Ascension* and one from HMS *Moorsom*: 'For gallantry, skill and good seamanship shown while serving in H.M. Ships *Ascension* and *Moorsom*, in a successful patrol against a U-boat under gale conditions.'

Commander William Jocelyn Moore of HMS *Ascension* was recommended for his part in the attack, in which he 'displayed outstanding zeal and ability'.

> His leadership, efficiency and tact have been largely responsible for the high state of efficiency of his group … on 25 November 1944 during a patrol by the 17th Escort Group lasting twenty-six days during which period six successive gales were encountered, Commander Moore in HMS *Ascension* made and attacked a contact which has subsequently been assessed as a probable kill.

Admiral Whitworth, Commander-In-Chief concurred with the recommendation, and on 2 June Commander Moore was awarded the Distinguished Service Cross.

Lieutenant John D. Little RNVR of HMS *Ascension* was Group ASDIC Officer and Anti-submarine Control Officer. The Cheshire man was recommended for

> … skill and efficiency in the performance of his duties … during a long and arduous patrol, and in the destruction of two U-boats by HMS *Ascension* with a part in the destruction of a third. The fact that Hedgehog hits were obtained in the first attack on each occasion reflects credit on his own skill and on the efficiency of his department.

Lieutenant John D. Little was also awarded the Distinguished Service Cross.

Petty Officer William Smart of HMS *Ascension* from Carnoustie was the ASDIC operator during the attack on U-*482*. He was recommended for

> … skill and proficiency in carrying out his duties as Higher Submarine Detector during long and arduous A/S patrols culminating in the sinking of two submarines

and participating in the destruction of a third. During the attacks he was the Recorder Number of the A/S team and responsible for the correct time to fire. He was also responsible for the initial detection of one of the U-boats.

He was awarded the Distinguished Service Medal.

Able Seaman Henry Mackay of HMS *Ascension* was from Aberdeen. He was put forward for showing

> ... skill and proficiency in carrying out his duties as Submarine Detector. The destruction of two U-boats, and participation in the destruction of a third during a long and arduous patrol reflect great credit on his ability as First Operator in the A/S action team. He was responsible for the initial detection, in most difficult conditions, of one of the U-boats destroyed.

Able Seaman Mackay also received the Distinguished Service Medal.

Able Seaman Thomas Arthur Jarman from Darwen in Lancashire was recommended for his role as Trainer in the Hedgehog team on HMS *Ascension*. He showed

> ... skill and proficiency in the performance of his duties ... during a long patrol which was notable for the bad weather experienced, but in which two U-boats were destroyed and a part played in the destruction of another. The fact that Hedgehog hits were obtained in the first attack in all three instances, one of which was during a half gale, reflects great credit on his skill and efficiency.

He too was awarded the Distinguished Service Medal.

Lieutenant Commander John Parker Stewart RNR of HMS *Moorsom* was from Perth. He had already been awarded the DSC and was recommended for a further award for

> ... efficiency and devotion to duty ... during an arduous patrol ... Since the formation of the Group the conduct of this ship has been exemplary and he has always been of great assistance in intelligently anticipating the wishes of the Senior Officer.

Lieutenant Stewart was Mentioned in Dispatches.

These six men were awarded for their part in the destruction of an enemy ship that they had not seen, carrying an unknown number of men whose names they would never know. But that was the nature of the Battle of the Atlantic, for both sides. Locate and hunt, attack and sink, then move on to the next one. U-*482* became just another submarine that did not return to base, and was never heard from again.

The life-line is firm
thanks to the
MERCHANT NAVY

EPILOGUE

The Battle of the Atlantic was not won by any Navy or Air force, it was won by the courage and fortitude and determination of the British and Allied Merchant Navy.

Admiral Leonard Murray, RCN, Retd.

The sinking of four merchant ships and a Royal Navy corvette off the north coast of Ireland in the late summer of 1944 was an enormous blow to the Allies, and not only because of the tragic loss of life and costly loss of shipping and materials. It was also that the attacks underlined the fact that the U-boats could still strike, and strike hard. Advances in detection technology such as High Frequency Direction Finding and ASDIC meant that the U-boats had all but lost their invisibility, which was their greatest weapon; compared to surface ships their hulls were fragile and they stood no chance in normal naval combat. Sonar-equipped escort ships were able to sail ahead of a convoy and sweep the water for submarines before the enemy had any chance of getting near to the precious merchant ships. Developments in aircraft design had given planes increased range and the introduction of MAC ships meant that convoys could sail with their own air cover; this meant that they could send up aircraft to patrol over a much larger area to look out for enemy submarines. Improvements in anti-submarine weaponry had resulted in more accurate and dependable devices such as the Squid and Hedgehog, which ensured that when a U-boat was detected it had little chance of survival. In short, by 1944 the tide had completely turned against the U-boats and it seemed impossible that they could ever regain the upper hand.

What was so unusual and alarming about the events in the North Channel was that it had not been just a single instance of a submarine sneaking past the Allies' defences and delivering a lucky torpedo before being chased away by the counterattack. This had been a *series* of swift, unexpected attacks by an unidentified enemy that had slid through their defences, attacked without warning and then escaped undetected on four separate occasions.

In reality the success of U-*482* turned out to be very much a one-off, and in fact was one of the last successful U-boat patrols of the war. Her success was not the beginning of a new chapter in the war and did not represent any real change in the fortunes of the Kriegsmarine; afterwards U-boat successes continued to decline just as the Allies continued to gather strength. But for a brief time it looked to both sides as though it might have been the start of another phase in the Battle of the Atlantic.

Matuschka was the first commander to achieve any significant success with a snorkel-fitted U-boat and when U-*482* signalled her accomplishments in the North Channel to U-boat command it gave them cause for optimism. Dönitz wrote that the new technology 'showed very positive results'. He found cause for optimism in the initial success that the snorkel brought in the inshore campaign, 'Gratifying successes were also achieved in coastal waters in the Irish Sea, at the western exit to the Channel and off Cherbourg.'

At a time when the Kriegsmarine had grown terribly dejected after months and months of defeat it is easy to see why the sudden success of U-*482* was looked upon as a return to glory. Dönitz wrote, 'thanks to the effectiveness of the schnorchel and the indomitable enterprise of our U-boat captains and crews, what had started as a purely defensive delaying action was transformed into an offensive campaign in the enemy's coastal waters.' More U-boats were ordered towards inshore areas of operations in an attempt to emulate the success of U-*482*.

For the Allies, what made the losses even more shocking was that all of the ships had been sailing in convoy with significant escort protection, and despite being nearly home, had been sunk right on their own doorstep. There had been an extensive sweep of the area for U-boats and none had been found.

Ultimately the successful operations of Kapitänleutnant Matuschka and U-*482* – particularly the sinkings of *Empire Heritage* and *Pinto* from HX-305 – led to significant tactical changes in the way convoys were protected at sea and the way U-boats were dealt with in the event of an attack. They were changes that remained in place for the rest of the war. It was decided that the support group ships that joined up with convoys on a temporary basis to give additional support to the escort would no longer be placed under command of the senior officer of the close escort group as had been the case. The support groups were made up of additional ships that would help protect convoys when sailing through dangerous areas or when they had come under prolonged attack. It had always made sense for them to come under the command of the senior officer of the escort because he had the best tactical knowledge of the convoy and what had occurred within it. Convoys had often been the target of prolonged attacks from 'wolfpacks' made up of several enemy ships so it was necessary for the support groups to supplement the protection offered by the close escort because there were often more U-boats than they were able to deal with on their own. In the event of an attack, the ships of the close escort could not break away from a convoy to chase off a U-boat because it would leave the convoy ships undefended, but the support group had no actual escort responsibilities and so could immediately take off in search of the enemy even if the hunt should last for several hours or even days.

By 1944, however, the wolfpacks were long finished and the U-boats were operating alone, meaning this system of protection had become outdated. Rather than searching out a convoy in the mid-Atlantic and chasing it down the U-boats were remaining in shallow coastal waters and lying in wait for the convoy to come to them. This new approach was referred to as 'static tactics' by the Admiralty.

It was acknowledged that the support groups were likely to have much better local knowledge of the coastal area of operations than the senior officer of the escort who was simply passing through, and this meant better knowledge of the surrounding waters, tides, bottom conditions and wreck locations. Because it could be difficult for an ASDIC operator to differentiate between wrecks or large rocks and submerged U-boats, accurate geographical data and wreck charting became crucial. In the case of HX-305, had the support group ships been able to detach from the convoy immediately and head to the attack site rather than waiting for orders from the senior officer, they very likely would have prevented the attack on *Pinto* and probably located *U-482*. Therefore in the aftermath of the attack on *Empire Heritage* and *Pinto* it was decided that the support groups should remain independent of the close escort and that the senior officer of each group would retain authority over his own ships at all times.

In September the Royal Navy went on to officially acknowledge that the U-boats were likely to be using 'static tactics' from then on. It was a massive change in the Navy's attitude to the U-boats. It was considered that after an attack a U-boat would most likely submerge to the seabed and try to remain undetected until the danger had passed, rather than attempt to break away and flee as they would always have done previously. Lying still amongst the rocks and wrecks of the shallow coastal waters was potentially much safer because it would make them more difficult to detect by sonar. Admiral Max Horton,

Commander-in-Chief of Western Approaches broadcast a message to all forces in September 1944: 'When a ship in convoy is torpedoed in waters where a U-boat can bottom it should be assumed that it will do so provided immediate scaring tactics are adopted.' Lieutenant Storey wrote in his report about the attack on HX-305, 'Technique employed by U-boat appears to have been to remain submerged beneath survivors, ultimately probably bottoming.' Counter to this theory, Kapitänleutnant Matuschka did not bottom after the attack on HX-305 but in fact quickly left the scene and ultimately escaped while the escorts searched for him around the attack site.

The most important thing as far as the Allies were concerned was that there should never be any delay in their response to U-boat activity, as there had been in the case of *Empire Heritage*. The Admiralty wanted a swift and effective response to force the U-boat down or scare it off, and so prevent further attacks. It was believed that making the support groups independent of the convoy escort would go a long way to speeding up their response. It was also recommended that there should always be escort ships stationed astern of a convoy so that in the event of a U-boat being detected they would be able to simply accelerate towards the attack site without having to spend time turning and manoeuvring back through the convoy. The Admiralty broadcast a message in October 1944 informing all ships of the tactics the U-boats were believed to be employing.

> U-boats can now operate inshore and are likely to adopt static tactics in place of the mobile tactics which we have been used to dealing with. Static tactics involve the use of curly and gnat torpedoes fired from U-boats which endeavour to lie in wait on the course of convoys. When no targets are available U-boats are likely to move with great caution and charge by snort mainly by night. On approach of a hunting force [the U-boat] will probably bottom or may drift with tide near bottom.

'Curly torpedoes' was the British name for the German FAT and later LUT torpedoes which could be programmed to change direction after a set distance.

The new tactical procedures developed by the Allies in autumn 1944 remained relatively unchanged for the rest of the war. Some operational procedures were modified to suit certain situations but the main principles remained – a quick response to all U-boat activity and a concentrated attack to locate and destroy the enemy before he was able to attack or escape. This counter-attack was then to be sustained if necessary by the ships of the support group who could leave the ships of the close escort protecting the convoy and continue hunting the enemy.

The impact of U-482's momentous first patrol went far beyond the loss of five Allied ships – it made the Admiralty look hard at the way they were dealing with the U-boat threat in these days of snorkelling, bottoming and inshore attacks. Ultimately the success of U-482 led to a faster and more aggressive anti-submarine strategy, a better organised support system for the convoys and the laying of more anti-submarine minefields, particularly in the North Channel.

There is no single explanation for U-482's triumphs. It was certainly not a weakness on the part of the convoy system itself, which had proved itself time and time again to be the safest way for merchant ships to travel during wartime, and despite the findings of the Board of Inquiry, the blame cannot be wholly laid at the door of the senior officer of the escort, even though his formation of the convoy and the position of his ships undoubtedly left some weak areas that allowed the U-boat to get through. It would also be too easy to attribute the success to Kapitänleutnant Matuschka and praise him as a tactical genius who, by some sixth sense, managed to avoid all the convoy defences, all the anti-submarine patrols and all the ships that were sent to hunt him down. It would be equally futile to blame the Allied anti-submarine technology or to imply that it was insufficient to protect the convoys; they were without doubt capable of detecting and defeating U-482. Neither could the advances in German U-boat technology such as the T5 torpedo or the snorkel be given the full credit though they certainly contributed to the eventual success of the attacks; the snorkel may have allowed her to carry out tmost of her patrol submerged but many other snorkel-fitted boats achieved nothing.

It was a combination of elements that allowed U-482 to locate and stalk the three convoys as they approached the Northern Channel and that allowed her to remain undetected as she did so. The aggressive attitude of the U-boat commander certainly made a difference, but so did the fact that the escort screen happened to be weak in some areas – a fact Matuschka could not have known as he approached the convoy. The fact that there had been no losses amongst the HX convoys so far that year may have meant the attitude of the convoy escort had become too relaxed as they approached British waters. Perhaps the earlier success of the young U-boat commander gave him the added confidence to try for further triumphs when others might have considered they had pushed their luck far enough. Following the attack on *Empire Heritage*, there is no doubt that it took far too long to organise a proper search for the attacker and that delay almost certainly allowed the second attack to take place. Though *Pinto* and *Northern Wave* attended the wreck site promptly, they were unsupported by other forces for a considerable time. In fact it was fortunate that *Northern Wave* did not become a third victim of U-482. A badly organised convoy escort and significant flaws in communications within the convoy both gave the U-boat the chance it needed to escape unhindered.

The skill and determination of Kapitänleutnant Matuschka cannot be overlooked despite the fact that he was undoubtedly helped by some good luck. Matuschka had discipline, initiative and professionalism, and managed to turn each situation into an opportunity to attack. Incredibly, each of these opportunities resulted in the sinking of an Allied ship.

There were 23 U-boats lost in September 1944 and just thirteen Allied ships. Four of these ships were among the victims of U-*482*. Ultimately the losses of *Jacksonville*, *Hurst Castle*, *Fjordheim*, *Empire Heritage* and *Pinto* were a tragedy in a war filled with tragedies, and on balance they probably had more to do with the skill, aggression and extraordinary good fortune of the commander and crew of U-*482* than with the failings of the Allied technology, the convoy tactics, or the senior officer of the escort.

I have already made some mention of the contribution made by the Shetland seaman during the Second World War, and convoy HX-305 was no different. Ten of the crewmen of the *Empire Heritage* were Shetlanders, some had been at sea together since before the war. They were friends and comrades, linked forever by their small island community. When *Empire Heritage* sank there were only 48 men saved, 25 crewmen, 20 Distressed British Seamen, two naval gunners and a signalman; 110 men lost their lives, more than two-thirds of those aboard. Four Shetlanders were amongst the dead. They were the ship's master Captain James Campbell Jamieson OBE, Able Seaman George Robertson, Seaman Peter F. Johnson and Storekeeper John D. Smith.

The other six Shetlanders were amongst the 25 crewmen that survived. They were Chief Mate John R. Reid, Able Seaman George Irvine, Able Seaman John Sinclair, Able Seaman James Duncan, Able Seaman William H. Coutts and Bo'sun James Peterson – my grandfather and the initial inspiration for this book.

APPENDIX I

ALLIED U-BOAT LOSSES OVER 15,000 GRT

Altogether there were 21 merchant ships lost above 15,000 GRT – over 400,000 tonnes in total. The vast majority were lost in the early years of the Battle of the Atlantic when the U-boat threat was at its worst. Only two were lost after December 1942, the last of which was *Empire Heritage* in September 1944.

Date Lost	Name	Tonnage	Type	Men	Dead	Attacker
6/6/1940	RMS *Carinthia*	20.277	merchant cruiser	450	4	U-46
13/6/1940	HMS *Scotstoun*	17.046	merchant cruiser	352	7	U-25
2/7/1940	*Arandora Star*	15.501	steam passenger	1673	805	U-47
10/8/1940	HMS *Transylvania*	16.923	merchant cruiser	336	36	U-56
27/8/1940	HMS *Dunvegan Castle*	15.007	merchant cruiser	277	27	U-46
28/10/1940	*Empress of Britain*	42.348	steam passenger	623	45	U-32
3/11/1940	HMS *Laurentic*	18.724	merchant cruiser	417	49	U-99
2/12/1940	HMS *Forfar*	16.402	merchant cruiser	193	172	U-99
7/3/1941	*Terje Viken*	20.638	whale factory	107	2	U-99
13/4/1941	HMS *Rajputana*	16.644	merchant cruiser	323	40	U-108
3/2/1942	*Amerikaland*	15.355	motor merchant	39	5	U-106
12/9/1942	*Laconia*	19.695	troop transport	2741	1658	U-156
10/10/1942	*Orcades*	23.456	troop transport	1065	48	U-172
10/10/1942	*Duchess of Atholl*	20.119	steam passenger	832	5	U-178
29/10/1942	*Kosmos II*	16.966	whale factory	150	33	U-624
11/11/1942	*Viceroy of India*	19.627	troop transport	454	4	U-407
14/11/1942	*Warwick Castle*	20.107	troop transport	462	96	U-413
7/12/1942	*Ceramic*	18.713	steam passenger	657	656	U-515
21/12/1942	*Strathallan*	23.722	troop transport	5122	11	U-562
17/3/1944	*Dempo*	17.024	troop transport	333	0	U-371
8/9/1944	*Empire Heritage*	15.702	whale factory	163	112	U-482

APPENDIX II

CONVOY HX-305

The table below shows the make-up of convoy HX-305, detailing the various sections that left from New York, Halifax and Sydney, Nova Scotia, and the escort ships that assisted during the various stages of the journey. The ships are grouped by nationality.

DEPARTED NEW YORK 25 AUGUST 1944

American

Julius Olsen
Richard M. Johnson
Edward E. Spafford
Henry Lomb
Arunah S. Abell
Hawkins Fudske
Joshua Thomas
George T. Angell
Edward A. Savoy
S. Wiley Wakeman
Frank A. Munsey
John T. Holt
Charles Bulfinch
James D. Trask
Simon Newcomb
James G. Birney
Martin Van Buren
Collin McKinney
John R. McQuigg

Panaman

W. R. Keever
James G. Blaine
Robert Y. Hayne
Thomas Nuttall
Jacob Perkins
William Tyler Page
Florence Martus
Frederick H. Newell
William Kent
Henry D. Lindsley
John Chester Kendall
Joseph I. Kemp
Thomas Say
Jean Baptiste Le Moyne
Andrew A. Humphreys
Irwin Russel
Cornwall
Alexander H. Stephens
John N. Maffitt

Horatio Allen
W. S. Jennings
John A. Quitman
J. Warren Keifer
Byron Darnton
Umgeni
Samfoyle

Norwegian
Brimanger
Abraham Lincoln
Ferncourt
Solfonn

British
City of Lyons
Desirade

Dutch
Sovac
Westland

Panamanian
North King

Dwight L. Moody
Agwidale
Matthew J. O'Brien
Henry Wells
Thomas Kearns
Pennsylvania

Marit II
Fosna
Leiv Eiriksson
Ivaran
Fernwood

Lucellum
Empire Heritage
Empire Cheer

Taria

JOINED FROM HALIFAX, NOVA SCOTIA (SAILED 27 AUGUST 1944)

American
Eugene Field
Marcus H. Tracy
Junipero Serra
Lot M. Morrill
Harriet Tubman
Robert R. Livingston

British
Ariguani
Empire Kangaroo

Dutch
Macoma

Morris Hillquit
Julien Poydras
Peter Donahue
Orland Loomis
Henry Wynkoop
Livingston

Empire MacDermott
Empire MacCabe
Dorelian

Norwegian
S rvard

JOINED FROM SYDNEY, NOVA SCOTIA (SAILED 28 AUGUST 1944)

British

Jamaica Producer
Dromore
Tudor Prince
Caxton

Empire Waimana
Orient City
Alder Park
Empire Yukon
Fort Nottingham

Dutch

Tiba

ESCORT SHIPS

Algoma
Arvida
Border Cities
Cobourg
Dunver
Guelph
Hespeler
Huntsville
Kamsack
Long Branch
Midland
Nene

New Westminster
Noranda
Northern Sky
Northern Wave
Orillia
Peterborough
Pinto
Portage
Runnymede
Simon Newcomb
The Pas
Wetaskiwin

The escort ships listed were all engaged with the convoy at some point of its journey but some were only with it for a day or two while others were with it for most of the voyage. It was common for escort ships at either side of the Atlantic to accompany an outbound convoy after leaving port up to a certain middle point on the voyage when they would return home, usually escorting an incoming convoy on their return. Therefore not all of these vessels were present when the convoy was attacked.

APPENDIX III

U-*482* CREW LIST

Name	Rank	Rank	Translation	Age
Assmann	Hermann	Matrosenobergefreiter	Leading Seaman	20
Banik	Gunter-Ernst	Oberfahnrich zur See	Midshipman	20
Barthau	Alfred	Sanitatsmaat	Doctor	23
Becker	Heinrich	Matrosenobergefreiter	Leading Seaman	21
Belter	Kurt-Paul-Eberhardt	Maschinistobergfreiter	Leading Seaman (Engines)	30
Blass	Karl	Maschinistobergfreiter	Leading Seaman (Engines)	20
Bruggemann	Wilhelm	Funkmaat	Petty Officer (Radio)	23
Buchenau	Wilhelm	Matrosenobergefreiter	Leading Seaman	20
Castelle	Hermann	Maschinistgefreiter	Able Seaman (Engines)	20
Cersovsky	Otto	Mechanikerobergofreiter	Torpedo Mechanic	21
Daissler	Rudolf	Maschinistgefreiter	Able Seaman (Engines)	19
Dobele	Friedrich-Karl	Obermaschinist	Chief Petty Officer (Engines)	30
Drautzburg	Josef	Matrosenobergefreiter	Leading Seaman	20
Eckle	Erhard	Bootsmanner	Boatswain	24
Engeln	Arnold	Steuermann	Helmsman	24
Fakin	Slato	Maschinistobergfreiter	Leading Seaman (Engines)	24
Graf	Wilhelm	Matrose	Ordinary Seaman	20
Hahn	Wilhelm-Johannes	Funkobergefreiter	Radio Operator	22
Hasenauer	Gustav	Maschinenmaat	Petty Officer (Engines)	23
Hiemann	Otto	Mechanikerobergofreiter	Torpedo Mechanic	20
Huth	Werner	Maschinistobergfreiter	Leading Seaman (Engines)	20
Ikemeyer	Josef	Maschinistgefreiter	Able Seaman (Engines)	19
Jankowski	Willi	Obersteuermann	Navigator	24
Kampen	Heinz	Maschinistobergfreiter	Leading Seaman (Engines)	22
Kattner	Horst	Maschinenmaat	Petty Officer (Engines)	24

Krosta	Erich	Maschinistgefreiter	Able Seaman (Engines)	18
Kupper	Alfred	Maschinistobergfreiter	Engine Crew	19
Lochtmann	Wilhelm	Bootsmanner	Boatswain	22
Mademann	Rudolf	Mechanikerobergofreiter	Torpedo Mechanic	20
Matuschka	Hartmut	Kapitänleutnant	Captain Lieutenant	29
Melder	Herbert	Maschinenmaat	Petty Officer (Engines)	22
Neuhaus	Heinz	Funkobergefreiter	Radio Operator	20
Neuheisel	Bernhard	Funkgefreiter	Radio Operator	19
Pakin	Slato	Maschinistobergfreiter	Leading Seaman (Engines)	24
Pohlmann	Walter	Matrosenobergefreiter	Leading Seaman	20
Roschak	Bruno	Maschinistgefreiter	Able Seaman (Engines)	20
Rossner	Werner	Maschinenmaat	Petty Officer (Engines)	22
Rudolph	Walter	Matrosenobergefreiter	Leading Seaman	20
Scheil	Gunther	Maschinistgefreiter	Able Seaman (Engines)	19
Schloifer	Hans-Georg	Oberleutnant zur See	First Lieutenant	23
Schubert	Gerhard	Obermaschinist	Chief Petty Officer (Engines)	29
Stahlberg	Werner	Leutnant zur See	Sub-Lieutenant	19
Stankowski	Hans	Mechanikermaat	Torpedo Mechanic Mate	25
Steinbach	Alfred	Matrosenobergefreiter	Leading Seaman	19
Stobner	Helmut	Bootsmanner	Boatswain	21
Strauss	Bruno	Matrosenobergefreiter	Leading Seaman	21
Vieth	Hans-Peter	Leitender Ingenieur	Chief Engineer	24
Zaun	Wilhelm	Funkmaat	Petty Officer (Radio)	22
Zell	Gerhard	Obermaschinist	Chief Petty Officer (engines)	24

APPENDIX IV

CASUALTIES

MERCHANT NAVY AND DEMS PERSONNEL LOST FROM *EMPIRE HERITAGE*, RECORDED ON PANEL 42 OF THE TOWER HILL MEMORIAL, LONDON

Name		Rank	Age	Home
Aitken	Robert Thomson	Deck Boy	19	Edinburgh
Aitken	Charles Forrester	Greaser	33	
Allen	John	Able Seaman		
Anderson**	Edward Douglas	2nd Radio Officer	29	Edinburgh
Award	Umar Muhammad	Baker		
Baker	Alan John	Boy	18	
Banks	John Johnston	3rd Officer	22	Renfrewshire
Barbour	Thomas Crawford	Cabin Boy	18	
Boardman	Ronald	Able Seaman	23	Liverpool
Bowen*	Ornan Jones	Convoy Signalman (RN)	23	Middlesex
Bradley	Leslie Norman Frederick	Assistant Steward	24	Liverpool
Brown	Eric Ritson	Chief Officer	31	Dunston-on-Tyne
Brown	Eric John Wallis	Chief Steward	38	
Chalmers	John Shiels	7th Engineer Officer	20	Midlothian
Cherrie	John McConnell	Greaser	34	
Church	John	Steward	38	Glasgow
Clark	Ralph	3rd Officer	28	Dundee
Colebourne	Henry	Fireman and Trimmer	30	
Colebourne	Stanley	Fireman	26	
Coleman	Thomas	2nd Engineer Officer	56	Rotherham
Connolly	James	Senior Ordinary Seaman	20	
Cordingley*	Edward Hulmes	Able Seaman (RN)		

Corfield	Edward	Fireman and Trimmer		
Coutts	Norman	Senior Ordinary Seaman	18	
Crawshaw	George Henry Collinson	Assistant Cook	22	
Devins	John	Pumpman	26	Glasgow
Dewar	John Buchanan	Fireman	30	Glasgow
Drummond	Gordon Murray	Cadet	18	Kirkcaldy
Easton	William Norman	Cadet	17	
Faith	Thomas Coundon	Cook	26	
Flight	James	6th Engineer Officer	24	Dundee
Forsyth	George	Senior Ordinary Seaman	22	London
Friend	Henry	Cook	22	
Gallagher	John	Galley Boy	17	North Shields
Garbe*	John	Able Seaman (RN)	20	Liverpool
Gardner	James	Donkeyman	24	
Gillian	George	Galley Boy	17	Greenock
Goring	Harry	Ordinary Seaman	23	
Hallett	John Henry	Chief Steward	43	
Haswell	George	Fireman		
Haymes	Albert Charles	Ordinary Seaman		
Hilton	Harold	Chief Cook	44	Liverpool
Hulley	Thomas Evan	Fireman	48	Glasgow
Hyde	William John	Fireman	52	
Jamieson	James	Master	49	Shetland
Jarvis*	Richard	Able Seaman (RN)	21	
Johnson	Peter Fraser	Junior Ordinary Seaman	18	Shetland
Jones	Joshua	Fireman and Trimmer	30	
Joyce	David John	Mess Room Boy	18	
Kelleher	Jeremiah	Mess Room Boy	18	Dublin
Mack	Henry Vincent	Trimmer	31	
Mahoney	Cornelius	Fireman and Trimmer	40	Dagenham
Mansell	William	2nd Cook and Baker		Montreal (Canada)
Marks	David Chapman	Sailor	29	Glasgow
Matheson	John Anderson	Able Seaman	24	Aberdeen
McCaghey	Patrick Joseph	Ordinary Seaman	31	Dublin
McDermott	Alfred Thomas	Greaser	29	London
McDevitt	Richard Sharpe	Greaser	43	Glasgow
McDonald	Lawrence John	Fireman and Trimmer	24	
McGrath	Patrick Joseph	Able Seaman	24	County Cork (Ireland)
McKenzie	Angus	Steward	21	Dundee

McKeown	James Coates	Able Seaman	31	
McNeillage	Reuben	Fireman	20	
Medlock*	Charles Sidney	Able Seaman (RN)	33	Clapham
Miller	John Vincent	Fireman	23	Liverpool
Muirden	Hector	Able Seaman	34	
Mullen	Joseph	Assistant Steward	21	Welwyn Garden City
Murdoch	William Christie	Donkeyman	29	
Murray	John George	5th Engineer Officer	24	
Nelhams	Percy John	Fireman	29	
Nelson	Stewart	Sailor	19	Midlothian
Newton	Dennis	Cabin Boy	20	
Nicoll	James Stanley	1st Radio Officer	19	Dundee
Niven	Duncan	Storekeeper	41	
O'Sullivan	Patrick	Fireman	30	Troon
Olsen	Sigvald	2nd Engineer Officer	57	
Ottolangui	George	Assistant Steward	23	London
Reynolds	Cecil	Fireman and Trimmer	20	Liverpool
Richards	John William	Steward	20	Cornwall
Robertson	George Fraser Jamieson	Able Seaman	25	Shetland
Root	William Thomas	Boatswain		
Rothwell	Bernard Eric	Boatswain	38	Liverpool
Ryan	Harold Edward	Fireman	18	Portsmouth
Sankey	Allan	Mess Room Boy	19	
Sharp	Joseph Wilkinson	Senior Ordinary Seaman	18	
Sheldrake	Douglas Haig	Carpenter	25	Ipswich
Simister	Eric	Assistant Steward	20	
Sisay	Alhaseine	Fireman and Trimmer	22	
Smith	John	Storekeeper	42	Shetland
Soutar	William Carnegie	4th Engineer Officer	24	Forfar
Stant	William Alfred	Greaser	67	
Stapleton	James Harold	Fireman and Trimmer	36	Liverpool
Tattersall	William	Fireman	54	
Taylor	John Henry	Greaser	34	
Thomson	Charles	3rd Radio Officer	17	Aberdeen
Thornton	James Robert	Senior Ordinary Seaman	20	
Togneri	Luigi Francisco	Surgeon	30	Edinburgh
Trotter	Charles Robert Pinkerton	Steward	24	
Tveitan	Johan Olsen	Pumpman	50	Sandefjord (Norway)
Tyson	Stephen James Mortimer	3rd Engineer Officer	42	Welwyn Garden City

Voase	Francis Edward	Fireman	21	Dagenham
Wilson	Garner	Fireman	37	
Wilson	George Lister	Fireman	22	County Durham
Winstanley	Donald Albert	Assistant Cook	18	

MERCHANT NAVY AND DEMS PERSONNEL LOST FROM *PINTO*, RECORDED ON PANEL 81 OF THE TOWER HILL MEMORIAL, LONDON

Name		Rank	Age	Home
Armitage	Joseph Vincent	3rd Radio Officer	19	Skipton
Bentley*	Leonard	Lance Bombardier (RN)	34	Salford
Binnie	James Givens Wilson	Boatswain	47	
Boggs	Laurence Stanley	Master	59	Lindfield (Australia)
Glassey	Edward Divene	Chief Steward	41	Monifieth
Hillan**	Michael	Donkeyman	38	Glasgow
Lawrence	Halford St Alban	Assistant Steward	19	
Semple	John	2nd Engineer Officer	27	
Sinclair	James Gillan	Assistant Steward	36	
Stephens*	Edward John	Petty Officer (RN)		Birmingham
Thomson**	Alexander Woodburn	Chief Engineer Officer	56	Airdrie

* Royal Navy personnel

** Rescued but died from injuries

Note: This information is taken from the Tower Hill Memorial in London which lists the names of Merchant Navy personnel lost during both World Wars. Therefore the above lists only include casualties who were either in the Merchant Navy or who were DEMS Gunners. Other casualties aboard both ships do not appear here.

BIBLIOGRAPHY

DOCUMENTS (NATIONAL ARCHIVES, KEW)

ADM 1/16168 Finding of Board of Enquiry into loss of SS *Empire Heritage* and the resue ship *Pinto*

ADM 1/29940 Awards to four officers and men of HMS *Northern Wave* and rescue ship *Pinto*

ADM 1/30263 Awards to six officers and men of HM ships *Ascension* and *Moorsom*

ADM 217/12 HMS *Northern Wave*: Report of Proceeding of Convoy HX-305

PUBLISHED WORKS

Blair, C *Hitler's U-boat War: The Hunted 1942–45* (Random House, 1996)

Busch, Fritz-Otto *The Story of the Prinz Eugen* (Futura Publications, 1975)

Chrisp, John *South of Cape Horn: A story of Antarctic Whaling* (Robert Hale, 1958)

Cremer, Peter *U-333: Story of a U-boat Ace* (The Bodley Head, 1984)

Doenitz, Karl *Memoirs: Ten Years and Twenty Days* (Phoenix, 2000)

Elliot, Gerald *A Whaling Enterprise: Salvesen in the Antarctic* (Michael Russell Publishing, 1998)

Hague, Arnold *The Allied Convoy System 1939–1945* (US Naval Institute, 2000)

Hague, Arnold *Convoy Rescue Ships 1940–1945* (World Ship Society, 1998)

Hutson, Harry C. *Grimsby's Fighting Fleet: Trawlers and U-boats During the Second World War* (Hutton Press, 1990)

Irvine, James W. *The Giving Years: Shetland and Shetlanders, 1939–1945* (Shetland Publishing, 1991)

Mitchell, W.H & Sawyer, L.A. *The Empire Ships: Record of British-built and Acquired Merchant Ships During the Second World War* (LLP Professional Publishing, 1990)

Padfield, Peter *War Beneath the Sea: Submarine Conflict, 1939–45* (John Wiley & Sons, 1995)

Robertson, R.B. *Of Whales and Men* (Knopf, 1954)

Somner, Graeme *From 70 North to 70 South: A History of the Christian Salvesen Fleet* (Christian Salvesen Ltd, 1984)

Turner, John Frayn *Fight for the Sea: Naval Adventures from World War II* (Naval Institute Press, 2001)

Vamplew, W. *Salvesens of Leith* (Scottish Academic Press, 1975)

Vause, Jordan *U-boat Ace: the Story of Wolfgang Luth* (St Martins, 1991)

Werner, Herbert *Iron Coffins: A U-boat Commander's War, 1939–45* (Phoenix, 1999)

Wilson, Ian *Donegal Shipwrecks* (Impact Printing, 1998)

Woodman, Richard *Arctic Convoys 1941–1945* (Pen & Sword, 2007)

WEBSITES

uboat.net
ubootwaffe.net
warsailors.com
convoyweb.org.uk
uboatarchive.net
deepimage.co.uk

INDEX